Muriel Davi

KETO DIET
BOOK
FOR BEGINNERS 2023

"All-in-One", Keto Diet Cookbook with the
Complete Guide to Understand Ketogenic Lifestyle
with Quick and **Healthy 450 Effortless Recipes
plus 16 Weeks Meal Plans!**

TABLE OF CONTENT

INTRODUCTION

Have you been wanting to finally lose the unnecessary weight, but felt that you were unable to for some reason? Are the words "w8loss" constantly inside your head, but once again for some reason you do not get round to working on it?

Now, you are probably asking, how does she know this. Well, that is because I know a great deal about losing w8 and finally achieving the "dream body," or the "dream physique".

I spent 20 years of my life overweight, all aggravated after giving birth to my son Manuel. I never gave importance to food and how it made my life heavy and slow. I went through periods of depression and loneliness without going out.

Like everyone else, I tried the band-aid solutions, never focusing on long-term goals. Strange, and restrictive diets did not help me, because all I wanted was to lose weight quickly without effort. That is why nothing worked. It was a never-ending loop until I discovered something – the Ketogenic Diet.

However, the process was not easy at all. It required quite some time until I realized the real benefits of the keto diet and how it actually works. I did not have enough information, and I easily mixed things up.

My motivation dropped, and I lost focus. The biggest mistake is not having the direction, the One Thing. But then everything changed. The strength came from my son's sweet face, the desire to stay close to him as long as possible with power and energy. I didn't want to be heavy anymore and be out of breath when I went shopping. I had said enough is enough.

That's why I created this manual to be easy to get started and never fail again to achieve your goals. The primary goal of this book is to provide you with the skills you need to make the ketogenic diet work more easily and naturally in your everyday life. To do this, I realized that there was a need to create a resource where people could find everything they needed: instructions, tips, meal plans, and recipes, without doing unnecessary and stressful research.

You need to know that the Ketogenic Diet will improve your lifestyle. It has helped me lose weight, but the benefits do not end there.

Over the years, I've become fascinated and talked to people who have used the Ketogenic Diet recommended by their nutritionist for anxiety and depression problems, restore brain function for people who have Alzheimer's and Dementia, fix Diabetes, lower cholesterol and treat chronic inflammation.

The fact that you are reading this book indicates that you are at least intrigued about how the Ketogenic Diet may assist you. Even better, maybe you are already aware of its advantages and are looking for diversified, rich, and flavourful dishes for a more enjoyable ketogenic journey.

Whatever the case may be, this cookbook will be able to provide you with practical culinary ideas to spice up your everyday meals.

I really hope that the information and concepts in this book are useful to you and that you have a successful ketogenic journey.

WHAT IS THE KETO DIET?

CHAPTER 1

As you'd already know, the Ketogenic Diet is a low-carb diet where you eliminate or minimize carbohydrates consumption. Proteins and fats replace the extra Carbohydrates: while you cut back on pastries and sugar.

How Does It Work?

See, when you consume less than 50 grams of Carbohydrates: per day, your body starts to run out of blood sugar (which is used as fuel to provide your body quick energy). Once there are no sugar reserves left, your body will start to utilize fat and protein for energy. This entire process is known as ketosis, and this is exactly what helps you lose weight.

Compared to other diets, keto has a better chance of helping you lose w8 more quickly. The diet is also incredibly popular as you're not encouraged to starve yourself. It would help if you worked towards a more high-fat and protein diet, which isn't as difficult as counting calories.

Is Keto Going Alright for People with Diabetes?

Now you're probably wondering, what do I do if I have diabetes? For starters, speak to your doctor. Talking to your doctor is important regardless of what kind of diet you choose. However, note that keto diets generally do work well to improve insulin sensitivity.

For better results, seek a doctor's help if you have diabetes. Keto diets can have a drastic impact on your body and overall lifestyle; hence, it's always better to seek professional guidance.

Macronutrients and Keto

Macronutrients

The food you consume provides nutrition to the body. Various types of nutrients are present in the food. They are broadly classified into macronutrients and micronutrients. Macronutrients are those nutrients required in significant quantities in the food to provide necessary energy and raw material to build different body parts. These are:

- Carbohydrates
- Proteins
- Fats

Carbohydrates

Carbohydrates are important energy sources for the body. In a Keto diet plan, you have to cut down your Carbohydrates: to eliminate this energy source and compel your body to spend the already present food stores in your body. These food stores are present as fat in your body. Once your body turns to these fat deposits in the body to energy, you start to lose weight.

Carbohydrates should not constitute more than 5–10% of your daily calorie intake.

Carbohydrates are present in a variety of foods. You should make sure that the small quota of carbohydrates you can consume comes from healthy carbohydrate sources like low-carb vegetables and fruits, e.g., broccoli, lemon, and tomatoes.

Proteins

Proteins are really important because they provide subunits, which are building blocks of the body. They produce various hormones, muscles, enzymes, and other working machinery of the body. They provide energy to the body as well.

No more than 20–25% of your daily caloric intake should come from proteins. As a rule of thumb, a healthy person should consume about 0.5–0.7 grams of proteins per pound of total body weight.

Many people who have adopted keto make a mistake by consuming much more protein than they should. This not only puts additional strain on their kidneys but is also very unhealthy for the digestive system.

Eat a good variety of proteins from various sources like tofu, fish, chicken, and other white meat sources, including seeds, nuts, eggs, and dairy (though you shouldn't fill your diet with cheese). Red meat like beef can be enjoyed less frequently. We also suggest you avoid processed meats, which are typically laden with artificial preservatives.

Processed meat refers to meat that's modified through a series of processes, which might include salting, smoking, and canning. It is also treated with preservatives, which is the worst process when it comes to meat variants typically including sausages, jerky, and salami. As these meats are not even considered healthy for normal diets, we suggest limiting your portions to only once or twice a week.

Fats

In keto, fats serve as the mainstay of your diet. It seems counterintuitive to consume what you want to eliminate from your body, but that is exactly how this strategy works.

But before you load your body with all types of fats, keep the following things in your mind:

1. You have to cut down on Carbohydrates: before this high-fat diet can be of any benefit to the body.
2. Fats should take up about 70–75% of your daily caloric intake.
3. Fats are of various types, and you have to be aware of the kind of fats you should consume.

Dietary fats can be divided into 2 kinds: healthy and harmful. Unsaturated fats belong to the healthier group, whereas saturated and trans-unsaturated fats belong to the unhealthier category. Aside from the differences in their health effects, these fats essentially differ in terms of chemical structure and bonding.

- **Saturated Fats**

  Saturated fats drive up cholesterol levels and contain harmful LDL cholesterol that can clog arteries anywhere in the body, especially the heart, and increase the risk of cardiovascular diseases. A diet high in saturated fat has an increased chance of reducing the risks of heart diseases. These fats are mainly contained in animal origin (except fish, which contains a small part). They are also present in plant-based foods, such as coconut oil. However, coconut oil contains medium-chain fatty acids, which are saturated fats different from animal origin, and therefore considered a healthy food.

  Saturated fats are mostly contained in:
  - Whole milk dairy products, including milk and cheese
  - Butter
  - Skin-on chicken
  - Red meat such as pork, lamb, and beef

  While there's no doubt that these foods are keto-friendly, they should not be consumed in large quantities, regardless of what diet you follow. It's also worth noting that some saturated fats are rated better in the health department than others. For instance, milk is healthier than consuming red meat. We suggest you limit butter and pork derived from animal fat as they overall tend to be unhealthy.

- **Unsaturated Fats**

  These 'good fats' contain healthy cholesterol. Unsaturated fats can most commonly be found in nuts, veggies, and fish. These fats keep your heart healthy and are a good substitution for saturated fats.

  Unsaturated fats can be divided into:

  Trans Fat: Trans fats, or trans-fatty acids, are a certain form of unsaturated fat. These unhealthy fats are manufactured through a partial hydrogenation food process. Moreover, some studies differentiate the health risks of those obtained industrially or transformed by cooking, from those naturally present in food (for example, vaccenic acid); the latter would be harmless or even beneficial to health.

  The industrial foods that contain these hydrogenated fats are mainly: fried foods (especially French fries), margarine, microwave popcorn, brioche, sweet snacks, and pretzels.

  While these foods may taste good, they're an unhealthy kind of fat and should be avoided.

  Trans fats are known to increase unhealthy cholesterol levels in the blood, thus increasing the risks of cardiovascular disease. The WHO (World Health Organization) has the aim of global elimination of industrially-produced trans fats from food supplies by 2023.

Calculating Your Daily Caloric Intake

Many people think that calculating your calories while you are on a keto diet is not very important, but it is always good to watch how many calories you consume a day. It would help if you calculated how many calories you consume every day by the idea of how much w8 you want to lose.

If your body needs 2,000 calories a day, but you consume only 1,200 calories, your body is in a caloric deficit, so it will have to tap into your body's fat reserves, and this will result in a loss of weight. There are various calculators available online that can be used to calculate your daily caloric intake taking into account your objectives, age, height, activity level, and other factors.

In general, if you want to lose weight, you need to subtract around 600 calories from your daily caloric needs. So less than 1,000–1,200 calories if you are a woman and less than 1,200–1,600 calories if you are a man.

Having a Meal Plan

When you have a complete meal plan laid out in front of you, you are in a better position to have an idea of what your diet would look like in the days to come. If you have to spontaneously decide what you will prepare to eat every time you are in the kitchen, your chances of going off the rails become pretty high.

You can start by calculating how many calories you are going to consume a day.

The next step would be to decide which macro-nutrients will have to be incorporated and in what proportion for your body to reach that goal. Remember that the rule of thumb is 75, 20, 5: for fats, proteins, and Carbohydrates: respectively.

CHAPTER 2

THE SCIENCE BEHIND THE KETO DIET

To bring the body into a Ketogenic condition, you need to follow a high-fat diet and small carbohydrates without any grains, or almost any. The composition will be roughly 80% fat and 20% protein. That will be the rule for the very first 2 days.

When the body absorbs Carbohydrates: it induces an insulin surge with the insulin emitted by the pancreas. Common sense assures us that if we then eliminate Carbohydrates: the insulin does not hold excess calories as the perfect fat. Now your body has no Carbohydrates: as an energy source, so your body should look for a new source.

If you decide to loose extra weight, this works well. The body must break down the extra fat and function with it, rather than Carbohydrates: as energy.

That particular condition is known as 'Ketosis.' This state, in which you want the body to be in, can make great sense in case you want to lose excess fat while keeping muscle.

Let's move on now to the portion of the diet and how to prepare it. With every pound of lean mass, you would need to ingest no less than one gram of protein. It will aid with strengthening and restoring muscle tissue during exercises. That means 65% protein and 30% fat.

Effectively, if you weigh 150 pounds, that means 150 g of protein a day. If you multiply it four times (number of calories equivalent to 600 calories in a gram of protein), any of the calories will come from fat. If the caloric maintenance is 3,000, you need to consume about 500, less that might imply that one day if you require 2,500 calories, about 1,900 calories should come from the fats!

To fuel the body, you have to consume fats, which will also burn up excess fat! That is the diet plan rule; you've got to consume fats! The downside of taking healthy fats and the keto diet is that you're not going to be thirsty. Fat processing of food is slow, operating to the benefit and making you feel satisfied.

You're going to be working on Monday–Friday, and then on the other days, you're going to have a 'carb-up.' When this process begins when the last exercise is on Friday, post-training, you need to take a liquid carbohydrate with your whey shake. This will help to produce an insulin surge, allowing us to provide the carbohydrates that the body urgently requires for restoring muscle mass and for glycogen stores to expand and refill.

Consume whatever you like during this specific process (carb-up): pizzas, crisps, spaghetti, and ice cream. Somehow, this will be beneficial for you because it can refresh the body for the week ahead and provide the food that your body requires.

Switch your focus on the no-carb and high-fat average protein diet program as Sunday starts. Holding the body in Ketosis and losing fat is the optimal remedy, by muscle.

An additional benefit of Ketosis is when you enter the ketosis state and burn the fat, the body will deplete carbohydrates. Packing up with Carbohydrates: can make you appear as full as before (but even fewer less body fat!), perfect for holiday activities if you visit the seaside or parties!

Let us recap on the diet schedule now.

Get in ketosis state by removing Carbohydrates: and taking moderate/low protein and high fat.

Take some fiber to keep the pipes as clear as ever; you should realize what I mean.

If the ketosis protein consumption has been collected, the lean mass per pound will be no less than that of one gram of protein.

So, it is! It does require determination not to eat Carbohydrates: during the week because certain products contain Carbohydrates: however, note that you would be greatly rewarded for the devotion.

You must not live on end days in Ketosis condition because it is dangerous and will wind up with yourself turning to make use of protein as a source of food that is a no-no.

Ketogenic diet systems are structured primarily to trigger a ketosis condition for the body. If the volume of glucose in the body is low, the whole body turns to fat as a source of energy replacement.

The body has main sources of fuel, one of which is:

Glucose

Free fatty acids (FFA) and, to a lesser degree, ketones from FFA Fat by-products are kept in the triglyceride type. Typically, they are split into long-chain fatty acids and glycerol.

The removal of glycerol from the triglyceride molecule enables the three free fatty acid (FFA) molecules to be used as energy to introduce the bloodstream.

The glycerol molecule goes into the liver, where three molecules of it combine to create one molecule of sugar. Additionally, when the body consumes fat, it creates glucose as a by-product. Its glucose may be used to power different regions of the brain and body parts that can't operate on FFA molecules.

However, though glucose on its triglycerides will travel through the blood, cholesterol takes a carrier to go through the bloodstream. In a carrier known as LDL or low-density lipoprotein, cholesterol and triglycerides are packed. Thus, the larger the LDL particles, the greater the number of triglycerides it has.

The general process of energy-burning of fat deposits produces CO_2, oxygen, and ketone-known components. The liver produces ketones out of the free essential fatty acids. Right now, they consist of 2 classes of atoms joined by a purposeful carbonyl unit.

The body cannot store ketones, and therefore they should be used or excreted at times. The body often excretes them as acetone through the breath and as acetoacetate through the urine.

The ketones may be used as a source of energy for body cells. The subconscious will use ketones to generate between 70–75 percent of the energy requirement.

As for alcoholic drinks, ketones take priority over carbohydrates as food resources. That means that they should be consumed first when filled with the bloodstream before glucose can be used as a fuel.

CHAPTER 3

THE MAIN FEATURES OF THE KETOGENIC DIET

Losing Weight

For most people, this is the foremost benefit of switching to keto! Their previous diet method may have stalled for them, or they were noticing weight creeping back on. With keto, studies have shown that people have been able to follow this diet and relay fewer hunger pangs and suppressed appetite while losing w8at the same time! You are minimizing your carbohydrate intake, which means fewer blood sugar spikes.

Often, those fluctuations in blood sugar levels make you feel more hungry and prone to snacking in between meals. Instead, by guiding the body towards ketosis, you are eating a more fulfilling diet of fat and protein and harnessing energy from ketone molecules instead of glucose. Studies show that low-carb diets effectively reduce visceral fat (the fat you commonly see around the abdomen that increases as you become obese). This reduces your risk of obesity and improves your health in the long term.

Reduce the Risk of Type 2 Diabetes

The problem with carbohydrates is how unstable they make blood sugar levels. This can be very dangerous for people who have diabetes or are pre-diabetic because of unstable blood sugar levels or family history. Keto is a great option because of the minimal intake of carbohydrates it requires. Instead, you are harnessing most of your calories from fat or protein, which will not cause blood sugar spikes and, ultimately, pressure the pancreas to secrete insulin. Many studies have found that diabetes patients who followed the keto diet lost more w8and ultimately reduced their fasting glucose levels.

This is monumental news for patients who have unstable blood sugar levels or are hoping to avoid or reduce their diabetes medication intake.

Improve Cardiovascular Risk Symptoms to Overall Lower Your Chances of Having Heart Disease

Most people assume that following a keto diet that is so high in fat content has to increase your risk of coronary heart disease or heart attack, but the research proves otherwise! Research shows that switching to keto can lower your blood pressure, increase your HDL good cholesterol, and reduce your triglyceride fatty acid levels.

That's because the fats you are consuming on keto are healthy and high-quality fats, so they reverse many unhealthy symptoms of heart disease. They boost your "good" HDL cholesterol levels and decrease your "bad" LDL cholesterol levels. It also decreases the level of triglyceride fatty acids in the bloodstream.

A high level of these can lead to stroke, heart attack, or premature death. And what are the high levels of fatty acids linked to?

Low Consumption of Carbohydrates

With the keto diet, you are drastically cutting your carbohydrates intake to improve fatty acid levels and improve other risk factors. A 2018 study on the keto diet found that it can improve 22 out of 26 risk factors for cardiovascular heart disease! These factors can be very important to some people, especially those who have a history of heart disease in their family.

Increases the Body's Energy Levels

Let's briefly compare the difference between the glucose molecules synthesized from a high carbohydrate intake versus ketones produced on the keto diet. The liver makes ketones and ~~use~~ uses fat molecules you already stored. This makes them much more energy-rich, and a lasting fuel source compared to glucose, a simple sugar molecule. These ketones can physically and mentally give you a burst of energy, allowing you to have greater focus, clarity, and attention to detail.

Decreases Inflammation in the Body

Inflammation on its own is a natural response by the body's immune system, but when it becomes uncontrollable, it can lead to an array of health problems, some severe, and some minor.

The health concerns include acne, autoimmune conditions, arthritis, psoriasis, irritable bowel syndrome, and even acne and eczema. Often, removing sugars and carbohydrates from your diet can help patients of these diseases avoid flare-ups—and the delightful news is keto does just that!

A 2008 research study found that keto decreased a blood marker linked to high inflammation in the body by nearly 40%. This is glorious news for people who may suffer from inflammatory disease and want to change their diet to see improvement.

Increases Your Mental Functioning Level

As we mentioned earlier, energy-rich ketones can boost the body's physical and mental alertness levels. Research has shown that keto is a much better energy source for the brain than simple sugar glucose molecules are. With nearly 75% of your diet coming from healthy fats, the brain's neural cells and mitochondria have a better energy source to function at the highest level.

Some studies have tested patients on the keto diet and found they had higher cognitive functioning, better memory recall, and less memory loss. The keto diet can even decrease the occurrence of migraines, which can be very detrimental to patients.

Heart Diseases

Keto diets help women over 50 to shed those extra pounds. Reducing any amount of w8greatly reduces the chances of a heart attack or any other heart complications. Through the carefully selected diet routine, you are not only losing w8and enjoying delicious meals, but you are significantly boosting your heart's health and reviving yourself from the otherwise dull state that you may have been in before.

Diabetes Control

Needless to say, the careful selection of ingredients, when cooked together, ~~provide~~ provides rich nutrients, free from any processed or harmful contents such as sugar. Add to that the fact that keto automatically controls your insulin levels. The result is a glucose level that is always under control, and continued control would lead to a day where you will say goodbye to the medications you might be taking for diabetes.

CHAPTER 4

WHAT TO EAT AND AVOID

I've had people complain about the difficulty of switching their ordinary grocery list to one that's Ketogenic-friendly. That is not the problem. The problem is, people's fridges are usually filled with food rich in carbohydrates, and they do not know of substitutes. That is why before you start you have to do a clean sweep. That's right, everything that's packed with carbohydrates should be identified and set aside to make sure that you are not overeating.

What to Eat on the Keto Diet

Fats and Oils

Because fats will be included as part of all your meals, we recommend that you choose the highest quality ingredients that you can afford. Some of your best choices for fat are:

- Ghee or Clarified butter
- Avocado
- Coconut Oil
- Butter
- Coconut Butter
- Fish rich in Omega-3 Fatty
- Acids like salmon, mackerel, trout, tuna, and shellfish
- Peanut Butter
- Chicken Fat
- Beef Dripping
- Non-hydrogenated Lard
- Macadamias and other nuts
- Egg Yolks

Protein

Those on a keto diet will generally keep fat intake high, carbohydrate intake low, and protein intake at a moderate level. Some on the keto diet for w8 loss have better success with higher protein and lower fat intake.

- Fresh meat: beef, veal, lamb, chicken, duck, pheasant, pork, etc.
- Deli meats: bacon, sausage, ham (make sure to watch out for added sugar and other fillers)
- Eggs: preferably free-range or organic eggs
- Fish: wild-caught salmon, cod, halibut, trout, tuna, etc.
- Other seafood: lobster, crab, oyster, clams, mussels, etc.
- Peanut Butter: this is a great source of protein, but make sure to choose a brand that contains no added sugar

Dairy

Compared to other weight-loss diets, the keto diet actually encourages you to choose dairy products that are full fat. Some of the best dairy products that you can choose are:

- Hard and soft cheese: cream cheese, mozzarella, cheddar, etc.
- Cottage cheese
- Double cream
- Sour cream
- Full-fat yogurt

Vegetables

Overall, vegetables are rich in vitamins and minerals that contribute to a healthy body. However, if you're aiming to avoid Carbohydrates, you should limit starchy vegetables such as potatoes, peas, corn, beans, and most legumes. Other vegetables that are high in carbohydrates, such as parsnips and butternut squash, should also be limited. Instead, stick with green leafy vegetables and other low-carb veggies. Choose local or organic varieties if it fits with your budget.

- Spinach
- Lettuce

- Spring greens
- Bok choy
- Kale
- Alfalfa sprouts
- Celery
- Tomato
- Broccoli
- Cauliflower

Fruits

Your choice of fruit on the keto diet is typically restricted to avocado and berries because fruits are high in carbohydrates and sugar.

Drinks

- Water
- Black coffee
- Herbal tea
- **Wine:** white wine and dry red wine are OK if they are only consumed occasionally.
- **Others**
- **Homemade mayo:** if you want to buy mayo from the store, make sure that you watch out for added sugar
- Homemade mustard
- Any type of spices or herbs
- Stevia and other non-nutritive sweeteners such as Swerve
- Ketchup (Sugar-free)
- Dark chocolate/cocoa

Foods to Avoid

1. Bread and Grains

Bread is a key food in many countries. You have loaves, bagels, tortillas, and the list goes on. However, no matter what form bread takes, they still contain a lot of Carbohydrates. The same applies to whole grain as well because they are made from refined flour. Depending on your daily carb limit, eating a sandwich or bagel can put your way over your daily limit. So, if you want to eat bread, it is best to make keto variants at home instead. Grains such as rice, wheat, and oats contain a lot of Carbohydrates: too. So limit or avoid that as well.

2. Fruits

Fruits are healthy for you. They are found to make you have a lower risk of heart disease and cancer. However, there are a few that you need to avoid in your keto diet. The problem is that some of those foods contain quite a lot of Carbohydrates, such as bananas, raisins, dates, mango, and pear. As a general rule, avoid sweet and dried fruits. Berries are an exception because they do not contain as much sugar and are rich in fiber. So, you can still eat some of them, around 50 grams. Moderation is key.

3. Vegetables

Vegetables are healthy for your body. The keto diet in general does not forbid or restrict the number of vegetables that should be eaten daily. Of course, as long as they are low in starch.

Vegetables that are high in fiber can aid with w8 loss. On the one hand, they make you feel full for longer, so they help suppress your appetite. Another benefit is that your body would burn more calories to break and digest them.

Moreover, they help control blood sugar levels and aid with bowel movements. But that also means you need to avoid or limit vegetables that are high in starch because they have more Carbohydrates: than fiber. That includes sweetcorn, potato, sweet potato, and beetroot.

4. Pasta

Pasta is also a staple food in many countries. It is versatile and convenient. As with any other suitable food, pasta is rich in Carbohydrates. So, when you are on your keto diet, spaghetti, or many different types of pasta are not recommended.

You can probably eat a small portion, but that is not suggested. Thankfully, that does not mean you need to give up on it altogether. If you are craving pasta, you can try some other alternatives that are low in Carbohydrates: such as spiralized veggies or shirataki noodles.

5. Cereal

Cereal is also a massive offender because sugary breakfast cereals contain a lot of Carbohydrates. That also applies to "healthy cereals." Just because they use other words to describe their product does not mean that you should believe them.

That also applies to porridge, whole-grain cereals, etc. So, if you get your cereal when you are doing keto, you are already way over your carb limit, and we haven't even added milk into the equation! Therefore, avoid whole-grain cereal or cereals that we mention here altogether.

CHAPTER 5

TIPS FOR WHO WANT TO START

Learn How to Count Your Macros

This is especially important at the beginning of your journey. As time goes on, you will learn how to estimate your meals without using a food scale.

Prepare Your Kitchen for Your Keto-friendly Foods

Once you've made a choice, it's time to get rid of all the foods in your kitchen that aren't allowed in the keto diet. To do this, check the nutritional labels of all the food ingredients. Of course, there's no need to throw everything away. You can donate foods you don't need to food kitchens and other institutions that give food to the needy.

Purchase Some Keto Strips for Yourself

These are important so you can check your ketone levels and track your progress. You can purchase keto strips in pharmacies and online. For instance, some of the best keto strips available on Amazon are Perfect Keto Ketone Test Strips, Smackfat Ketone Strips, and One Earth Ketone Strips.

Find an Activity You Enjoy

When you have done enough exercise, you will know what activities you like. One way to encourage yourself to exercise more regularly is by making it more entertaining than a chore. If possible, stick to your favorite activities, and you can get the most out of your exercises. Keep in mind that the activities you enjoy may not be effective or needed, so you need to find other exercises to compensate for, which you may not enjoy. For instance, if you like jogging, you can work your leg muscles, but your arms are not involved. So, you need to do pushups or other strength training exercises.

Check with a Healthcare Provider

Your dietitian can tell you whether a keto diet would work. Still, it helps to check in with your healthcare provider to ensure that you do not have any medical condition that prevents you from losing weight, such as hypothyroidism and polycystic ovarian syndrome. It helps to know well in advance whether your body is even capable of losing fat in the first place before you commit and see no result.

Hydrate Properly

That means drinking enough water or herbal tea and ditching sweetened beverages or other drinks that contain sugar altogether. Making the transition will be difficult for the first few weeks, but your body will thank you for it. There is nothing healthier than good old plain water, and the recommended amount is 9 litres a day.

Have the Right Mindset

Your mindset is one of the most important things you need to change when you've decided to follow the keto lifestyle. Without the right mindset, you might not stick with the diet long enough to enjoy all its benefits. Also, the proper mindset will keep you motivated to keep going no matter what challenges come your way.

Get Enough Sleep

Getting enough sleep helps your body regulate the hormones for it, so try to aim for 7 to 9 hours of sleep a night. You can get more restful sleep by creating a nighttime routine that involves not looking at a computer, phone, or TV screen for at least 1 hour before going to bed. You can drink warm milk or water to help your body relax or even do 10 to 20 minutes of stretching to get a restful sleep.

Keep a Food Log

Add the calories and divide them into three to get an average. Now that you know how many takes, you can figure out how much you need to pay on average per day to reach your goals.

CHAPTER 6

7-DAYS PLAN DETOX FOR WEIGHT LOSS

☑ Day One

Breakfast: Avocados Stuffed with Crab Salad

Lunch: Lemon Baked Salmon

Supper: Roasted Leg of Lamb

☑ Day Two

Breakfast: Banana Pancakes

Lunch: Garlic Chicken

Supper: Shrimp Scampi with Garlic

☑ Day Three

Breakfast: Tomato Eggs

Lunch: Buffalo Drumsticks and Chili

Aioli

Supper: Thai Beef Salad

☑ Day Four

Breakfast: Eggs with Leeks

Lunch: Roasted Lemon Chicken Sandwich

Supper: Salmon Keto Cutlets

☑ Day Five

Breakfast: Bacon & Egg Breakfast Muffins

Lunch: Courgette Sushi

Supper: Grilled Steak

☑ Day Six

Breakfast: Bacon & Avocado Omelet

Lunch: Low-Carb Broccoli Mash

Supper: Creamy Tuscan Garlic Chicken

☑ Day Seven

Breakfast: Avocados Stuffed with Crab Salad

Lunch: Easy Keto Smoked Salmon Lunch

Bowl

Supper: Cauliflower and Pumpkin

Casserole

IMPROVE YOUR KETOGENIC DIET WITH FITNESS

Can you remember when the last time you squatted? During PE at school? Or maybe you tried to do a workout a few months ago, but then you lost your motivation?

Every diet that you decide to follow must also include an adequate training regimen; they are 2 sides of the same coin, both important and necessary motivators.

It only takes a second to decide that it's worth it, 10 minutes for your first workout, and 2 weeks to feel the difference.

Everyone knows that doing physical activity improves wellbeing, but many are not familiar with all the benefits.

Here are the main benefits you can get when you start exercising:

- Lower risk of chronic diseases
- Mood and mental health improve
- Balanced energy levels during the day and better sleep quality
- Slowing down of aging processes
- Better brain health
- Positive effects on the microbiome
- Guaranteed sex life

My general advice is:

- **Cardio** (minimum amount of activity): at least 150 minutes of moderate activity during the week. You can replace them with 75 minutes of intense activity or a combination of both.
- **Train your strength** (highly recommended): exercises involving the main muscle groups 2 or more days a week.
- **For extra benefits:** all minimal cardio activity can add 300 minutes (moderate level) or 150 minutes (intense level) per week (or a combination of both).

Tips for Who Want to Start

It may sound challenging, but the good thing is that you can adapt these tips to your schedule. As long as cardio activities are performed for at least 10 minutes, you can divide your active minutes into how many training sessions you like. Depending on your personal goal, you can choose to start with cardio or strength training.

Types of Physical Activities

What are the most common types of physical activity?

Cardio: any activity that increases your heart rate and makes you breathe faster is considered cardio. Usually refers to activities aimed at improving endurance, such as:

- **Moderate level:** brisk walking, dancing, jumping, jogging, cycling, swimming, push-ups, etc.

- **Intense level:** running, fast cycling, fast walking uphill, fast swimming.

Strength training: any activity that uses endurance to increase muscle strength. Using your body weight as resistance has many benefits!

Flexibility and mobility training: exercises to maintain and improve passive (flexibility) and active (mobility) movement.

What Type of Physical Activity is Best for Losing Weight?

Any exercise that requires high effort (for you) will have similar effects—especially for a beginner. So the truth is that... it doesn't matter! Choose activities that you enjoy and that you can imagine continuing to do for more than a month or 2. After all, losing w8 depends on the calorie deficit. So be sure also to adjust your diet to get the results you want.

Tips to Start Working Out

The first step is to reach a level of fitness where you no longer feel you "hate sport." Here's how to do it:

Find the Inspiration and Set a Goal

How many times have you forced yourself to start a training plan to lose 5 kg, and you have not succeeded? Try a different approach and first decide what you want to improve. Think about what you would like to do—whether it's exercising for 30 minutes without stopping or participating in the next marathon, improving your fitness for more energy being more productive at work, and being able to keep up with your children.

CHAPTER 8

HEALTH TIPS

Nobody told you that life was going to be this way! But don't worry. There's still plenty of time to make changes and take care of your health. Here are a couple of tips that will allow you to lead a healthier life in your fifties:

Start Building on Immunity

Every day, our body is exposed to free radicals and toxins from the environment. The added stress of work and family problems doesn't make it any easier for us. To combat this, you must start consuming healthy veggies that contain plenty of antioxidants and build a healthier immune system.

This helps ward off unwanted illnesses and diseases, allowing you to maintain good health.

Adding more healthy veggies to your keto diet will help you obtain various minerals, vitamins, and antioxidants.

Consider Quitting Smoking

It's never too late to try to quit smoking, even if you are in your fifties. Once a smoker begins to quit, the body quickly starts to heal the previous damages caused by smoking.

Once you start quitting, you'll notice how you'll be able to breathe easier while acquiring a better sense of smell and taste.

Over some time, eliminating the habit of smoking can greatly reduce the risks of high blood pressure, strokes, and heart attack. Please note how these diseases are much more common among people in the fifties and above than in younger people.

Not to mention, quitting smoking will help you stay more active and enjoy better health with your friends and family.

Stay Social

We recommend you stay in touch with friends and family or become a part of a local community club. Some people find it comforting to get an emotional support animal.

Being surrounded by people you love will give you a sense of belonging and will improve your mood. It'll also keep your mind and memory sharp as you engage in different conversations.

Intermittent Fasting and Keto Diet

What Is Intermittent Fasting?

Intermittent fasting (IF) is one of the world's most popular fitness and health trends right now. It is being used to help people lose weight, enhance their health, and simplify their lives. Many studies have shown that it has profound impacts on your body and brain and could even increase longevity.

Intermittent fasting (IF) is a kind of eating pattern that varies between fasting and eating phases. It does not define which things to consume, but rather when to eat them. In this way, it is more correctly defined as an eating pattern than a diet in the classic sense.

There are various methods used to practice IF; they divide time into hours or divide time into days. Since the regiment's response varies from person to person, no process can be called the best.

Knowing that intermittent fasting cannot make you lose the additional pounds you may have instantaneously is essential, but it can prevent unhealthy addictions to meals. It's a nutritional practice that requires you to be determined to follow to get the maximum gain.

If you already have a minimum duration to eat due to your schedule, this regiment will suit you like a duck to water, but you will always need to be conscious of what you are eating if you are a foodie.

Choose the appropriate regiment after expert guidance. You should see it as a segment of your schedule to get healthy, but not the only component.

Intermittent fasting is for those who want to regulate their hormones and burn excess body fat.

This diet allows for healthier whole foods and an all-around diet, which is better than living off processed foods and sugars, which are unhealthy.

It can also benefit individuals who are sugar-addicted or those who ate eat empty calories.

Drinks and sodas with few nutrients, but full of calories, are included in these products.

Finally, people generally want to do better in life and enjoy a food plan that doesn't require too much planning or maintenance.

Even if intermittent fasting may not be for you reading this book will equip you with the necessary information required to help another person or to use it eventually in life.

Different Methods

IF regiments are numerous to the point that you can choose from any that you like. Always make sure to select a regimen that will fit in your schedule so that it is possible to maintain it.

There are several short methods for fasting, including:

The 12-Hour Fast

That's what the regular living routine is called as you eat three meals a day and fast at night as you sleep. The generally small breakfast would break the fast. It is called the traditional method. Any regiment can help you lose w8 only if you follow it correctly.

The higher the levels of insulin are as a result of more people adding regular eating and snacking. It can cause resistance to insulin and, ultimately, obesity. This fasting technique sets aside twelve hours in which the body has low insulin levels, reducing the likelihood of insulin resistance. It can't help you lose excess fat, but it can help prevent obesity.

The 16-Hour Fast

This fasting for 16 hours is followed by an 8-hour window where you can eat what you like. Luckily you can sleep through most of it, so it's not difficult to keep doing it. Because it requires only small changes like just skipping your lunch, it has an enormous advantage over others, such as the 12 hours fast.

The 20-Hour Fast

It's called the "warrior diet." It includes fasting all day long and eating a lot of calories at night. It's meant to keep you from having breakfast, lunch, and other meals for most of the day, so you're getting all your nutrients from dinner. It is a division scheme of 20:4 with four hours of food followed by twenty hours of fasting. It's one of the easiest to do as you're allowed to eat a huge meal of calorific value, so you're going to feel fuller for longer. Start your daytime calories and have a big evening dinner to relax in this diet. You're going to gradually reduce what you're eating during the day and eventually leave dinner as your only meal.

The longer you do these fasting regiments, the more you will be able to maintain a fast. You will come to find out that you will not always feel hungry. The excitement of benefits will make you increase your period of fasting by a couple of hours. Unknowingly, therefore, you are plunging into longer stages of fasting. You can adhere to your regiment religiously but eating an extra hour will not ruin your fasting or fat burning.

The easiest way to track your feeding is to do it once a day is because it doesn't require a lot of thought. It's just eating at that moment every day on one dinner so that you can use your mental energy on the more important stuff. Unfortunately, it can cause a plateau of weight loss, where you are not losing or gaining weight. That's because you're going to consume the same number of calories every day and significantly less on a typical working day than you would eat. That's the best way to maintain your weight. You will have to change your fasting regimen to lose fat after a while. Timing your meals and fasting windows will lead to optimal loss of fat instead of random fasting. Choose one that can be maintained and modified if necessary.

There are longer fasting regiments, these include:

The 24-Hour Fast

It's a scheme of eating breakfast, lunch, or dinner in a day and then eating the following day at the same time. If you decide to eat lunch, then it only involves skipping breakfast and dinner, so nothing is disrupted in your life. It saves time and money because you're not going to eat as much and piling up dishes will not be a worry of yours. Knowing that you are fasting will be a task for people unless they are very interested in eating methods. By eating unprocessed natural foods, you should have enough vitamins, minerals, and oxygen to avoid nutrient deficiencies. You can do this weekly, but twice or three times a week, it is suggested.

During such long fasts, you should not knowingly avoid eating calories. What you are taking should be high in fat, low in carbohydrates, and unprocessed; there's nothing you shouldn't eat. It would be best if you consumed until you are adequately fed as the duration of fasting lets you burn a bunch of fat, and it will be difficult overtime to try to cut more purposefully.

The 36-Hour Fast

You retain in this fast for one and a half days without eating. For instance, if you eat lunch today, you consume no meal until the day's breakfast after the following day. This fast should be done about three times a week for people with type 2 diabetes. After the person reaches the desired w8 and all diabetes medications are successfully removed, they can reduce the number of days of fasting to a level that will make it easier for them to do while maintaining their gains. Blood sugar should usually be checked as small or high.

The 42-Hour Fast

It is adding six hours to the 36 hours fast, resulting in a fast of forty-2 hours carried out about 2 times a week.

The 5:2 Fast

This technique is conducted to prevent you from totally abstaining from meals and having cycles of calorie consumption. These calories are reduced to a rate that leads to many hormonal advantages of fasting. It consists of five days of regular feeding with 2 days of fasting. With some protein and oil-based sauce or green vegetables and half an avocado, you can eat some vegetable salad during these fasting days; furthermore, do not eat any dinner. These days of fasting can be placed randomly or following each other in a week at specific times. This method is designed to create fasting for more people, as many find it challenging to avoid eating altogether. There's no exact time to follow; as soon as you want, you can follow it.

The Alternate-Day Fast

It may seem similar to the 5:2 fasting regimen, but it is not. It's fasting every day. This technique can be followed until you lose as much w8 as you want, then you can reduce days of fasting. It allows w8 loss to be maintained.

It is possible to move to different fasting regimens as your schedule can change. Intermittent fasting is not about a time-limiting eating window; it is flexible, so you can move your eating and fasting time to suit you, but don't keep changing them all the time; this reduces the effect of fasting on your body. You can even combine some fasting regiments like the 5:2 technique and the 24-hour fasting by having lunch before your fasting day at a particular moment and adding only lunch at the fasting lunch and doing the same for the following fasting day. With this, for twenty-four hours, you could not eat any calories and set your days of fasting as in the 5:2 method of fasting. Choose the fasting day technique that works well with you and can synchronize with your life.

A schedule allows you to create a routine after frequent fasting that makes it easier to integrate into your life. You can plan, but there's no problem if you can't. Even if you can't plan to fast, you should be open-minded to fasting to opportunities. You can fast every month or every year. Frankly, you won't lose w8 on losing annual fasts.

Intermittent and Keto Diet

You know all of the different ways to fast, and you know what the ketogenic diet is. The primary purpose of intermittent fasting is to not eat as much during the day. Intermittent fasting can boost your fat burning. When your body is in a fasted state, your body will turn to your fat stores for energy. It is when the body starts forming ketones to fuel you and your brain. Now, the ketogenic diet does the same thing without any fasting. However, many people find they don't feel as hungry when following a keto diet. It means that they start fasting simply because they don't feel like they need to eat.

You don't have to fast when on keto, and you don't have to follow keto when fasting. You can choose whichever method, but some people will find that fasting becomes easier on a ketogenic diet.

People who follow a ketogenic diet will have lower insulin levels and blood glucose levels. They have a reduced appetite because of the effects of the ketogenic diet. It means that they won't have any sugar crashes, and they won't feel as hungry.

If you maintain a regular diet, high in Carbohydrates, and fast, you may experience an increase in hunger hormones, and your blood glucose may drop quickly. It could end up causing you to feel irritable, shaky, and weak. It could mean that you feel hungry all of the time. It doesn't always happen, though.

Using both ketogenic diet and intermittent fasting for w8 loss is a great idea, but remember, you can use them separately.

HOW TO PREPARE YOUR KITCHEN

Before I move on to the recipes, I want to list some of the most-used gadgets to cook keto-friendly meals. I'm not proposing that you have to have all of this in your Kitchen to follow the ketogenic diet successfully, so please don't go out and buy anything you won't use.

You'll see I'm not listing cutlery and crockery and other ingredients commonly found in a kitchen. I think in your 50 years on earth; you've spent enough time in a kitchen to know the basics required to cook food.

Kitchen Scales

Out of all the things on the list, this is one I would highly recommend buying. In the beginning, you won't be able to eyeball your macros as the more experienced keto dieters can. You will have to use a kitchen scale to weigh your food to know how much you are eating. You can then punch these numbers into a Carb and calorie tracker app, and it will let you know if you're on track.

Storage and Food Prep Containers

Essential for meal prepping and storing leftovers.

Slow Cooker

If you plan on prepping your meals in advance, I suggest investing in a slow cooker. Cook a large amount of food right away and then divide it into portions for the week. If meal prepping is not your thing, you can still use the slow cooker to prepare a keto-friendly meal in a fraction of the time.

Spiralizers

It is a nifty little gadget if you want to fool your eyes into thinking you're eating pasta. You can spiral different veggies into forms and sizes that resemble spaghetti, fettuccine, or other shapes.

Egg Cooker

Okay, you'll soon come to find that you'll be eating more eggs than usual. They're high in fat and protein and low in Carbohydrates, and that makes eggs a great snack. Boil a few eggs, pop them in the fridge and enjoy when you're feeling a little hungry.

Immersion Blender

This is a baby food processor that you can hold in your hands to blitz up smoothies, make your Hollandaise sauce, ground nuts, or whip some cream to add to your coffee. Just make sure you buy one with multiple attachments.

Frying Pan/Skillet

You'll be eating a lot of steaks, so why not get a frying pan or skillet to cook it in?

Roasting Pan

A whole chicken or beef roast surrounded by veggies, roasted in the oven, and then covered in a creamy cheese sauce. It doesn't sound like you're on a diet. A roasting tray is a perfect container to make delicious meals in the oven.

Safety First

As this guide ends and you get ready to try out some top keto recipes, just a reminder to put your safety first. It's possible to get so carried away in what you're doing and forget some standard safety rules. It is dangerous when you're working with open flames, boiling water, steam, and knives.

I think many people don't know how to handle knives safely because they try to mimic the cutting techniques they see on

TV. I remember I once showed off my non-existent chopping skills and almost lost a finger.

So, allow me to talk you through a quick crash course in knife safety:

- Always use a cutting board. Don't cut anything while holding it in your hand.
- Do not leave knives lying around in the sink. Clean them as soon as possible and put them away.

- Don't store knives lose in a drawer. You may be reaching for something else and then get a nasty surprise.
- Dull knives cause more injuries. Always use a sharp knife.
- On the hand that's holding the item that is being cut, curl your fingers under. If you keep them straight, they'll be in the way.
- Always point the knife away from you; blade facing down. Don't run or fool around with a knife in your hand.
- Keep your focus while you're chopping, dicing, or mincing.
- If you drop a knife, don't try to catch it. Please step back and let it fall.

"Okay, have a look through the recipes, find one you like, and head to the kitchen! I hope you found the Keto knowledge in this guide helpful and feel that you now know enough to start the Ketogenic diet confidently.

I promise you—this diet will change your life for the better."

BREAKFAST

1. Blueberry Oatmeal with Nuts

Preparation Time: 10 minutes	**Cooking Time:** 6 to 8 hours	**Servings:** 6

Ingredients:

- 1 tablespoon coconut oil (melted)
- 60 grams chopped pecans
- 60 grams sliced almonds
- 1 avocado, chopped
- 120 ml. coconut milk
- 120 grams coconut, shredded
- 250 ml. water
- 56 grams protein powder
- 30 grams granulated erythritol
- ¼ teaspoon ground cinnamon
- ¼ teaspoon nutmeg, ground
- 60 grams blueberries

Directions:

1. Melt the coconut oil and coat the inside of the slow cooker with it.
2. Put all ingredients except for the blueberries in the slow cooker and stir until thoroughly mixed.
3. Cook covered on low heat for about 6 to 8 hours.
4. Divide the oatmeal among six serving bowls and garnish with the blueberries before serving.

TIP: To add more flavours to this oatmeal, serve topped with a spoonful of plain Greek yogurt.

Nutrition:
Calories: 298 **Fat:** 12.2g **Carbohydrates:** 45g **Protein:** 8.5g

2. Keto Bombs with Salmon and Goat Cheese

Preparation Time: 10 minutes	**Cooking Time:** 0 minutes	**Servings:** Makes 12 fat bombs

Ingredients:

- 60 grams butter
- 60 grams goat cheese
- 56 grams smoked salmon
- 2 teaspoons lemon juice, squeezed
- A pinch of pepper, ground

Directions:

1. Line a baking tray with baking paper. Set aside.
2. Make the fat bombs: Mix the butter, goat cheese, smoked salmon, pepper, and lemon juice in a bowl. Stir well to incorporate.

3. Scoop mounds of the mixture onto the parchment-lined baking tray.
4. Transfer the fat bombs to the fridge for 2 to 3 hours until firm but not completely solid.
5. Remove from the fridge and let chill at room temperature for 8 minutes before serving.

TIP: You can store the fat bombs in a sealed airtight container in the fridge for up to 1 week.

Nutrition (per 1 bomb):
Calories: 122 **Fat:** 10g **Carbohydrates:** 2g **Protein:** 4g

3. Salmon Cakes with Fried Pork Rind

Preparation Time: 10 minutes	**Cooking Time:** 12 minutes	**Servings:** 4

Ingredients:

Salmon Cakes:

- 170 grams wild salmon, dried
- 1 egg, lightly beaten
- 2 tablespoons pork rinds (crushed)
- 3 tablespoons mayonnaise
- Pink Himalayan Salt
- Pepper

Mayo Dipping Sauce:

- 1 tablespoon ghee
- ½ tablespoon Dijon mustard

Directions:

1. Mix the salmon, beaten egg, pork rinds, mayo, salt, and pepper in a large bowl until well combined.
2. Make the salmon cakes: on a lightly floured surface, form a patty with some of the salmon mixture in your palm. Repeat with the remaining salmon mixture until you have made X salmon cakes.
3. Melt the ghee in a large pan over a medium-high heat.
4. Fry the patties for about 6 minutes until golden brown on both sides, flipping once.
5. Remove from the heat and place on a plate lined with kitchen paper. Set aside.
6. Combine the remaining mayo and mustard in a small bowl. Stir well.
7. Serve the salmon cakes with the mayo dipping sauce on the side.

TIP: If you don't have a large pan that fits all the patties, you can cook them in batches.

Nutrition (per cake):
Calories: 121   **Fat:** 6g   **Carbohydrates:** 0g   **Protein:** 15g

4. Artichoke Caponata with Grilled Salmon Fillets

 Preparation Time:
15 minutes

 Cooking Time:
20 minutes

 Servings:
4

Ingredients:

CAPONATA:
- ½ tablespoon olive oil
- 2 celery stalks (chopped)
- 1 tablespoon garlic (chopped)
- 1 onion (chopped)
- 60 grams marinated artichoke hearts (chopped)
- 2 tomatoes (chopped)
- 2 tablespoons dry white wine
- 30 grams apple cider vinegar
- 2 tablespoons chopped pecans
- 30 grams pitted green olives (chopped)
- 120 grams salmon fillets
- Freshly ground black pepper (to taste)
- 2 tablespoons chopped fresh basil (for garnish)

Directions:

1. Make the caponata: heat olive oil in a nonstick pan over a medium heat until shimmering.
2. Add the celery, garlic, and onion to the pan and sauté for 4 minutes or until the onion becomes translucent.
3. Add in the artichoke hearts, tomatoes, dry white wine, vinegar, pecans, and olives to the pan.
4. Sauté to mix well and bring to the boil.
5. Turn down the heat to low and simmer for 6 minutes or until the liquid is reduced by one-third. Take the pan off the heat and set aside.
6. Preheat the grill to a medium-high heat.
7. On a clean work surface or board, brush the salmon fillets with olive oil, and sprinkle the salt and pepper over to season.
8. Arrange the salmon on the preheated grill trays and grill for 8 minutes or until cooked through.
9. Flip the salmon halfway through.
10. Transfer the salmon into four plates and pour the caponata over each.

 TIP: To make it a complete meal, you can serve it with roasted green beans and spicy chicken stew.

 Nutrition:
Calories: 340.9   **Fat:** 25.3g   **Carbohydrates:** 4.1g   **Protein:** 24.2g

5. Avocados Stuffed with Crab Salad

 Preparation Time:
20 minutes

 Cooking Time:
0 minutes

 Servings:
2

Ingredients:

Crab salad:
- 60 grams of cream cheese
- 130 grams of (Dungeness) crab meal
- 30 grams chopped (peeled English cucumber)
- 30 grams chopped red pepper
- 1 teaspoon chopped coriander
- 60 grams spring onions (chopped)
- Pinch of sea salt and freshly ground black pepper (to taste)

Stuffed Avocados:
- 1 avocado (peeled, halved lengthwise, and pitted)
- ½ teaspoon freshly squeezed lemon juice

Directions:

1. Make the crab salad: place the cream cheese, crab meat, cucumber, red pepper, coriander, spring onions, salt, and pepper in a medium bowl. Mix well until blended. Set aside.
2. Rub the cut parts of the avocado with fresh lemon juice.
3. Using a spoon, stuff each avocado halves with the crab salad. Serve immediately or cover it with cling film and refrigerate until ready to serve.

 TIP: The crab salad can be made ahead of time and refrigerated until you want to stuff the avocado halves.

 Nutrition:
Calories: 204   **Fat:** 19g   **Carbohydrates:** 2g   **Protein:** 6g

6. Bacon & Avocado Omelet

 Preparation Time:
5 minutes

 Cooking Time:
5 minutes

 Servings:
1

Ingredients:

- 1 slice of crispy bacon
- 2 organic eggs
- 25 grams grated parmesan cheese
- 30 grams ghee
- 1 avocado
- 50 grams spinach
- 100 grams tomatoes

Instructions

4. Cook bacon in a nonstick pan until crisp, stirring regularly.
5. Remove the grease from the pan. Add the cherry tomatoes and the spinach. Cook until the spinach has wilted, and the cherry tomatoes are soft, approximately 1 minute, over a medium heat.
6. Take out of the pan and put aside. Wipe out the skillet.
7. Whisk eggs with kosher salt and black pepper to taste.
8. In a pan over a medium-high heat, melt the butter. Cook for approximately 5 seconds after adding the eggs.
9. Lift cooked egg up around sides to enable the uncooked egg to flow below, approximately 2 minutes, until omelet is set but the top is still wet.
10. Arrange bacon, spinach, tomatoes, and avocado on one side of the omelet and fold over gently.
11. Reduce the heat to low and simmer for another 1 to 2 minutes, or until the chicken is cooked through. Serve the omelet immediately on a platter.

Nutrition:
Calories: 516 **Fat:** 18g **Carbohydrates:** 2g **Protein:** 34g

7. Bacon & Cheese Frittata

Preparation Time: 5 minutes	**Cooking Time:** 5 minutes	**Servings:** 6

Ingredients:
- 120 grams Heavy cream
- 6 eggs
- 5 slices of bacon
- 2 green onions
- 115 grams Cheddar cheese

Directions:
1. Preheat the oven to 175°C, fan 155°C. Lightly grease a 7x11-inch baking dish.
2. Place bacon in a large pan and cook over a medium-high heat, turning occasionally, until evenly browned, about 10 minutes. Drain bacon slices on kitchen paper and crumble.
3. Beat eggs, milk, butter, salt, and ground pepper in a bowl; pour into prepared baking dish. Sprinkle with onions, bacon, and Cheddar cheese.
4. Bake in preheated oven until a knife inserted near the center comes out clean, 25 to 30 minutes.

Nutrition:
Calories: 249 **Fat:** 19g **Carbohydrates:** 3g **Protein:** 14g

8. Bacon & Egg Breakfast Muffins

Preparation Time: 15 minutes	**Cooking Time:** 30 minutes	**Servings:** 12

Ingredients:
- 5 large eggs
- 125grams crisp-cooked bacon, crumbled
- 130 grams grated cheddar, or any cheese you like
- Salt and fresh cracked pepper, to taste
- 1/2 teaspoon Italian seasoning and 1/2 teaspoon crushed chili pepper flakes (optional)

Directions:
1. Preheat the oven to 200°C, fan 180°C, gas 6.
2. Grease a 6-cup muffin tin with oil or non-stick cooking spray and set aside.
3. Set aside. In a large mixing bowl, add eggs and whisk together with salt and black pepper.
4. Stir in cooked bacon, cheddar cheese, Italian seasoning, and red chili pepper flakes (if using). Divide evenly into muffin cups filling each about 2/3 full.
5. Top with more bacon and cheese if you like.
6. Bake the egg muffins in preheated oven for 12-15 minutes, or until set.
7. Allow to cool a bit and serve your cheesy bacon egg muffins immediately, or enjoy cold, or at room temp.

Nutrition:
Calories: 397 **Fat:** 21g **Carbohydrates:** 29g **Protein:** 22g

9. Bacon Hash

Preparation Time: 5 minutes	**Cooking Time:** 10 minutes	**Servings:** 2

Ingredients:
- 700 grams potatoes
- 2 tablespoons olive oil
- 200 grams diced bacon
- 2 spring onions
- 4 large eggs
- 90 grams shredded mozzarella
- Pepper
- Salt

Directions:
1. Preheat oven to 200°C, fan 180°C, gas 6. Arrange the potatoes in a single layer in a oven proof pan or dish (or baking sheet). Spray with a light coating of cooking oil spray and bake for about 30 minutes, mixing them around halfway through cook time, until they are crisp and golden.
2. Remove from oven, add the bacon, and place back into the oven for a further 10 minutes or until the bacon is crispy.
3. Make four wells in the hash, crack an egg into each well and arrange the mozzarella around each egg. Place pan back into the oven until the whites are set and the eggs are cooked to your liking.
4. Serve immediately.

Nutrition:
Calories: 230 **Fat:** 24 grams **Carbohydrates:** 9 grams
Protein: 23 grams

10. Bagels with Cheese

Preparation Time: 10 minutes	**Cooking Time:** 15 minutes	**Servings:** 6

Ingredients:
- 210 grams mozzarella cheese
- 1 teaspoon baking powder
- 85 grams Cream cheese
- 200 grams Almond flour
- 2 eggs

Directions:
1. Shred the mozzarella and combine with the flour, baking powder, and cream cheese. Microwave for one minute. Mix well.
2. Cool and add the eggs. Break into six parts and shape into round bagels.
3. Bake for 12 to 15 minutes. Serve.

Nutrition:
Calories: 13g **Fat:** 11g **Carbohydrates:** 51g **Protein:** 13g

11. Baked Apples

 Preparation Time: 10 minutes   **Cooking Time:** 1 hour   **Servings:** 4

Ingredients:
- 4 teaspoons keto-friendly sweetener
- 1,75 teaspoon cinnamon
- 130 grams chopped pecans
- 4 apples

Directions
1. Set the oven temperature at 190°C, fan 170°C, gas 5.
2. Mix the sweetener, cinnamon, and pecans.
3. Core the apple and stuff with the sweetener, cinnamon and pecans mixture.
4. Add enough water into the baking dish. Bake for 45 minutes to 1 hour. Serve.

Nutrition:
Calories: 147   **Fat:** 0g   **Carbohydrates:** 36g   **Protein:** 1g

12. Eggs with Leeks

 Preparation Time: 10 minutes   **Cooking Time:** 20 minutes   **Servings:** 2

Ingredients:
- 1½ tablespoon rapeseed oil, plus a splash extra
- 2 trimmed leeks, sliced
- 2 garlic cloves, sliced
- 1/2 teaspoon coriander seeds
- 1/2 teaspoon fennel seeds
- Pinch of chilli flakes, plus extra to serve
- 200 grams spinach
- 2 large eggs
- 2 tablespoons Greek yogurt
- Squeeze of lemon

Directions:
5. Heat the oil in a large frying pan. Add the leeks and a pinch of salt, then cook until soft. Add the garlic, coriander, fennel and chilli flakes. Once the seeds begin to crackle, tip in the spinach and turn down the heat. Stir everything together until the spinach has wilted and reduced, then scrape it over to one side of the pan. Pour a little oil into the pan, then crack in the eggs and fry until cooked to your liking.
6. Stir the yogurt through the spinach mix and season. Pile onto two plates, top with the fried egg, squeeze over a little lemon and season with black pepper and chilli flakes to serve.

Nutrition:
Calories: 231g   **Fat:** 16g   **Carbohydrates:** 11g   **Protein:** 10g

13. Banana Pancakes

 Preparation Time: 10 minutes   **Cooking Time:** 15 minutes   **Servings:** 3

Ingredients:

- Butter
- 2 bananas
- 4 eggs
- 1 teaspoon cinnamon
- ½ teaspoon baking soda (optional)

Directions:
1. Mix all the ingredients together until well combined.
2. Melt a knob of butter in a pan over a medium heat and cook about 4 pancakes per batch (depending on the size of the pan).
3. Allow the pancakes to cook about 1-2 minutes per side. I like to cover the pan while the pancakes cook on the first side before flipping. This allows the top to steam a little bit, making it fluffier and also easier to flip.
4. Serve immediately as is, or with a dollop of coconut cream and fresh strawberries.

Nutrition:
Calories: 124g   **Fat:** 7g   **Carbohydrates:** 13g   **Protein:** 6g

14. Turkey Scramble

 Preparation Time: 10 minutes   **Cooking Time:** 15 minutes   **Servings:** 2

Ingredients:
- 450 grams organic ground turkey
- 6 organic eggs
- 120 grams Keto-friendly salsa

Directions:
1. Grease the pan, then add the turkey and simmer.
2. Fold in the salsa and simmer for two to three minutes.
3. Put the eggs to the top of the turkey base.
4. Cook for seven minutes. Serve.

Nutrition:
Calories: 280   **Fat:** 17g   **Carbohydrates:** 5g   **Protein:** 25g

15. Brunch BLT Wrap

 Preparation Time: 5 minutes   **Cooking Time:** 15 minutes   **Servings:** 1

Ingredients:
- 4 bacon slices
- 2 Romaine lettuce leaves
- 68 grams tomatoes
- 2 teaspoons Mayo
- Pepper

Directions:
1. Cook the bacon until crispy in a pan.
2. Spread mayonnaise on one side of the lettuce.
3. Add the bacon and tomato.
4. Roll up the lettuce and serve.

Nutrition:
Calories: 409 calories   Fat: 25g   **Carbohydrates:** 31g   **Protein**: 15g

16. Cheesy Bacon & Egg Cups

 Preparation Time: 10 minutes   **Cooking Time:** 20 minutes   **Servings:** 6

Ingredients:
- 6 bacon slices
- 6 large eggs
- 200 grams cheese
- 1 spinach
- Pepper

Directions:
1. Pre heat the oven to 200°C, fan 180°C, gas 6.
2. Cook the bacon on a medium heat. Grease the muffin tins. Put a slice of bacon in each muffin cup.
3. Mix the eggs and combine with the spinach. Add the batter to tins and sprinkle with cheese. Add salt and pepper.
4. Bake for 15 minutes. Serve.

 Nutrition: **Calories:** 156 **Fat:** 11g **Carbohydrates:** 0,6g **Protein:** 11g

17. Coconut Keto Porridge

 Preparation Time: 15 minutes   **Cooking Time:** 10 minutes   **Servings:** 1

Ingredients:
- 1 egg, beaten
- 1 tablespoon coconut flour
- ¼ teaspoon ground psyllium husk powder
- ¼ teaspoon salt
- 28 grams butter
- 4 tablespoons coconut cream

Directions:
1. In a small bowl, combine the egg, coconut flour, psyllium husk powder and salt.
2. Over a low heat, melt the butter and coconut cream. Slowly whisk in the egg mixture, combining until you achieve a creamy, thick texture.
3. Serve with coconut milk or cream. Top your porridge with a few fresh or frozen berries and enjoy!

 Nutrition: **Calories:** 301 **Fat:** 17g **Carbohydrates:** 31g **Protein:** 6g

18. Cream Cheese Eggs

 Preparation Time: 5 minutes   **Cooking Time:** 5 minutes   **Servings:** 1

Ingredients:
- 1 tablespoon butter
- 2 eggs
- 2 tablespoons soft cream cheese with chives

Directions:
1. Warm-up a pan and melt the butter.
2. Whisk the eggs with the cream cheese.
3. Cook until done to your liking. Serve.

 Nutrition: **Calories:** 184 **Fat:** 13g **Carbohydrates:** 1,6g **Protein:** 13g

19. Creamy Basil Baked Sausage

Preparation Time: 5 minutes **Cooking Time:** 5 minutes **Servings:** 12

Ingredients:
- 1,5 kg Italian sausage
- 220 grams cream cheese
- 50 ml. double cream
- 100 grams Basil pesto
- 100 grams Mozzarella

Directions:
1. Set the oven at 200°C, fan 180°C, gas 6.
2. Put the sausage in the dish and bake for 30 minutes.
3. Combine the double cream, pesto, and cream cheese. Pour the sauce over the casserole and top it off with the cheese.
4. Bake for 10 minutes. Serve.

 Nutrition: **Calories:** 160 **Fat:** 12g **Carbohydrates:** 2g **Protein:** 12g

20. Almond Coconut Egg Wraps

 Preparation Time: 5 minutes   **Cooking Time:** 5 minutes **Servings:** 4

Ingredients:
- 5 organic eggs
- 1 tablespoon coconut flour
- Sea salt
- 2 tablespoons almond meal

Directions:
1. In a blender pulse the ingredients together.
2. Warm-up a pan on a medium-high heat.
3. Cook the mixture for 6 minutes, 3 minutes per side.
4. Serve.

 Nutrition: **Calories:** 120 **Fat:** 8g **Carbohydrates:** 3g **Protein:** 8g

21. Banana Waffles

 Preparation Time: 30 minutes   **Cooking Time:** 30 minutes **Servings:** 4

Ingredients:
- 4 eggs
- 1 banana
- 100 ml. coconut milk
- 100 grams almond flour
- Salt
- 1 tablespoon psyllium husk powder
- ½ teaspoon vanilla extract
- 1 teaspoon baking powder
- 1 teaspoon ground cinnamon
- Butter

Directions:
1. Mix all of the ingredients together and let sit for a while.

2. Make in a waffle maker or fry in a frying pan with coconut oil or butter.
3. Serve with hazelnut spread or whipped coconut cream and some fresh berries, or just have them as is with melted butter. You can't go wrong!

 Nutrition:
Calories: 197   **Fat:** 3g   **Carbohydrates:** 37g   **Protein:** 7g

22. Keto Coffee

Preparation Time: 5 minutes	**Cooking Time:** 5 minutes	**Servings:** 1

Ingredients:

- 2 tablespoons ground coffee
- 45 grams double cream, whipped
- 1 teaspoon ground cinnamon
- 470 ml. of water

Directions:

1. Start by mixing the cinnamon with the ground coffee.
2. Pour in hot water and whip the cream.
3. Serve with cinnamon.

 Nutrition:
Calories: 155   **Fat:** 14g   **Carbohydrates:** 1g   **Protein:** 1g

23. Keto Waffles with Blueberries

Preparation Time: 15 minutes	**Cooking Time:** 10 to 15 minutes	**Servings:** 8

Ingredients:

- 8 eggs
- 140 grams melted butter
- 1 teaspoon vanilla extract
- 2 teaspoons baking powder
- 43 grams coconut flour
- Topping:
- 40 grams butter
- 30 grams blueberries

Directions:

1. Mix the butter and eggs, put in the remaining ingredients except those for the topping.
2. On a medium-high heat make the waffles. Leave them aside and add blueberries and butter on top.

 Nutrition:
Calories: 188   **Fat:** 14g   **Carbohydrates:** 4g   **Protein:** 10g

24. Tomato Eggs

Preparation Time: 30 minutes	**Cooking Time:** 60 minutes	**Servings:** 4

Ingredients:

- 900g ripe vine tomatoes
- 3 garlic cloves
- 3 tbsp olive oil
- 4 large free range eggs
- 2 tbsp chopped parsley and/or chives

Directions:

1. Preheat the oven to fan 180C/ conventional 200C/gas 6. Cut the tomatoes into quarters or thick wedges, depending on their size, then spread them over a fairly shallow 1.5 litre ovenproof dish. Peel the garlic, slice thinly and sprinkle over the tomatoes. Drizzle with the olive oil, season well with salt and pepper and stir everything together until the tomatoes are glistening.
2. Slide the dish into the oven and bake for 40 minutes until the tomatoes have softened and are tinged with brown.
3. Make four gaps among the tomatoes, break an egg into each gap and cover the dish with a sheet of foil. Return it to the oven for 5-10 minutes until the eggs are set to your liking. Scatter over the herbs and serve piping hot with thick slices of toast or warm ciabatta and a green salad on the side.

 Nutrition:
Calories: 204   **Carbohydrates:** 7g   **Fat:** 16g   **Protein:** 13g

25. Mushroom Omelette

Preparation Time: 15 minutes	**Cooking Time:** 5 minutes	**Servings:** 1

Ingredients:

- 3 eggs
- 30 grams cheese
- 30 grams butter
- ¼ onion, chopped
- 4 large mushrooms
- Vegetables by choice
- Salt
- Pepper

Directions:

1. Beat the eggs, put in some salt and pepper.
2. Cook the mushroom and onion. Put the egg mixture into the pan and cook on a medium heat.
3. Put the cheese on top of the still-raw portion of the egg.
4. Pry the edges of the omelet and fold it in half. Serve.

 Nutrition:
Calories: 484   **Fat:** 23g   **Carbohydrates:** 5g   **Protein:** 20g

26. Chocolate Sea Salt Smoothie

Preparation Time: 15 minutes	**Cooking Time:** 5 minutes	**Servings:** 2

Ingredients:

- 1 avocado
- 470 ml. almond milk
- 1 tablespoon tahini
- 30 grams cocoa powder
- 1 scoop Keto chocolate base

Directions:

1. Combine all the ingredients in a high-speed blender.
2. Add ice and serve!

 Nutrition:
Calories: 386   **Fat:** 4g   **Carbohydrates:** 53g   **Protein:** 15g

27. Courgette Lasagna

Preparation Time: 20 minutes	Cooking Time: 1 hour 20 minutes	Servings: 9

Ingredients:

- 4 large courgettes
- 1 kg. minced beef
- 500 ml. pasta sauce
- 220 grams ricotta cheese
- 130 grams shredded parmesan regianno
- 220 grams mozzarella
- 1 egg
- salt and pepper
- small handful fresh parsley and basil, chopped

Directions:

1. Preheat the oven to 200°C, fan 180°C, gas 6.
2. Slice the courgette lengthwise into thin slices, as thin or thick as you'd like. Set aside.
3. Add the minced beef to a large pan over a medium high heat. Finely break down the minced beef with a spatula and pan fry it until browned and no longer pink.
4. Pour the pasta sauce on top of the minced beef (leave 60 grams aside) and stir together, then remove from heat.
5. In a medium bowl, make the ricotta mix by stirring together the ricotta cheese, parmesan, egg, salt and pepper.
6. Spread half of the pasta sauce onto the bottom of your 9x13-inch casserole dish.
7. Add your courgette slices on top of the pasta sauce. They can overlap or you can place them side-by-side.
8. Top the courgette with half of the pasta sauce, and evenly spread half of the ricotta mix on top of that.
9. Add half of grated mozzarella on top of the ricotta, along with a sprinkle of chopped parsley and basil.
10. Repeat these layers one more time.
11. Top the lasagna with a final layer of courgette slices, a sprinkle of chopped parsley and basil, half of the mozzarella cheese.
12. Place the lasagna in the oven and cook for 40-45 minutes. Grill for a couple of minutes to get a nice golden top.
13. Garnish with whole basil leaves and serve.

Nutrition:
Calories: 275   **Fat:** 12g   **Carbohydrates:** 17g   **Protein:** 26g

28. Vegan Keto Scramble

Preparation Time: 15 minutes	Cooking Time: 10 to 15 minutes	Servings: 1

Ingredients:

- 400 grams firm tofu
- Avocado oil
- 1 onion, chopped
- 1/5 tablespoon nutritional yeast
- ½ teaspoon turmeric
- ½ teaspoon garlic powder
- 130 grams baby spinach
- 3 grape tomatoes
- 85 grams vegan cheddar cheese
- Salt

Directions:

1. Sauté the chopped onion until it caramelizes.
2. Crumble the tofu on the pan. Grease avocado oil onto the mixture with the dry seasonings. Stir.
3. Fold the baby spinach, cheese, and chopped tomato. Cook for a few more minutes. Serve.

Nutrition:
Calories: 108   **Fat:** 4g   **Carbohydrates:** 2g   **Protein:** 10g

29. Bavarian Cream with Vanilla and Hazelnuts

Preparation Time: 15 minutes	Cooking Time: 0 minutes	Servings: 3

Ingredients:

- 54 grams mascarpone
- 7 grams Soy lecithin
- 2 grams Hazelnuts
- 8 grams Fruit mousse
- vanillin

Directions:

1. Prepare the mousse by mixing the mascarpone at room temperature sweetened with one or 2 drops of liquid saccharin and flavored with a pinch of vanillin. Add the lecithin, blending the mixture well.
2. Put the Bavarian cream in a dessert bowl and decorate with the fruit puree and chopped hazelnuts.
3. Chill and serve.

Nutrition:
Calories: 318   **Fat:** 25g   **Carbohydrates:** 17g   **Protein:** 6g

30. Vanilla Mousse

Preparation Time: 15 minutes	Cooking Time: 0 minutes	Servings: 5

Ingredients:

- 30 grams Mascarpone
- 70 grams Cream
- 4 grams Butter
- 3 grams Rusk rich in fiber
- 40 grams Cheese
- vanillin

Directions:

1. Prepare the mousse with mascarpone and butter.
2. Sweeten with liquid saccharin and sprinkle with a little decaffeinated coffee granules.
3. Serve the cheese separately with the buttered rusk and the hot drink prepared with cream and barley coffee sweetened with saccharin.

Nutrition:
Calories: 215   **Fat:** 17g   **Carbohydrates:** 17g   **Protein:** 1g

31. Blueberry Bavarian Cream

 **Preparation Time:** 15 minutes	**Cooking Time:** 0 minutes	**Servings:** 3

Ingredients:

- 40 grams Mascarpone
- 5 grams Soy lecithin
- 10 grams Hazelnuts
- 10 grams Blueberries

Directions:

1. Prepare the mousse by mixing the mascarpone at room temperature sweetened with one or 2 drops of liquid saccharin and flavored with a pinch of vanillin.
2. Add the lecithin, blending the mixture well.
3. Put the Bavarian cream in a dessert bowl and decorate it with chopped blueberries and hazelnuts. Chill and serve.

 Nutrition:
Calories: 180 **Fat:** 1g **Carbohydrates:** 40g **Protein:** 4g

32. Strawberry Bavarian

Preparation Time: 15 minutes	**Cooking Time:** 0 minutes	**Servings:** 5

Ingredients:

- 260 grams fresh strawberries
- 30 grams powdered sugar
- 2 eggs
- 60 g granulated sugar
- 200 ml. whole milk
- 13 grams gelatin
- 200 ml. whipping cream

Directions:

1. Separate egg yolks from whites. Combine the yolks with the granulated sugar and beat for a couple of minutes with an electric mixer. Stir in the milk and set on a medium heat. Stir the mixture until it reaches boiling temperature, it will thicken slightly. Remove from the heat when done.
2. Soak the gelatin and prepare it according to package instructions. Stir gelatin into egg custard. Let cool to room temperature making sure not to leave it too long or the gelatin will harden this mixture before the other ingredients are added.
3. Clean and cut the strawberries, combine with powdered sugar. Blend until smooth. Stir into custard mixture when it has reached room temperature.
4. Whip the cream to soft peaks and fold into Bavarian cream mixture. Divide strawberry Bavarian cream into 4 molds and refrigerate for a minimum of 2 hours before serving.

 Nutrition:
Calories: 153 **Fat:** 6g **Carbohydrates:** 24g **Protein:** 2g

33. Almond Mousse

Preparation Time: 15 minutes	**Cooking Time:** 0 minutes	**Servings:** 2

Ingredients:

- 3 sheets gelatin vanilla bean
- 2 eggs
- 250 milliliters
- 100 grams ground almonds
- 2 tablespoons almond liqueur
- 80 grams sugar
- 80 milliliters double cream
- 4 tablespoons almonds

Directions:

1. Soak gelatine in plenty of cold water. Slit vanilla pod lengthwise and scrape out seeds. Separate eggs.
2. Slowly heat milk in a pot. Add ground almonds and vanilla seeds, bring to a boil and set aside.
3. Whisk egg yolks with almond liqueur and 30 grams (approximately 1 ounce) of sugar over hot water bath until foamy.
4. Gradually add milk to egg yolk mixture, whisking constantly, until mixture thickens. Add gelatine and dissolve, stirring.
5. Cool cream, whisking, in ice water bath. Add 60 ml. of cream. Beat egg whites until stiff and fold into mixture. Pour cream into 6 glasses and refrigerate for 2 hours.
6. Add remaining cream and remaining sugar into pan and caramelize slightly. Add whole almonds and coat with caramel, stirring. Place on waxed paper and cool.
7. Place caramelized almonds on top of mousse and serve.

 Nutrition:
Calories: 251 **Fat:** 19g **Carbohydrates:** 12g **Protein:** 6g

34. Nougat

Preparation Time: 15 minutes	**Cooking Time:** 0 minutes	**Servings:** 4

Ingredients:

- 100 grams whole blanched almonds
- 100 grams peeled pistachios
- 100g peeled hazelnuts
- 2 sheets edible rice paper
- icing sugar for dusting
- 150 grams clear honey
- 300 grams white caster sugar
- 100 grams liquid glucose
- 2 medium egg whites

Directions:

1. Heat oven to 180°C, fan 160°C, gas 4. Scatter the nuts over a baking tray and toast in the oven for 10 mins, then set aside (they don't need to cool). Cut the two pieces of rice paper to fit a 20 x 20cm square tin. Line the tin with one sheet of rice paper, brush the sides of the tin with oil, then dust the tin with icing sugar.
2. Put the honey into a saucepan, then in another saucepan tip in the sugar, glucose and 100ml of water. Put the egg whites in the very clean bowl of a tabletop mixer with a whisk attachment and whisk on a low speed. Heat and boil the honey until it reaches 121°C on a digital cooking thermometer, then straightaway pour the honey over the egg whites and set the speed to medium. While the whites and honey are whisking, bring the sugar and water to the boil and keep boiling until the syrup reaches 145°C exactly on a digital cooking thermometer. Pour the hot syrup

in a slow, steady stream into the beating egg white mixture. Continue beating for about 10 minutes until you have a thick, glossy, firm meringue. It's hard to over-whisk at this stage but easy to under-whisk, so keep going until the meringue looks like sticky chewing gum.

3. Use a spatula to stir though the nuts (which should still be warm), the vanilla extract and a small pinch of salt. Scrape the mixture into the lined tin, then smooth over to spread the mixture out evenly (if you have an offset spatula, now is the time to use it). Finally, top with the remaining sheet of rice paper and press down. Leave the nougat to set for at least 2 hours or overnight.

4. To turn out and portion, use a spatula to loosen the edges of the nougat away from the tin, then invert the tin on to a clean board and use a sharp serated, hot knife to portion into bars or squares. The nougat will keep, stored in an airtight container, for up to a month.

 Nutrition:
Calories: 55 (per serving)   **Carbohydrates:** 12g
Fat: 0g   **Protein:** 0g

35. Chocolate Crepes

 Preparation Time: 15 minutes | **Cooking Time:** 10 minutes | **Servings:** 4

Ingredients:
- 36 grams Whole egg
- 5 grams Dark chocolate
- 34 grams Mascarpone
- 17 grams Butter

Directions:
1. Beat the egg. Cook the crepes in a non-stick pan.
2. Prepare the filling by mixing mascarpone and butter at room temperature, sweetening with one or 2 drops of liquid saccharin.
3. Melt the dark chocolate in a bain-marie and mix it with the mascarpone cream.
4. Stuff the crepes and serve with a cup of decaffeinated tea without sugar.

 Nutrition:
Calories: 150   **Fat:** 8g   **Carbohydrates:** 19g   **Protein:** 2g

36. Rusk with Walnut Cream

 Preparation Time: 15 minutes | **Cooking Time:** 10 minutes | **Servings:** 1

Ingredients:
- 8 rusks
- 5 teaspoon condensed milk
- 60 grams sugar
- 1 liter milk
- 4 drops vanilla essence

Directions:
1. Take a saucepan and add the milk. Heat it over a high flame. Once the milk starts to boil, add sugar and mix well.
2. Boil till it reduces to 3/4th and pour 1/4 of the boiled milk over 2 rusks and blend together in a mixer for 5 minutes. Add

condensed milk and vanilla essence. Blend again for 2 more minutes.
3. Add this to the remaining milk and transfer to freezer safe ice cream bowls. Put it in the freezer for 1 hour or until set. Place one scoop on each rusk, garnish with mint leaves and serve.

 Nutrition:
Calories: 97   **Fat:** 4g   **Carbohydrates:** 12g   **Protein:** 1g

37. Bavarian Coffee with Hazelnuts

 Preparation Time: 15 minutes | **Cooking Time:** 10 minutes | **Servings:** 1

Ingredients:
- 67 grams Mascarpone
- 11 grams Hazelnuts
- Coffee
- Saccharin

Directions:
1. Prepare the hot drink by heating the water.
2. Weigh the hazelnuts and pass them to the mixer then add them by mixing with the mascarpone held for a few moments at room temperature.
3. Add the remaining part of soluble decaffeinated coffee.
4. Sweeten with saccharin.

 Nutrition:
Calories: 20   **Fat:** 1g   **Carbohydrates:** 3g   **Protein:** 0g

38. Bavarian Strawberry Butter

 Preparation Time: 15 minutes | **Cooking Time:** 0 minutes | **Servings:** 1

Ingredients:
- 50 grams Fresh cream
- 30 grams Butter
- 15 grams Hazelnuts
- 13 grams Strawberries
- Fish glue
- Saccharin
- Vanilla flavour
- 37 grams Cheese

Directions:
1. Soak a piece of gelatin in hot water.
2. Put it in the Bavarian container and add the exact amount of cream. Add the butter, softened to room temperature.
3. Sweeten with liquid saccharin and add the vanilla flavor.
4. Chill and serve with strawberries, a small leaf of mint, and the coarsely chopped hazelnuts. Serve the cheese separately with a cup of jasmine tea sweetened with saccharin.

 Nutrition:
Calories: 100   **Fat:** 7g   **Carbohydrates:** 5g   **Protein:** 1g

39. Cheese Platters

 **Preparation Time:**
15 minutes

 Cooking Time:
0 minutes

 Servings:
1

Ingredients:

- 45 grams Ricotta cheese
- 35 grams Cheese
- 22 grams Hazelnuts
- 30 grams Mascarpone cheese
- 26 grams Butter
- Saccharin and orange flavor

Directions:

1. Weigh the cheeses' exact quantity and serve them on a small wooden cutting board with hazelnuts in the center.
2. Prepare the mascarpone pastry by weighing the precise amount of mascarpone and softened butter at room temperature. Is more detailed required for this part?

 Nutrition:
Calories: 220   **Carbohydrates:** 6g   **Fat:** 4g   **Protein:** 12g

40. Hazelnut Bavarian with Hot Coffee Drink

 Preparation Time:
15 minutes

 Cooking Time:
0 minutes

 Servings:
1

Ingredients:

- 85 grams Mascarpone cheese
- 21grams Hazelnuts
- 3 grams Butter
- 15 grams Wild strawberries
- 150 ml. water
- Coffee
- Saccharin

Directions:

1. Prepare the drink by heating 150 ml of water.
2. Add a teaspoon of decaffeinated coffee and saccharin.
3. Prepare the Bavarian by mixing mascarpone, butter, and hazelnuts passed in the mixer at room temperature, sweetening.
4. Garnish with wild strawberries and chill. Serve.

 Nutrition:
Calories: 263   **Carbohydrates:** 10g   **Fat:** 5g   **Protein:** 4g

41. Muffins and Coffee

 Preparation Time:
5 minutes

 Cooking Time:
0 minutes

 Servings:
1

Ingredients:

- 50 grams Sugar-free muffins
- 12 grams Butter
- 47 grams White flour
- 45 grams Cream with 35% fat
- Coffee

Directions:

1. Prepare the hot coffee drink by mixing the white flour, cream, and American coffee in a mug. Sweeten to taste.
2. Butter the sugar-free muffin.
3. Serve.

 Nutrition:
Calories: 284   **Fat:** 24g   **Carbohydrates:** 4g   **Protein:** 9g

42. French Toast with Coffee Drink

 Preparation Time:
15 minutes

Cooking Time:
10 minutes

 Servings:
1

Ingredients:

- 24 grams cream with 35% fat
- 14 grams egg
- 15 grams sweet cheese
- 12 grams low carb bread without crust
- 11 grams butter
- For the hot drink:
- 10 grams White flour
- 80 grams Cream with 35% fat
- Saccharin

Directions:

1. In a small bowl, scramble the egg, cream, finely grated cheese in the mixer.
2. Toast the bread in butter, turn it several times and pour the mixture over it.
3. Garnish with chopped fresh parsley.
4. Prepare the hot drink by shaking the white flour with the cream.
5. Add the soluble decaffeinated coffee and saccharin.

 Nutrition:
Calories: 229   **Carbohydrates:** 12g   **Fat:** 5g   **Protein:** 1g

43. Cheese Crepes

 Preparation Time:
15 minutes

 Cooking Time:
20 minutes

 Servings:
5

Ingredients:

- 170 grams cream cheese
- 43 grams Parmesan cheese
- 6 large organic eggs
- 1 teaspoon granulated erythritol
- 1 ½ tablespoon coconut flour
- 1/8 teaspoon xanthan gum
- 2 tablespoons unsalted butter

Directions:

1. Pulse the cream cheese, Parmesan cheese, eggs, and erythritol using a blender.
2. Place the coconut flour and xanthan gum and pulse again.
3. Now, pulse at medium speed. Transfer and put aside for 5 minutes.
4. Melt butter over a medium-low heat.
5. Place 1 portion of the mixture and tilt the pan to spread into a thin layer.
6. Cook for 160 grams minutes.
7. Flip the crepe and cook for 15-20 seconds more. Serve.

 Nutrition:
Calories: 297   Fat: 25g   **Carbohydrates:** 3.5g   Protein: 13.7g

44. Ricotta Pancakes

Preparation Time: 10 minutes	**Cooking Time:** 20 minutes	**Servings:** 4

Ingredients:

- 4 organic eggs
- 65 grams ricotta cheese
- 65 grams vanilla whey protein powder
- ½ teaspoon organic baking powder
- Salt
- ½ teaspoon liquid stevia
- 2 tablespoons unsalted butter

Directions:

1. Whisk all the ingredients in the blender.
2. Melt butter over a medium heat.
3. Put the batter in a pan and spread it evenly. Cook for 2 minutes.
4. Flip and cook again for 1–2 minutes. Serve.

 Nutrition:
Calories: 195 **Fat:** 11g **Carbohydrates:** 20g **Protein:** 13g

45. Yogurt Waffles

Preparation Time: 15 minutes	**Cooking Time:** 25 minutes	**Servings:** 5

Ingredients:

- 65 grams golden flax seeds meal
- 65 grams almond flour
- 1 ½ tablespoons granulated erythritol
- 1 teaspoon vanilla whey protein powder
- ¼ teaspoon baking soda
- ½ teaspoon organic baking powder
- ¼ teaspoon xanthan gum
- Salt
- 1 organic egg
- 1 ½ teaspoons unsalted butter
- 2 tablespoons unsweetened almond milk
- 85 grams plain Greek yogurt

Directions:

1. Preheat the waffle iron and then grease it.
2. Mix the flour, erythritol, protein powder, baking soda, baking powder, xanthan gum, and salt.
3. Beat the egg white until it has stiff peaks. In a third bowl, add 2 egg yolks, whole egg, almond milk, butter, yogurt, and beat.
4. Put egg mixture into the bowl with the flour mixture and mix.
5. Gently, fold in the beaten egg whites. Place 30 grams of the mixture into preheated waffle iron and cook for about 4–5 minutes. Serve.

 Nutrition:
Calories: 236 **Fat:** 18g **Carbohydrates:** 14g **Protein:** 9g

46. Broccoli Muffins

Preparation Time: 15 minutes	**Cooking Time:** 20 minutes	**Servings:** 6

Ingredients:

- 2 tablespoons unsalted butter
- 6 large organic eggs
- 60 grams double cream
- 60 grams Parmesan cheese
- Salt
- Pepper
- 160 grams broccoli
- 2 tablespoons parsley
- 60 grams Swiss cheese

Directions:

1. Warm up the oven to 190°C, fan 160°C, gas 4, then grease a 12-cup muffin tin.
2. Mix together the eggs, cream, Parmesan cheese, salt, and black pepper.
3. Divide the broccoli and parsley into the muffin cup.
4. Top with the egg mixture, and then Swiss cheese.
5. Bake for 20 minutes. Cool for about 5 minutes. Serve.

 Nutrition:
Calories: 230 **Fat:** 14g **Carbohydrates:** 5g **Protein:** 14g

47. Pumpkin Bread

Preparation Time: 15 minutes	**Cooking Time:** 1 hour	**Servings:** 16

Ingredients:

- 210 grams almond flour
- 1 ½ teaspoons organic baking powder
- 60 grams pumpkin pie spice
- ½ teaspoon pumpkin pie spice
- ½ teaspoon cinnamon
- ½ teaspoon cloves
- ½ teaspoon salt
- 230 grams cream cheese
- 6 organic eggs
- 1 teaspoon coconut flour
- 130 grams powdered erythritol
- 1 teaspoon stevia powder
- 1 teaspoon organic lemon extract
- 130 grams pumpkin puree
- 60 ml. coconut oil

Directions:

1. Preheat the oven to 190°C, fan 170°C, gas 5.
2. Grease 2 bread loaf tins.
3. Mix almond flour, baking powder, spices, and salt in a small bowl.
4. In a second bowl, add the cream cheese, 1 egg, coconut flour, 30 grams of erythritol, and 1.21 teaspoon of the stevia, and beat.
5. In a third bowl, add the pumpkin puree, oil, 5 eggs, erythritol, and a spoon of the stevia and mix.
6. Mix the pumpkin mixture into the bowl of the flour mixture.
7. Place about 60 grams of the pumpkin mixture into each loaf pan.
8. Top each pan with the cream cheese mixture, plus the rest pumpkin mixture.
9. Bake for 50–60 minutes. Cold for 10 minutes. Slice and serve.

Nutrition:
Calories: 179 **Fat:** 4g **Carbohydrates:** 33g **Protein:** 3g

48. Eggs in Avocado Cups

 Preparation Time: 10 minutes | **Cooking Time:** 20 minutes | **Servings:** 4

Ingredients:

- 2 avocados
- 4 organic eggs
- Salt
- Ground black pepper
- 4 tablespoons cheddar cheese
- 2 slices of cooked bacon
- 1 tablespoon spring onions

Directions:

1. Preheat the oven to 200°C, fan 180°C, gas 6. Remove the flesh from the avocado.
2. Place avocado halves into a small baking dish.
3. Crack an egg in each avocado half and sprinkle with salt plus black pepper.
4. Top each egg with cheddar cheese evenly.
5. Bake for 20 minutes. Serve with bacon and spring onions.

Nutrition:
Calories: 343 **Fat:** 30g **Carbohydrates:** 20g **Protein:** 12g

49. Cheddar Scramble

 Preparation Time: 10 minutes | **Cooking Time:** 8 minutes | **Servings:** 6

Ingredients:

- 2 eggs
- 80 grams cheddar cheese, grated (or Monterey Jack)
- ½ teaspoon olive oil (or butter)
- salt and pepper to taste
- 1 slice wholegrain bread (toasted)

Directions:

1. Put a frying pan onto a medium heat and put in the butter or oil.
2. Break the eggs into a bowl and beat with a fork.
3. Grate the cheese and set aside.
4. Tip the beaten eggs into the frying pan.
5. Layer the cheese on top.
6. The eggs will start to solidify almost straight away – as soon as they do use a spatula and 'pull' the eggs in from the side to the middle.
7. Repeat the pulling in several times.
8. It doesn't take long, the idea behind this is you'll have soft, lightly cooked fresh eggs. It's hard to undercook an egg really, but very easy to overcook. 2 – 3 minutes cooking time is all you'll need.
9. When the egg has no 'watery' bits left, you're done! Quickly remove from heat and transfer to plate – preferably on top of some lovely, hot, unbuttered bread.

10. Add some salt and pepper to taste. Done!

Nutrition:
Calories: 250 **Fat:** 22g **Carbohydrates:** 20g **Protein:** 18g

50. Keto Pizza Wraps

 Preparation Time: 10 minutes | **Cooking Time:** 15 minutes | **Servings:** 2

Ingredients:

- 2 large eggs
- ½ tablespoon butter
- ½ tablespoon tomato sauce
- 14 grams mozzarella cheese, shredded
- 45 grams salami, sliced

Directions:

1. Heat a large, non-stick frying pan to a medium heat. Add the butter.
2. Crack the eggs into a bowl, and whisk until smooth in color.
3. Slowly pour the eggs into the pan, allowing the mixture to go right to the edges.
4. Cook until the edges begin to lift off the side of the frying pan. Using a spatula all around the edge, lift the egg from the pan.
5. Flip and cook on the other side for 30 seconds.
6. Remove from the pan. Layer tomato sauce, mozzarella cheese, and salami in the middle. Roll it together into a wrap.

Nutrition:
Calories: 348 **Fat:** 18g **Carbohydrates:** 22g **Protein:** 6g

51. Green Veggies Quiche

 Preparation Time: 20 minutes | **Cooking Time:** 20 minutes | **Servings:** 4

Ingredients:

- 6 organic eggs
- 60 ml. unsweetened almond milk
- Salt
- Pepper
- 250 grams baby spinach
- 60 grams green pepper
- 1 spring onion
- 30 grams coriander
- 1 tablespoon chives
- 3 tablespoons mozzarella cheese

Directions:

7. Preheat the oven to 200°C, fan 180°C, gas 6.
8. Grease a pie dish. Beat eggs, almond milk, salt, and black pepper. Set aside.
9. In another bowl, add the vegetables and herbs then mix.
10. Place the veggie mixture and top with the egg mixture in the pie dish.
11. Bake for 20 minutes. Remove then sprinkle with the Parmesan cheese.
12. Slice and serve.

Nutrition:
Calories: 176 **Fat:** 12g **Carbohydrates:** 24g **Protein:** 9g

52. Chicken & Asparagus Frittata

 Preparation Time:
15 minutes

 Cooking Time:
12 minutes

 Servings:
4

Ingredients:

- 60 grams grass-fed chicken breast
- 40 grams Parmesan cheese
- 6 organic eggs
- Salt
- Ground black pepper
- 40 grams boiled asparagus
- 30 grams cherry tomatoes
- 30 grams mozzarella cheese

Directions:

1. Warm up the grill of the oven, then mix Parmesan cheese, eggs, salt, and black pepper in a bowl.
2. Melt butter, then cook the chicken and asparagus for 2–3 minutes.
3. Add the egg mixture and tomatoes and mix. Cook for 4–5 minutes.
4. Remove then sprinkle with the Parmesan cheese.
5. Place the wok under the grill and grill for 3–4 minutes. Slice and serve.

Nutrition:
Calories: 158 **Fat:** 9g **Carbohydrates:** 22g **Protein:** 10g

53. Southwest Scrambled Egg Bites

 Preparation Time:
10 minutes

 Cooking Time:
23 minutes

 Servings:
4

Ingredients:

- 5 eggs
- 1/2 teaspoon hot pepper sauce
- 43 grams tomatoes
- 3 tablespoons green chilies
- 1 teaspoon black pepper
- Salt
- 2 tablespoons non-dairy milk

Directions:

1. Mix both the eggs and milk in a large cup.
2. Add the hot sauce, pepper, and salt.
3. Add small, chopped chilies and chopped tomatoes.
4. Fill each of the muffin cups 3/4 full with the egg mixture.
5. Put the trivet in the pot and pour in 120 ml. of water.
6. Put the muffin tray on the trivet. Set on high for 8 minutes. Let it cool before serving.

Nutrition:
Calories: 124 **Fat:** 7g **Carbohydrates:** 2g **Protein:** 6g

54. Bacon Egg Bites

 Preparation Time:
10 minutes

 Cooking Time:
22 minutes

 Servings:
9

Ingredients:

- 130 grams cheese
- 1/2 green pepper
- 60 grams cottage cheese
- 4 slices bacon
- Pepper
- Salt
- 130 grams red onion
- 130 ml. water
- 30 grams whipping cream
- 30 grams egg whites
- 4 eggs

Directions:

1. Blend egg whites, eggs, cream, cheese (cottage), shredded cheese, pepper, and salt for 30 to 45 seconds in a blender. Put the egg mixture into mini muffin cups.
2. Top each with bacon, peppers, and onion.
3. Cover the muffin tray tightly with foil.
4. Place the trivet in the pot and pour in 120 ml. of water.
5. Put the tray on the trivet. Set to steam for 12 minutes. Cooldown before serving.

Nutrition:
Calories: 155 **Fat:** 8g **Carbohydrates:** 16g **Protein:** 9g

55. Cheese and Egg Bites

 **Preparation Time:**
5 minutes

 Cooking Time:
8 minutes

 Servings:
3

Ingredients:

- 1 handful of mushrooms
- 1 onion
- 3 green peppers
- 1/8 teaspoon hot sauce
- Pepper, salt, mustard, garlic powder
- 60 grams cheese cheddar
- 60 grams cheese cottage
- 2 deli ham slices
- 4 eggs

Directions:

1. Whisk eggs, then add the cheddar and cottage cheese.
2. Add the ham, veggies, and seasonings, mix.
3. Pour the mixture into greased silicone molds. Put the trivet with before the molds in the pot then fill with 250 ml. of water.
4. Steam for about 8 minutes. Transfer, cool down before serving.

Nutrition:
Calories: 177 **Fat:** 4g **Carbohydrates:** 14g **Protein:** 7g

56. Cheddar & Bacon Egg Bites

 Preparation Time:
10 minutes

 Cooking Time:
8 minutes

 Servings:
7

Ingredients:

- 120 grams mature cheddar cheese
- 1 teaspoon parsley flakes
- 4 eggs
- 4 tablespoons cream
- Hot sauce
- 120 ml. water
- 60 grams cheese

- 4 slices bacon

Directions:

1. Blend the cream, cheddar, and eggs in the blender; for 30 seconds.
2. Stir in the parsley. Grease silicone egg bite molds.
3. Divide the crumbled bacon between them. Put the egg batter into each cup. With a piece of foil, cover each mold.
4. Place the trivet with the molds in the pot then fill with 120 ml. of water. Steam for 8 minutes.
5. Remove, let rest for 5 minutes. Serve, sprinkled with black pepper, and optional hot sauce.

 Nutrition:
Calories: 170 **Fat:** 14g **Carbohydrates:** 3g **Protein:** 12g

57. Avocado Pico Egg Bites

Preparation Time: 15 minutes	**Cooking Time:** 10 minutes	**Servings:** 7

Ingredients:

- Egg bites:
- 200 grams cheese cottage
- 60 grams cheese Mexican blend
- 1/4 teaspoon chili powder
- 1/4 teaspoon cumin
- 1/4 teaspoon garlic powder
- 4 eggs
- Pepper
- Salt
- Pico de Gallo:
- 1 avocado
- 1 jalapeno
- Salt
- Half an onion, chopped
- 5 grams coriander
- 2 tablespoons lime juice
- 4 Roma tomatoes

Directions:

1. Mix all of the Pico de Gallo ingredients except for the avocado. Gently fold in the avocado.
2. Blend all the egg bites ingredients in a blender.
3. Take 1 teaspoon of Pico de Gallo into each egg bite silicone mold.
4. Place the trivet in the pot then fill with 120 ml. of water.
5. Put the molds in the trivet. Set to high for 10 minutes.
6. Remove.
7. Serve topped with cheese and Pico de Gallo.

 Nutrition:
Calories: 118 **Fat:** 23g **Carbohydrates:** 13g **Protein:** 10g

58. Salmon Scramble

Preparation Time: 10 minutes	**Cooking Time:** 5 minutes	**Servings:** 1

Ingredients:

- 2 teaspoon vegetable oil
- 8 eggs
- 115 grams crumbled smoked salmon

- 2 tablespoons cream cheese, softened
- 75 grams chopped spring onions, divided

Directions:

1. Heat the oil in a large frying pan over a medium heat. Combine the eggs and salmon and mix lightly with a fork. Cook until just beginning to scramble.
2. Add the cream cheese and mix until everything is a smooth texture. Add 1/2 the spring onions and stir into the scrambled eggs. Cook long enough to heat through.
3. Serve the salmon scrambled eggs on a plate and garnish with the remaining spring onions.

 Nutrition:
Calories: 352 **Fat:** 14g **Carbohydrates:** 12g **Protein:** 8g

59. Mexican Scrambled Eggs

Preparation Time: 5 minutes	**Cooking Time:** 10 minutes	**Servings:** 6

Ingredients:

- 6 eggs
- 2 jalapeños
- 1 tomato
- 90 grams cheese
- 2 tablespoons butter

Directions:

1. Warm-up butter over a medium heat in a large pan.
2. Add tomatoes, jalapeños, and green onions then cook for 3 minutes.
3. Add eggs and continue for 2 minutes. Add cheese and season to taste. Serve.

 Nutrition:
Calories: 230 **Fat:** 17g **Carbohydrates:** 18g **Protein:** 12g

60. Caprese Omelette

Preparation Time: 10 minutes	**Cooking Time:** 10 minutes	**Servings:** 2

Ingredients:

- 6 eggs
- 2 tablespoons olive oil
- 460 grams cherry tomatoes, halved
- 1 tablespoon dried basil
- 160 grams mozzarella cheese

Directions:

4. Mix the basil, eggs, salt, and black pepper in a bowl.
5. Place a large pan with oil over a medium heat.
6. Once hot, add tomatoes and cook.
7. Top with egg and cook.
8. Add cheese, adjust heat to low, and allow to fully set before serving.

Nutrition:
Calories: 533 **Fat:** 43g **Carbohydrates:** 4g **Protein:** 30g

61. Sausage Omelette

 Preparation Time: 10 minutes | **Cooking Time:** 15 minutes | **Servings:** 2

Ingredients:

- 230 grams gluten-free sausage
- 60 grams double cream
- Salt
- Black pepper
- 8 large organic eggs
- 130 grams cheddar cheese
- ¼ teaspoon red pepper flakes

Directions:

1. Warm-up oven to 190°C, fan 170°C, gas 5. Grease a baking dish. Cook the sausage for 8–10 minutes.
2. Put the rest of the ingredients in a bowl and beat. Remove sausage from the heat. Place cooked sausage in the baking dish then top with the egg mixture. Bake for 30 minutes. Slice and serve.

Nutrition:
Calories: 320 **Fat:** 14g **Carbohydrates:** 20g **Protein:** 14g

62. Brown Hash with Courgette

 Preparation Time: 10 minutes | **Cooking Time:** 20 minutes | **Servings:** 2

Ingredients:

- 1 small onion
- 6 to 8 mushrooms
- 250 grams grass-fed minced beef
- 1 pinch salt
- 1 pinch ground black pepper
- 1 teaspoon smoked paprika
- 2 eggs
- 1 avocado
- 10 black olives

Directions:

1. Warm-up air fryer for 175°C.
2. Grease a pan with coconut oil.
3. Add the onions, mushrooms, salt plus pepper to the pan.
4. Add the minced beef, smoked paprika and eggs. Mix, then place the pan in Air Fryer.
5. Set to cook for 18 to 20 minutes with a temperature, of 190°C.
6. Serve with chopped parsley and chopped avocado!

Nutrition:
Calories: 300 **Fat:** 12g **Carbohydrates:** 20g **Protein:** 11g

63. Crunchy Radish & Courgette Hash Browns

 Preparation Time: 10 minutes | **Cooking Time:** 10 minutes | **Servings:** 6

Ingredients:

- 1 teaspoon onion powder
- 60 grams courgette
- 130 grams cheddar cheese
- 60 grams radishes
- 3 egg whites
- Pepper
- Salt

Directions:

1. Mix the egg whites in a bowl. Stir in the radishes, courgette, seasonings, and cheese.
2. Shape into 6 patties.
3. Pre heat a pan over a medium-high heat.
4. Grease. Cook the patties.
5. Adjust to a medium-low heat and cook for a further 3 to 5 minutes. Serve.

Nutrition:
Calories: 125 **Fat:** 5g **Carbohydrates:** 12g **Protein:** 6g

64. Fennel Quiche

 Preparation Time: 15 minutes | **Cooking Time:** 18 minutes | **Servings:** 4

Ingredients:

- 300 grams fennel
- 120 grams spinach
- 5 eggs
- 60 grams almond flour
- 1 teaspoon olive oil
- 1 teaspoon butter
- 1 teaspoon salt
- 30 grams double cream
- 1 teaspoon ground black pepper

Directions:

1. Combine the chopped spinach and chopped fennel in a big bowl.
2. Whisk the egg in a separate bowl.
3. Combine the whisked eggs with the almond flour, butter, salt, double cream, and ground black pepper.
4. Warm-up air fryer to 190°C.
5. Grease.
6. Then add the spinach-and fennel mixture and pour in the whisked egg mixture.
7. Cook for 18 minutes. Remove then chill. Slice and serve.

Nutrition:
Calories: 249 **Carbohydrates:** 9.4g **Protein:** 11.3g **Fat:** 19.1g

65. Turkey Hash

 Preparation Time: 10 minutes | **Cooking Time:** 25 minutes | **Servings:** 5

Ingredients:

- 380 grams cauliflower florets
- 1 small onion
- Salt
- Ground black pepper
- 30 grams double cream
- 2 tablespoons unsalted butter
- 1 teaspoon dried thyme
- 450 grams cooked turkey meat

Directions:

1. Put the cauliflower in salted boiling water and cook for 4 minutes.
2. Then chop the cauliflower and set it aside.
3. Dissolve the butter over a medium heat in a large pan and sauté onions for 4-5 minutes.
4. Add thyme, salt, and black pepper and sauté again for 1 minute. Stir in cauliflower and cook for 2 minutes. Stir in turkey and cook for 5-6 minutes. Stir in the cream and cook for 2 minutes more. Serve.

 Nutrition:
Calories: 169 **Fat:** 14g **Carbohydrates:** 6g **Protein:** 18g

66. Crustless Veggie Quiche

Preparation Time: 10 minutes	**Cooking Time:** 30 minutes	**Servings:** 6

Ingredients:

- 250 grams Monterey Jack cheese
- 1 red pepper
- 60 ml. coconut milk
- Salt
- Basil
- 120 grams tomatoes
- 1 courgette
- 80 grams mushrooms
- 60 grams arrowroot flour
- Black pepper
- 2 spring onions
- 8 eggs

Directions:

1. Whisk the milk, egg, flour, pepper, and salt in a large bowl.
2. Mix in the veggies and 120 grams of cheese. Pour the mixture into a heatproof container.
3. Cover it with foil. Place the trivet in the pot then fill with 120 ml. of water.
4. Cook on high for 30 minutes. Remove and uncover.
5. Top with the rest of the cheese.
6. Cover then rest for 2 minutes. Serve!

 Nutrition:
Calories: 212 **Fat:** 14g **Carbohydrates:** 7g **Protein:** 12g

67. Crustless Broccoli & Cheddar Quiche

Preparation Time: 10 minutes	**Cooking Time:** 25 minutes	**Servings:** 4

Ingredients:

- 120 grams cheddar cheese
- 60 grams non-dairy milk
- Black pepper
- Kosher salt
- 6 eggs
- 1 broccoli head
- 3 spring onions
- Salt

Directions:

1. Grease the soufflé dish.
2. In a bowl, whisk the milk, eggs, pepper, and salt. Stir in the cheese, broccoli, and spring onions.

3. Pour the mixture into the greased dish.
4. Place the trivet in the pot then fill with 190 ml. of water.
5. Set to a medium-high heat for 25 minutes. Slice and serve.

 Nutrition:
Calories: 296 **Fat:** 20g **Carbohydrates:** 5g **Protein:** 15g

68. Keto Courgette Bread

 **Preparation Time:** 10 minutes	**Cooking Time:** 50 minutes	**Servings:** 4

Ingredients:

- 220 grams almond flour
- ½ teaspoon Kosher salt
- ½ teaspoon Ground Cinnamon
- 60 grams Granular Sweetener
- 1 teaspoon Baking soda
- 2 Large Eggs, Beaten
- 30 grams Melted butter
- 220 grams Grated Courgette with skin

Directions:

1. Preheat oven to 220°C, fan 200°C, gas 7. Grease a 9x5 loaf tin with butter or cooking spray.
2. In a large bowl, combine the almond flour, salt, cinnamon, swerve, and baking soda.
3. Wrap the grated courgette in a kitchen towel and squeeze out as much liquid as you can. Discard liquid and add courgette to the dry ingredients followed by the eggs and melted butter. Stir batter until combined. See notes for instructions on adding walnuts, chocolate chips, or blueberries.
4. Pour batter into greased loaf tin and bake in the oven for 60 minutes or until a toothpick comes out clean. Let cool before serving. Slice into 12 slices. See notes for freezing, making muffins, and for a savory bread.

 Nutrition:
Calories: 267 **Fat:** 23g **Carbohydrates:** 11g **Protein:** 4g

69. Keto Almond Bread Recipe

Preparation Time: 10 minutes	**Cooking Time:** 30 minutes	**Servings:** 6

Ingredients:

- 2 eggs
- 130 grams almond flour
- 1/5 teaspoons baking powder
- 2 tablespoons olive oil
- 1 teaspoon powdered mustard
- Spices
- 1 teaspoon coarse salt
- 1 teaspoon immediate gluten-free yeast

Directions:

1. Pre heat the oven to 190°C, fan 170°C, gas 5.
2. Combine eggs, almond flour, baking powder, mustard powder, salt, and olive oil.

3. Place the mixture on a small, greased baking sheet.
4. Bake for 30 minutes.
5. Slice and serve.

 Nutrition:
Calories: 270 **Fat:** 27g **Carbohydrates:** 3g **Protein:** 6g

70. Quick Keto Toast

Preparation Time: 10 minutes	Cooking Time: 5 minutes	Servings: 4

Ingredients:

- 45 grams almond flour
- 1/2 teaspoon baking powder
- 1/8 teaspoon salt
- 1 egg
- 1 tablespoon ghee

Directions:

1. Pre heat the oven to 200°C, fan 180°C, gas 6.
2. Put all the bread components in a container and mix well.
3. Microwave the mixture for 90 seconds.
4. Cool down and cut it into four slices.
5. Bake in the oven for 4 minutes.
6. Serve with additional ghee.

 Nutrition:
Calories: 270 **Fat:** 27g **Carbohydrates:** 3g **Protein:** 6g

71. Keto Loaf of Bread

Preparation Time: 10 minutes	Cooking Time: 60 minutes	Servings: 6

Ingredients:

- 140 grams Almond Flour
- 60 grams Coconut Flour
- 2 teaspoon baking powder
- 1/4 teaspoon Sea salt
- 5 tablespoons Butter
- 12 large Egg whites
- Erythritol
- xanthan gum

Directions:

1. Preheat the oven to 160 degrees Celsius. Line an 8 1/2 x 4 1/2 in (22×11 cm) loaf tin with parchment paper, with extra hanging over the sides for easy removal later.
2. Combine the almond flour, coconut flour, baking powder, erythritol, xanthan gum, and sea salt in a large food processor. Pulse until combined.
3. Add the melted butter. Pulse, scraping down the sides as needed, until crumbly.
4. In a very large bowl, use a hand mixer to beat the egg whites and cream of tartar (if using), until stiff peaks form. Make sure the bowl is large enough because the whites will expand a lot.
5. Add 1/2 of the stiff egg whites to the food processor. Pulse a few times until just combined. Do not over-mix!
6. Carefully transfer the mixture from the food processor into the bowl with the egg whites, and gently fold until no streaks

remain. Do not stir. Fold gently to keep the mixture as fluffy as possible.
7. Transfer the batter to the lined loaf tin and smooth the top. Push the batter toward the center a bit to round the top.
8. Bake for about 40 minutes, until the top is golden brown. Tent the top with aluminum foil and bake for another 30-45 minutes, until the top is firm and does not make a squishy sound when pressed. Internal temperature should be 200 degrees. Cool completely before removing from the tin and slicing.

 Nutrition:
Calories: 117 **Fat:** 15g **Carbohydrates:** 5g **Protein:** 4g

72. Blueberry Loaf

Preparation Time: 10 minutes	Cooking Time: 70 minutes	Servings: 6

Ingredients:

- 300 grams Almond Flour
- 1 tablespoon Coconut Flour
- Baking powder
- 7 tablespoons Truvia
- Oil
- 4 tablespoons double cream
- 1 teaspoon vanilla
- 2 eggs
- 100 grams blueberries

Directions:

1. Pre heat the oven to 145°C.
2. Combine almond flour, coconut flour, baking powder, and six tablespoons of Truvia.
3. Mix oil, whipping cream, and vanilla.
4. Mix damp and dry ingredients
5. Wash blueberries and add 15 grams. of Truvia and stir.
6. Put blueberries on top of the batter.
7. Bake for 1 hour and 10 minutes, turning the loaf tin at 30 minutes. Cool before serving.

 Nutrition:
Calories: 149 **Fat:** 7g **Carbohydrates:** 21g **Protein:** 2g

73. Simple Loaf of Bread

Preparation Time: 10 minutes	Cooking Time: 60 minutes	Servings: 6

Ingredients:

- 350 grams almond flour
- Olive oil
- 50 ml. almond milk
- 3 eggs
- 2 tablespoons baking powder.
- 1 teaspoon baking soda.
- Salt

Directions:

1. Pre heat the oven to 140°C.
2. Grease the bread tin. Mix all the ingredients. Bake for 60 minutes.
3. Leave to cool.
4. Serve.

Nutrition:
Calories: 266   **Fat:** 2g   **Carbohydrates:** 32g   **Protein:** /g

74. Keto Chocolate Bread

 Preparation Time: 10 minutes   **Cooking Time:** 45 minutes   **Servings:** 5

Ingredients:

- 300 grams finely milled almond flour measured and sifted
- 100 grams sugar substitute
- 30 grams cocoa powder
- 1 1/2 teaspoons of baking powder
- 1/4 teaspoon of sea salt
- 120 grams cream cheese, room temperature
- 4 eggs, room temperature
- 4 tablespoons of unsalted butter, room temperature
- 100 grams baking chocolate (melted)
- 1 teaspoon of instant coffee (optional for enhancing chocolate)

Directions:

1. Preheat oven to 220°C, fan 200°C, gas78.
2. Grease an 8-inch loaf tin and line with parchment paper for easier release.
3. In a medium-size bowl combine all the dry ingredients (except sugar substitute) and set them aside.
4. In a large mixing bowl beat with a hand whisk, on high, the softened butter and sugar substitute until light and fluffy.
5. Add the cream cheese and combine well until fully incorporated.
6. Add the eggs one at a time making sure to mix well after each addition.
7. Add all the dry ingredients mixing well until fully combined.
8. Lastly, add the melted baking chocolate in a stream and beat the mixture until fully mixed.
9. Bake the bread for 50-60 minutes or until an inserted toothpick comes out clean.
10. Allow cooling for 10 minutes before taking it out of the mold. Then place on a cooling rack to fully cool before slicing.
11. Store leftovers in the refrigerator for up to 5 days or freeze for up to 3 weeks.

Nutrition:
Calories: 198   **Carbohydrates:** 9g   **Fat:** 16g   **Protein:** 7g

75. Sunflower Bread

 Preparation Time: 120 minutes   **Cooking Time:** 15 minutes   **Servings:** 15

Ingredients:

- 1 ¾ teaspoon fresh yeast
- 30 ml. water
- 380 grams ground rye flour
- 250 grams wheat flour
- 200 grams rye sourdough starter
- Salt
- 3 tablespoons honey
- 85 grams sunflower seeds
- 1 tablespoon cumin

Directions:

1. Melt the yeast in a little water. Add all ingredients, mix well.
2. Let the dough rise for 1 to 2 hrs.
3. Divide the dough into fifteen small rolls. Put them on the baking sheet and also let them prove until doubled in size. Knead the dough after it has increased, and shape into a long roll.
4. Cut the dough into fifteen pieces. Form into rounded loaves.
5. Bake at 190°C, fan 170°C, gas 5 for 10 minutes. Slice and serve.

Nutrition:
Calories: 140   **Fat:** 4g   **Carbohydrates:** 12g   **Protein:** 3g

76. Collagen Keto Bread

 Preparation Time: 20 minutes   **Cooking Time:** 40 minutes   **Servings:** 15

Ingredients:

- 60 grams Unflavored Grass-Fed Collagen Protein
- 6 tablespoons almond flour
- 5 pastured eggs
- 1 tablespoon unflavored fluid coconut oil
- 1 teaspoon aluminum-free baking powder
- 1 teaspoon xanthan gum
- Pinch of Himalayan pink salt
- A squeeze of stevia

Directions:

1. Pre heat the oven to 220°C, fan 200°C, gas 7.
2. Grease the glass loaf pan with coconut oil.
3. In a large bowl, add the egg whites, set them aside.
4. In a little bowl, blend the dry components and set them aside.
5. In a further little dish, whisk together the damp ingredients, egg yolks, and liquid coconut oil.
6. Include the dry and the damp components to the egg whites and blend till well mixed.
7. Bake for 40 minutes.
8. Slice before serving.

Nutrition:
Calories: 177   **Fat:** 7g   **Carbohydrates:** 14g   **Protein:** 15g

77. Keto Breakfast Pizza

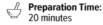 **Preparation Time:** 20 minutes   **Cooking Time:** 15 minutes   **Servings:** 2

Ingredients:

- 250 grams grated cauliflower
- 2 tablespoons coconut flour
- Salt
- 4 eggs
- 1 tablespoon psyllium husk powder
- Toppings: smoked salmon, avocado, natural herbs, spinach, olive oil

Directions:

1. Pre heat the oven to 220°C, fan 200°C, gas 7.
2. Line a pizza tray with baking paper.

3. In a mixing bowl, add all ingredients except toppings and mix up.
4. Leave for 5 minutes.
5. Thoroughly put the breakfast pizza base onto the pan.
6. Cook for 15 minutes.
7. Garnish with toppings. Serve.

 Nutrition:
Calories: 454 **Fat:** 31g **Carbohydrates:** 26g **Protein:** 22g

78. Cauliflower Bread

 Preparation Time: 20 minutes | **Cooking Time:** 35 minutes | **Servings:** 2

Ingredients:

- 250 grams grated cauliflower
- 1-2 tablespoons coconut flour
- Salt
- 4 eggs
- 1/2 teaspoon garlic powder
- 1/2 tablespoon psyllium husk
- 3-4 pieces' bacon
- ¼ springtime onion, chopped.
- 1 avocado

Directions:

1. Pre heat the oven to 220°C, fan 200°C, gas 7
2. Mix the 250 grams of grated cauliflower, salt, 2 eggs, 15 grams of coconut flour, psyllium, garlic powder, and flour.
3. Divide the cauliflower and mix well to combine.
4. Place each cauliflower ball onto one of the lined cooking trays, shape the blend into even rectangular shapes.
5. Cook in the oven for 15 minutes.
6. Bake with the bacon for an additional 10 minutes.
7. Boil water in a little pan, including the dash of apple cider vinegar plus salt.
8. Split 2 eggs into the boiling water to poach. Cook.
9. Transfer the cauliflower bread then serve with the poached eggs, crispy bacon, spring onion, and avocado.

 Nutrition:
Calories: 412g **Fat:** 38g **Carbohydrates:** 14g **Protein:** 27g

79. Coconut Flour Donuts

 Preparation Time: 15 minutes | **Cooking Time:** 18 minutes | **Servings:** 8

Ingredients:

- 43 grams coconut flour
- 43 grams Swerve Sweetener
- 3 tablespoons cocoa powder
- 1 teaspoon baking powder
- Salt
- 4 eggs
- 30 grams butter, softened
- ½ teaspoon vanilla essence
- 6 tablespoons brewed coffee
- Glaze:
- 30 grams powdered Swerve Sweetener
- 11 teaspoon cocoa powder
- 15 grams heavy cream
- 4 grams vanilla essence
- 30ml. water

Directions:

1. Pre heat the oven to 220°C, fan 200°C, gas 7 and grease the donut frying pan.
2. Mix the coconut flour, sweetener, cacao powder, baking powder, and salt. Then the eggs, melted butter, and vanilla essence. Stir in the cold coffee.
3. Separate the batter amongst the wells of the donut pan. Bake 16 to 20 minutes. Cool down.
4. Glaze: In a medium shallow bowl, mix the powdered sugar and cocoa powder. Add the hefty cream and vanilla and whisk. Put water up until the glaze thins out. Serve.

 Nutrition:
Calories: 150 **Fat:** 9g **Carbohydrates:** 18g **Protein:** 5g

80. Tofu Mushrooms

 Preparation Time: 5 minutes | **Cooking Time:** 10 minutes | **Servings:** 3

Ingredients:

- 1 block tofu
- 120 grams mushrooms
- 4 tablespoons butter
- 4 tablespoons Parmesan cheese
- Salt
- Ground black pepper

Directions:

1. Toss tofu cubes with melted butter, salt, and black pepper in a mixing bowl.
2. In a pan, over a medium-high heat, sauté tofu for 5 minutes. Stir in cheese and mushrooms.
3. Sauté for another 5 minutes. Serve.

 Nutrition:
Calories: 215 **Fat:** 19g **Carbohydrates:** 3g **Protein:** 12g

81. Onion Tofu

 Preparation Time: 8 minutes | **Cooking Time:** 5 minutes | **Servings:** 3

Ingredients:

- 2 blocks tofu
- 2 onions
- 2 tablespoons butter
- 120 grams cheddar cheese
- Salt
- Ground black pepper

Directions:

1. Rub the tofu with salt and pepper in a bowl.
2. Add melted butter and onions to a pan to sauté for 3 minutes.
3. Toss in tofu and stir cook for 2 minutes. Stir in cheese and cover the pan for 5 minutes on a low heat. Serve.

 Nutrition:
Calories: 198 **Fat:** 13g **Carbohydrates:** 6g **Protein:** 11g

82. Spinach Rich Ballet

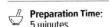 **Preparation Time:** 5 minutes	**Cooking Time:** 30 minutes	**Servings:** 4

Ingredients:

- 680 grams baby spinach
- 40 grams coconut cream
- 400 grams cauliflower
- 2 tablespoons unsalted butter
- Salt
- Ground black pepper

Directions:

1. Pre heat the oven at 220°C, fan 200°C, gas 7.
2. Melt butter, then toss in spinach to sauté for 3 minutes.
3. Divide the spinach into four ramekins.
4. Divide cream, cauliflower, salt, and black pepper in the ramekins.
5. Bake for 25 minutes. Serve.

 Nutrition:
Calories: 190 **Fat:** 13g **Carbohydrates:** 5g **Protein:** 15g

83. Pepperoni Egg Omelette

Preparation Time: 5 minutes	**Cooking Time:** 20 minutes	**Servings:** 4

Ingredients:

- 15 pepperonis
- 6 eggs
- 2 tablespoons butter
- 4 tablespoons coconut cream
- Salt and ground black pepper

Directions:

1. Whisk eggs with pepperoni, cream, salt, and black pepper in a bowl.
2. Add 60 grams of the butter to a warm-up pan.
3. Now pour 60 grams of the batter in this melted butter and cook for 2 minutes on each side. Serve.

 Nutrition:
Calories: 145 **Fat:** 11g **Carbohydrates:** 15g **Protein:** 8.9 g

84. Nut Porridge

Preparation Time: 10 minutes	**Cooking Time:** 15 minutes	**Servings:** 4

Ingredients:

- 120 grams cashew nuts
- 120 grams pecan
- 30 grams stevia
- 4 teaspoons coconut oil
- 260 ml. water

Directions:

1. Grind the cashews and peanuts in a processor.
2. Stir in stevia, oil, and water. Add the mixture to a saucepan and cook for 5 minutes on high. Adjust on low for 10 minutes. Serve.

 Nutrition:
Calories: 260 **Fat:** 23g **Carbohydrates:** 13g **Protein:** 7g

85. Parsley Soufflé

Preparation Time: 5 minutes	**Cooking Time:** 6 minutes	**Servings:** 1

Ingredients:

- 2 eggs
- 1 red chili pepper
- 2 tablespoons coconut cream
- 1 tablespoon parsley
- Salt

Directions:

1. Blend all the soufflé ingredients to a food processor.
2. Put it in the soufflé dishes, then bake for 6 minutes at 220°C.
3. Serve.

 Nutrition:
Calories: 108 **Fat:** 9g **Carbohydrates:** 2g **Protein:** 6g

86. Bok Choy Samba

Preparation Time: 5 minutes	**Cooking Time:** 15 minutes	**Servings:** 3

Ingredients:

- 1 onion
- 4 Bok choy
- 4 tablespoons coconut cream
- Salt
- Ground black pepper
- 60 grams Parmesan cheese

Directions:

1. Toss Bok choy with salt and black pepper.
2. Add oil to a large pan and sauté onion for 5 minutes.
3. Stir in Bok choy and cream. Stir for 6 minutes.
4. Toss in cheese and cover the pan to cook on low for 3 minutes. Serve.

 Nutrition:
Calories: 112 **Fat:** 4.9g **Carbohydrates:** 1.9g **Protein:** 3g

87. Eggs with Watercress

Preparation Time: 10 minutes	**Cooking Time:** 5 minutes	**Servings:** 6

Ingredients:

- 6 organic eggs
- 1 medium ripe avocado
- 43 ml. watercress
- ½ tablespoon lemon juice
- Salt

Directions:

1. Put water into the pot with the trivet inside.
2. Spread the watercress in the trivet.
3. Cook for 3 minutes with high pressure.

4. Drain the steamed watercress.
5. Toss the watercress with lemon juice, salt, avocado, and yolks in a bowl.
6. Mix and mash.
7. Divide the egg yolk mixture at the center of all the egg whites. Serve.

 Nutrition:
Calories: 132 **Fat:** 10.9g **Carbohydrates:** 3.3g
Protein: 6g

88. Banana Porridge

 Preparation Time: 10 minutes | **Cooking Time:** 5 minutes | **Servings:** 2

Ingredients:
- 60 grams walnuts
- 1 banana
- hot water
- 2 tablespoons coconut butter
- ½ teaspoon cinnamon powder
- 2 teaspoons maple syrup

Directions:
1. Pulse all the ingredients together using a blender, then transfer them to a saucepan.
2. Warm-up over a medium heat for 5 minutes, then transfer it into a large bowl and serve.

 Nutrition:
Calories: 269 **Fat:** 14g **Carbohydrates:** 21g **Protein:** 8g

89. Mushroom Sandwich

 Preparation Time: 5 minutes | **Cooking Time:** 10 minutes | **Servings:** 1

Ingredients:
- 2 Portobello mushroom caps
- 2 lettuce leaves
- 2 avocado slices
- 250 grams pound turkey meat, cooked
- Olive oil

Directions:
1. Cook the turkey meat, and for 4 minutes, transfer and drain excess oil.
2. Warm-up pan with the olive oil, add mushroom caps, cook for 2 minutes on each side.
3. Remove then arrange 1 mushroom cap on a plate, add turkey, avocado slices, lettuce leaves, and serve.

 Nutrition:
Calories: 521 **Fat:** 15g **Carbohydrates:** 5g **Protein:** 47g

90. Pepper Sandwich

 Preparation Time: 5 minutes | **Cooking Time:** 10 minutes | **Servings:** 2

Ingredients:
- 250 grams pepper
- ½ tablespoon avocado oil
- 3 eggs
- 430 grams turkey breast
- Olive oil

Directions:
1. Warm-up oil over a medium-high heat, add peppers, stir and cook for 5 minutes
2. Warm up another pan over a medium heat, add the turkey meat, stir, cook for 3-4 minutes, transfer.
3. Mix the eggs, put to the pan with the peppers, cook for 7-8 minutes. Serve.

 Nutrition:
Calories: 411 **Fat:** 12g **Carbohydrates:** 19g **Protein:** 44g

91. Mushroom and Salmon Sliders

 Preparation Time: 10 minutes | **Cooking Time:** 15 minutes | **Servings:** 3

Ingredients:
- 3 Portobello mushroom caps
- 280 grams turkey meat
- 3 eggs
- 300 grams smoked salmon
- Olive oil

Directions:
1. Warm up a pan over medium-high heat, add the turkey, cook for 4 minutes, transfer.
2. Warm-up a pan with the olive oil over a medium heat, place egg rings in the pan, crack an egg in each, cook for 6 minutes, and transfer.
3. Warm up the pan again, add mushroom caps, cook for 5 minutes, and transfer.
4. Top each mushroom cap with turkey slices, salmon, and eggs and serve.

 Nutrition:
Calories: 315 **Fat:** 12g **Carbohydrates:** 3g **Protein:** 33g

92. Beef and Butternut Squash One Pot

 Preparation Time: 10 minutes | **Cooking Time:** 20 minutes | **Servings:** 3

Ingredients:
- 430 grams beef
- 2 tablespoons ghee
- 3 garlic cloves
- 2 celery stalks
- 1 onion
- Sea salt
- Black pepper
- ½ teaspoon coriander
- 1 teaspoon cumin
- 1 teaspoon garam masala
- 1/2 grams butternut squash
- 3 eggs
- 1 small avocado
- 430 grams spinach

Directions:

1. Warm up a pan with the ghee over medium heat, add onion, garlic, celery, a pinch of salt and pepper, cook for 3 minutes. Add beef, cumin, garam masala, and coriander, cook for 5 minutes more.
2. Add butternut squash flesh and spinach, stir and make 3 holes in this mix.
3. Break an egg into the pan then bake at 220°C, fan 200°C, gas 7, for 15 minutes. Serve with avocado on top.

 Nutrition:
Calories: 594 **Fat:** 35g **Carbohydrates:** 19g **Protein:** 54g

93. Turkey and Veggies Mix

Preparation Time: 10 minutes	**Cooking Time:** 15 minutes	**Servings:** 4

Ingredients:

- 20 ounces of turkey meat
- 4 tablespoons coconut oil
- 1 small green bell pepper
- 60 grams onion
- 2 garlic cloves
- 250 grams sweet potato
- 1 avocado
- 3 eggs
- 250 grams spinach

Directions:

1. Warm up a pan with the oil, add onion, stir and cook for 3 minutes.
2. After that, add the garlic and pepper, cook for 1 minute. Put the ground turkey, cook for 15 minutes more. Put the sweet potato and cook for 4 minutes. Put the spinach, cook for 2 minutes. Make 3 holes in the batter, break an egg in each, place pan un- der a preheated grill, and cook for 3 minutes. Top with avocado slices and serve.

 Nutrition:
Calories: 619 **Fat:** 34g **Carbohydrates:** 29g **Protein:** 49g

94. Pork Pot

Preparation Time: 10 minutes	**Cooking Time:** 20 minutes	**Servings:** 4

Ingredients:

- 200 grams mushrooms
- 450 grams pork
- Olives
- 2 courgettes
- ½ teaspoon garlic powder
- ½ teaspoon basil
- Sea salt
- Black pepper
- 2 tablespoons Dijon mustard

Directions

1. Warm up a pan with the oil over a medium-high heat, add mush- rooms, cook for 4 minutes.
2. Put courgettes, salt, and black pepper cook for 4 minutes more.
3. Add pork, garlic powder, and basil, cook for 10 minutes.
4. Put the mustard, stir, and cook for 3 more minutes. Transfer and serve.

 Nutrition:
Calories: 226 **Fat:** 8g **Carbohydrates:** 5g **Protein:** 3g

LUNCH

95. Roasted Lemon Chicken Sandwich

Preparation Time: 15 minutes	Cooking Time: 1 hour 30 minutes	Servings: 12

Ingredients
- A whole chicken, 1kg
- 5 tablespoons of butter
- 1 lemon (cut into wedges)
- 1 tablespoon garlic powder
- Salt
- Pepper
- 2 tablespoons mayonnaise
- Keto-friendly bread

Directions:
1. Preheat the oven to 220°C, fan 200°C, gas 8.
2. Grease a deep baking dish with butter.
3. Ensure that the chicken is patted dry and that the gizzards have been removed.
4. Combine the butter, garlic powder, salt, and pepper.
5. Rub the entire chicken with it, including in the cavity.
6. Place the lemon and onion inside the chicken and place the chicken in the prepared baking dish.
7. Bake for about 160 minutes, depending on the size of the chicken.
8. Baste the chicken often with the drippings. If the drippings begin to dry, add water. The chicken is done when a thermometer inserted into the thickest part of the thigh, reads 170°C, or when the juices run clear when the thickest part of the thigh is pierced.
9. Allow the chicken to cool before slicing.
10. To assemble the sandwich, shred some of the breast meat and mix with mayonnaise.
11. Place the mixture between the two slices of bread.

 TIP: To save the chicken, refrigerated for up to 5 days or freeze for up to 1 month.

 Nutrition:
Calories: 214 **Fat:** 11.8g **Carbohydrates:** 1.6g **Protein:** 24.4g

96. Keto-Friendly Pan Pepperoni Pizza

Preparation Time: 10 minutes	Cooking Time: 6 minutes	Servings: 4

Ingredients:

For crust
- 60 grams almond flour
- ½ teaspoon of baking powder
- 8 large egg whites (whisked into stiff peaks)
- Salt
- Pepper

Toppings
- 3 tablespoons unsweetened tomato sauce
- 60 grams shredded cheddar cheese
- 60 grams of pepperoni

Directions:
1. Gently incorporate the almond flour into the egg whites. Ensure that no lumps remain.
2. Stir in the remaining crust ingredients.
3. Heat a nonstick pan over a medium heat. Spray with nonstick spray.
4. Pour the batter into the heated pan to cover the bottom of the pan.
5. Cover the pan with a lid and cook the pizza crust for about 4 minutes or until bubbles appear on the top.
6. Flip the dough and add the toppings, starting with the tomato sauce and ending with the pepperoni.
7. Cook the pizza for two more minutes.
8. Allow the pizza to cool slightly before serving.

 TIP: It can be stored in the refrigerator for up to 5 days and frozen for up to 1 month.

 Nutrition:
Calories: 175 **Fat:** 12g **Carbohydrates:** 1.9g **Protein:** 14.3g

97. Cheesy Chicken Cauliflower

Preparation Time: 5 minutes	Cooking Time: 10 minutes	Servings: 4

Ingredients:
- 250 grams of cauliflower florets (chopped)
- 60 grams of red pepper (chopped)
- 120 grams of roasted chicken, shredded (Lunch Recipes: Roasted Lemon Chicken Sandwich)
- 30 grams of shredded cheddar cheese
- 1 tablespoon of butter
- 1 tablespoon of sour cream
- Salt and pepper (to taste)

Directions:
1. Stir fry the cauliflower and peppers in the butter over a medium heat until the veggies are tender.
2. Add the chicken and cook until the chicken is warmed through.
3. Add the remaining ingredients and stir until the cheese is melted.

4. Serve warm.

 Nutrition:
Calories: 144 **Fat:** 8.5g **Carbohydrates:** 4g **Protein:** 13.2g

98. Lemon Baked Salmon

Preparation Time: 10 minutes	**Cooking Time:** 30 minutes	**Servings:** 4

Ingredients:

- 450 grams salmon
- 1 tablespoon of olive oil
- Salt and pepper to taste
- 1 tablespoon of butter
- 1 lemon (thinly sliced)
- 1 tablespoon of lemon juice
- Lemon sliced

Directions:

1. Preheat your oven to 220°C, fan 200°C, gas 8.
2. Grease a baking dish with olive oil and place the salmon skin-side down.
3. Season the salmon with salt and pepper then top with the lemon slices.
4. Slice half the butter and place it over the salmon.
5. Bake for 20 minutes or until the salmon flakes easily.
6. Melt the remaining butter in a saucepan. When it starts to bubble, remove it from the heat and allow it to cool before adding the lemon juice.
7. Drizzle the lemon butter over the salmon and serve warm.

 Nutrition:
Calories: 211 **Fat:** 13.5g **Carbohydrates:** 1.5g **Protein:** 22.2g

99. Baked Salmon

Preparation Time: 10 minutes	**Cooking Time:** 10 minutes	**Servings:** 4

Ingredients:

- Cooking spray
- 3 cloves of garlic (minced)
- 30 grams butter
- 1 teaspoon of lemon zest
- 2 tablespoons of lemon juice
  4 salmon fillets
- Salt
- Pepper
- 2 tablespoons parsley, chopped

Directions:

1. Preheat your oven to 220°C, fan 200°C, gas 8.
2. Grease the pan with cooking spray.
3. In a bowl, mix the garlic, butter, lemon zest, and lemon juice.
4. Sprinkle salt and pepper on salmon fillets.
5. Drizzle with the lemon butter sauce.
6. Bake in the oven for 12 minutes.
7. Garnish with parsley before serving.

 Nutrition:
Calories: 345 **Fat:** 22.7g **Carbohydrates:** 1.2g **Protein:** 34.9g

100. Buttered Cod

Preparation Time: 5 minutes	**Cooking Time:** 5 minutes	**Servings:** 4

Ingredients:

- 450 grams cod fillets
- 6 tablespoons butter
- ¼ teaspoon of garlic powder
- ¾ teaspoon of ground paprika
- Lemon slices
- Salt
- Pepper
- Parsley, chopped

Directions:

1. Mix the garlic powder, paprika, salt, and pepper in a bowl.
2. Season cod pieces with seasoning mixture.
3. Add 10 grams butter in a pan over a medium heat.
4. Melt half of the butter.
5. Add the cod and cook for 2 minutes per side.
6. Top with the remaining slices of butter.
7. Cook for 3 to 4 minutes.
8. Garnish with parsley and lemon slices before serving.

 Nutrition:
Calories: 295 **Fat:** 19g **Carbohydrates:** 1.5g **Protein:** 30.7g

101. Tuna Salad

Preparation Time: 5 minutes	**Cooking Time:** 0 minute	**Servings:** 2

Ingredients:

- 2 cans of tuna
- 56 gams mayonnaise
- 1 stalk of celery, diced
- 2 tablespoons red onion, diced
- 1 tablespoon chopped parsley, chives and/or other herbs
- 0.5 tablespoon Dijon mustard

Directions:

1. Drain the liquid from the tuna cans. Then, add the tuna, mayonnaise, diced celery, diced red onion, herbs, Dijon mustard, salt and pepper to a mixing bowl.
2. Stir all of the ingredients together until well combined.
3. Enjoy the tuna salad plain out of a bowl, wrapped up in lettuce, or in a sandwich.

 Nutrition:
Calories: 130 **Fat:** 7.8g **Carbohydrates:** 8.5g **Protein:** 8.2g

102. Keto Frosty

Preparation Time: 45 minutes	**Cooking Time:** 0 minute	**Servings:** 4

Ingredients:

- 60 grams of double cream
- 2 tablespoons of cocoa powder (unsweetened)
- 3 tablespoons of swerve
- 1 teaspoon of pure vanilla extract

- Salt to taste

Directions:

1. In a bowl, combine all the ingredients.
2. Use a hand mixer and beat until you see stiff peaks forming.
3. Place the mixture in a Ziploc bag.
4. Freeze for 35 minutes.
5. Serve in bowls or dishes.

 Nutrition:
Calories: 164 **Fat:** 17g **Carbohydrates:** 2.9g **Protein:** 1.4g

103. Coconut Crack Bars

Preparation Time: 2 minutes	**Cooking Time:** 3 minutes	**Servings:** 20

Ingredients:

- 380 grams of coconut flakes (unsweetened)
- 120 grams of coconut oil
- 30 grams of maple syrup

Directions:

1. Line a baking tray with parchment paper.
2. Put coconut in a bowl.
3. Add the oil and syrup.
4. Mix well.
5. Pour the mixture into the pan.
6. Refrigerate until firm.
7. Slice into bars before serving.

 Nutrition:
Calories: 147 **Fat:** 14g **Carbohydrates:** 12g **Protein:** 6g

104. Strawberry Ice Cream

Preparation Time: 1 hour and 20 minutes	**Cooking Time:** 0 minute	**Servings:** 4

Ingredients:

- 200 ml. coconut milk
- 200 grams frozen strawberries
- 2 tablespoons swerve
- 60 grams of fresh strawberries

Directions:

8. Put all the ingredients except the fresh strawberries in a blender.
9. Pulse until smooth.
10. Put the mixture in an ice cream maker.
11. Use the ice cream maker according to directions.
12. Add the fresh strawberries a few minutes before the ice cream is done.
13. Freeze for 1 hour before serving.

 Nutrition:
Calories: 320 **Fat:** 25g **Carbohydrates:** 25g **Protein:** 2.9g

105. Trout and Chili Nuts

 **Preparation Time:** 10 minutes	**Cooking Time:** 0 minutes	**Servings:** 3

Ingredients:

- 1.5 kg of rainbow trout
- 300 grams of shelled walnuts
- 1 bunch of parsley
- 9 cloves of garlic
- 7 tablespoons Olive oil
- 2 fresh hot peppers
- Lemon juice, 2 lemons

Directions:

1. Clean and dry the trout, then place them on a baking tray.
2. Chop the walnuts, parsley, and chili peppers then mash the garlic cloves.
3. Mix the ingredients by adding olive oil, lemon juice, and a pinch of salt.
4. Stuff the trout with some of the sauce and use the rest to cover the fish.
5. Bake at 180°C, fan 180°C, gas 4 for 30/40 minutes.
6. Serve the trout hot or cold.

 Nutrition:
Calories: 226 **Fat:** 5g **Carbohydrates:** 7g **Protein:** 8g

106. Five Greens Smoothie

Preparation Time: 10 minutes	**Cooking Time:** 25 minutes	**Servings:** 3

Ingredients:

- 6 kale leaves (chopped)
- 3 stalks celery (chopped)
- 1 ripe avocado (skinned, pitted, sliced)
- 120 grams of ice cubes
- 250 grams of spinach (chopped)
- 1 large cucumber (peeled and chopped)
- Chia seeds to garnish

Directions:

1. In a blender, add the kale, celery, avocado, and ice cubes, and blend for 45 seconds.
2. Add the spinach and cucumber, and process for another 45 seconds until smooth.
3. Pour the smoothie into glasses, garnish with chia seeds, and serve the drink immediately.

 Nutrition:
Calories: 124 **Fat:** 7.8g **Carbohydrates:** 2.9g **Protein:** 3.2g

107. Turkey and Cream Cheese Sauce

Preparation Time: 15 minutes	**Cooking Time:** 25 minutes	**Servings:** 5

Ingredients:

- 2 tablespoons butter
- 1 kg of turkey breast
- 350 grams cream
- 40 grams cheese
- 1 tablespoon tamari soy sauce

- Pepper
- Salt
- Capers

Directions:

1. Pre heat the oven at 170°C, fan 150°C, gas 3, then dissolve half the butter in an iron pan.
2. Rub the breast of the turkey with pepper and salt. Fry for five minutes.
3. Bake for ten minutes.
4. Add the drippings of turkey in a pan, cream cheese, and whipping cream. Simmer. Put pepper, soy sauce, and salt. Sauté the small capers in remaining butter.
5. Slice and serve with fried capers and cream cheese sauce.

 Nutrition:
Calories: 810   **Fat:** 50g   **Carbohydrates:** 6.9g   **Protein:** 47.6g

108. Baked Salmon and Pesto

Preparation Time: 15 minutes	Cooking Time: 30 minutes	Servings: 4

Ingredients:

- For the green sauce:
- 4 tablespoons green pesto
- 130 grams mayonnaise
- Half a Greek yogurt
- Pepper
- Salt
- For the salmon:
- 350 grams salmon
- 4 tablespoons green pesto
- Pepper
- Salt

Directions:

1. Put the fillets on a greased baking tray, skin side down. Add pesto on top. Add pepper and salt.
2. Bake at 200°C, fan 180°C, gas 6 for thirty minutes.
3. Combine all the listed ingredients for the green sauce in a bowl.
4. Serve the baked salmon with green sauce on top.

 Nutrition:
Calories: 1010   **Protein:** 51.6g   **Carbohydrates:** 3.1g   **Fat:** 87.6g

109. Keto Chicken with Butter and Lemon

Preparation Time: 15 minutes	Cooking Time: 1 hour & 30 minutes	Servings: 2

Ingredients:

- A whole chicken
- Pepper and salt
- 2 teaspoons barbecue seasoning
- 1 teaspoon water
- 1 lemon
- 2 onions
- 500 ml. water

Directions:

1. Pre heat the oven at 170°C, fan 150°C, gas 3. Grease the baking tray.
2. Rub the chicken with pepper, salt, and barbecue seasoning. Put In the baking dish.
3. Arrange lemon wedges and onions surrounding the chicken put slices of butter.
4. Bake for 1 hour and 30 minutes. Slice and serve.

 Nutrition:
Calories: 980.3   **Fat:** 38g   **Carbohydrates:** 55g   **Protein:** 57g

110. Garlic Chicken

Preparation Time: 15 minutes	Cooking Time: 40 minutes	Servings: 4

Ingredients:

- 50 grams butter
- 500 grams chicken drumsticks
- Pepper
- Salt
- lemon juice
- 2 tablespoons olive oil
- 7 garlic cloves
- 60 grams parsley, chopped

Directions:

1. Pre heat the oven to 250°C, fan 230°C, gas 11.
2. Put the chicken in a baking dish. Add pepper and salt.
3. Add olive oil with lemon juice over the chicken. Sprinkle parsley and garlic on top.
4. Bake for 40 minutes. Serve.

 Nutrition:
Calories: 540   **Fat:** 38.6g   **Protein:** 41g   **Carbohydrates:** 3.1g

111. Salmon Skewers Wrapped with Prosciutto

Preparation Time: 15 minutes	Cooking Time: 4 minutes	Servings: 4

Ingredients:

- 30 grams basil
- 450 grams salmon
- Black pepper
- 100 grams prosciutto
- 1 tablespoon olive oil
- 8 skewers

Directions:

1. Start by soaking the skewers in a bowl of water.
2. Cut the salmon fillets lengthwise. Thread the salmon using skewers.
3. Coat the skewers in pepper and basil. Wrap the slices of prosciutto around the salmon.
4. Warm-up oil in a grill pan. Grill the skewers for four minutes. Serve.

 Nutrition:
Calories: 670.5   **Carbohydrates:** 1.2g   **Fat:** 61.6g   **Protein:** 27.2g

112. Buffalo Drumsticks and Chili Aioli

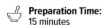 **Preparation Time:** 15 minutes	**Cooking Time:** 40 minutes	**Servings:** 4

Ingredients:

- For the chili aioli:
- 60 grams mayonnaise
- 1 tablespoon smoked paprika powder
- One clove garlic
- For the chicken:
- 300 grams chicken drumsticks
- 2 tablespoons white wine vinegar
- Olive oil
- 2 tablespoons tomato paste
- Salt
- 1 tablespoon paprika powder
- 1 tablespoon tabasco
- Salt

Directions:

1. Pre heat the oven at 200°C, fan 180°C, gas 6.
2. Combine the listed marinade ingredients. Marinate the chicken drumsticks for ten minutes.
3. Arrange the chicken drumsticks in the tray. Bake for 40 minutes.
4. Combine the listed ingredients for the chili aioli in a bowl. Serve.

 Nutrition:
Calories: 567.8 **Fat:** 43.2g **Carbohydrates:** 2.2g
Protein: 41.3g

113. Slow Cooked Roasted Pork and Creamy Gravy

Preparation Time: 15 minutes	**Cooking Time:** 8 hours & 15 minutes	**Servings:** 6

Ingredients:

- For the creamy gravy:
- 200 grams whipping cream
- Roast juice
- For the pork:
- 450 grams pork roast
- Salt
- Bay leaf
- Five black peppercorns
- 600 ml. water
- 2 tablespoons thyme
- 2 cloves garlic
- 5 grams ginger, grated
- 10 grams Paprika powder
- Olive oil
- Black pepper

Directions:

5. Pre heat your oven to 150°C, fan 130°C, gas 1.
6. Add the meat, salt, water to a baking dish. Put peppercorns, thyme, and bay leaf. Put in the oven for 8 hours. Remove. Reserve the juices. Adjust to 200°C, fan 180°C, gas 6.
7. Put ginger, garlic, pepper, herbs, and oil. Rub the herb mixture on the meat. Roast the pork for fifteen minutes.
8. Slice the roasted meat. Strain the meat juices in a bowl. Boil for reducing it by half.
9. Add the cream. Simmer for 20 minutes. Serve with creamy gravy.

 Nutrition:
Calories: 586.9 **Fat:** 50.3g **Carbohydrates:** 2.6g **Protein:** 27.9g

114. Bacon-Wrapped Meatloaf

Preparation Time: 15 minutes	**Cooking Time:** 1 hour	**Servings:** 4

Ingredients:

- For the meatloaf:
- 2 tablespoons butter
- One onion
- 450 grams minced beef
- 60 grams double cream
- 30 grams cheese
- 1 large egg
- 10 grams oregano
- Salt
- Black pepper
- 1 pack of bacon
- For the gravy:
- 60 grams double cream
- 1/2 tablespoon tamari soy sauce

Directions:

1. Pre heat your oven to 200°C, fan 180°C, gas 6.
2. Dissolve the butter in a pan. Add the onion. Cook for four minutes. Keep aside.
3. Combine onion, minced meat, and the remaining ingredients, except for the bacon, in a large bowl.
4. Make a firm loaf. Use bacon strips for wrapping the loaf.
5. Bake the meatloaf for 45 minutes.
6. Put the juices from the baking dish and cream, then boil. Simmer for ten minutes. Add the soy sauce. Slice and serve with gravy.

 Nutrition:
Calories: 1020.3 **Fat:** 88.9g **Carbohydrates:** 5.6g **Protein:** 46.7g

115. Lamb Chops and Herb Butter

Preparation Time: 15 minutes	**Cooking Time:** 4 minutes	**Servings:** 4

Ingredients:

- 8 lamb chops
- Olive oil
- Butter
- Pepper
- Salt
- For the herb butter:
- 60 grams butter
- One clove garlic
- ½ tablespoon Garlic powder
- 4 tablespoons parsley
- Salt
- 1 teaspoon lemon juice

Directions:

1. Season the lamb chops with pepper and salt.
2. Warm-up olive oil and butter in an iron pan. Add the lamb chops. Fry for four minutes.
3. Mix all the listed ingredients for the herb butter in a bowl. Cool.
4. Serve with herb butter.

Nutrition:
Calories: 722.3 **Fat:** 61.5g **Carbohydrates:** 0.4g **Protein:** 42.3g

116. Crispy Cuban Pork Roast

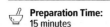 **Preparation Time:** 15 minutes	**Cooking Time:** 4 minutes	**Servings:** 6

Ingredients:

- 2 kg. pork shoulder
- Salt
- 2 teaspoons cumin
- 1 teaspoon black pepper
- 2 tablespoons oregano
- 1 red onion
- 4 garlic cloves
- Orange juice
- Lemon juice
- 60 ml. olive oil

Directions:

1. Rub the pork shoulder with salt in a bowl. Mix all the remaining ingredients of the marinade in a blender.
2. Marinate the meat for 8 hours. Cook for 40 minutes. Warm-up your oven to 200°C, fan 180°C, gas 6. Roast the pork for 30 minutes.
3. Remove the meat juice. Simmer for 20 minutes. Shred the meat.
4. Pour the meat juice. Serve.

 Nutrition:
Calories: 910.3 **Fat:** 69.6g **Carbohydrates:** 5.3g **Protein:** 58.3g

117. Keto Barbecued Ribs

Preparation Time: 15 minutes	**Cooking Time:** 1 hour & 10 minutes	**Servings:** 4

Ingredients:

- 60 grams Dijon mustard
- Apple cider vinegar
- Butter
- Salt
- 1.5 kg spareribs
- 2 tablespoons Paprika powder
- 2 teaspoons Chili powder
- 2 teaspoons Garlic powder
- 2 teaspoons Onion powder
- 2 teaspoons Cumin
- 2 teaspoons Black pepper

Directions:

1. Warm up a grill for 30 minutes.
2. Mix vinegar and Dijon mustard in a bowl, add the ribs and coat.
3. Mix all the listed spices. Rub the mix all over the ribs. Put aside. Put ribs on an aluminum foil. Add some butter over the ribs. Wrap with foil. Grill for 1 hour. Remove and slice.
4. Put the reserved spice mix. Grill again for 10 minutes. Serve.

 Nutrition:
Calories: 980 **Fat:** 80.2g **Carbohydrates:** 5.8g **Protein:** 54.3g

118. Turkey Burgers and Tomato Butter

Preparation Time: 15 minutes	**Cooking Time:** 15 minutes	**Servings:** 4

Ingredients:

- For the chicken patties:
- 1 kg chicken (by choice)
- 1 egg
- Half an onion, chopped
- Salt
- Pepper
- ½ teaspoon thyme
- 40 grams butter
- For the fried cabbage:
- 1 kg green cabbage
- 50 grams butter
- Salt
- Pepper
- For the tomato butter:
- 50 grams butter
- 1 tablespoon tomato paste
- 1 teaspoon red wine vinegar
- Pepper
- Salt

Directions:

1. Pre heat your oven to 150°C, fan 130°C, gas 1.
2. Combine the listed ingredients for the patties in a large bowl. Shape the mixture into patties.
3. Fry the chicken patties for five minutes, each side. Keep warm in the oven.
4. Warm-up butter in a pan. Put the cabbage, plus pepper and salt. Fry for five minutes.
5. Whip the ingredients for the tomato butter in a bowl using an electric mixer.
6. Serve with a dollop of tomato butter from the top.

 Nutrition:
Calories: 830.4 **Fat:** 71.5g **Carbohydrates:** 6.7g
Protein: 33.6g

119. Keto Hamburger

Preparation Time: 15 minutes	**Cooking Time:** 70 minutes	**Servings:** 4

Ingredients:

- For the burger buns:
- 260 grams almond flour
- 60 grams ground psyllium husk powder
- 20 grams baking powder
- Salt
- Water
- 2 tablespoons apple cider vinegar
- 3 egg whites
- 5 grams sesame seeds
- For the hamburger:
- 1 kg beef
- Olive oil
- Salt
  Pepper
- 1 whole lettuce
- 1 tomato
- 1 red onion
- 50 grams mayonnaise
- 10 grams bacon

Directions:

1. Pre heat your oven to 150°C, fan 130°C, gas 1.
2. Mix the listed dry ingredients for the buns in a bowl. Boil the water. Put egg whites, water, and vinegar into the dry mix. Mix.
3. Make individual pieces of buns, put sesame seeds on the top. Bake for 60 minutes
4. Fry the slices of bacon. Keep aside.
5. Mix beef, pepper, and salt in a bowl. Make patties. Grill the beef patties for 5 minutes, each side.
6. Combine mayonnaise and lettuce in a bowl. Cut the buns in half. Add beef patty, lettuce mix, onion slice, and a tomato slice. Top with bacon slices. Serve.

Nutrition:
Calories: 1070.3 **Fat:** 85.3g **Carbohydrates:** 6.1g **Protein:** 53.4g

120. Chicken Wings and Blue Cheese Dressing

 Preparation Time: 70 minutes

 Cooking Time: 25 minutes

 Servings: 4

Ingredients:

- 30 grams mayonnaise
- 30 grams sour cream
- 3 teaspoons lemon juice
- Salt
- Garlic powder
- 50 grams whipping cream
- 85 grams blue cheese
- For the chicken wings:
- 1 kg chicken wings
- Olive oil
- ¼ teaspoon garlic powder
- 1 clove garlic
- Black pepper
- Salt
- 20 grams parmesan cheese

Directions:

1. Mix all the blue cheese dressing ingredients in a bowl. Chill for 40 minutes.
2. Combine the chicken with olive oil and spices. Marinate for 30 minutes.
3. Bake in the oven for 25 minutes. Toss the chicken wings with parmesan cheese in a bowl.
4. Serve with blue cheese dressing by the side.

Nutrition:
Calories: 839.3 **Fat:** 67.8g **Carbohydrates:** 2.9g **Protein:** 51.2g

121. Salmon Burgers with Lemon Butter and Mash

 Preparation Time: 70 minutes

 Cooking Time: 15 minutes

 Servings: 4

Ingredients:

- For the salmon burgers:
- 1kg salmon
- 1 egg
- Half an onion, yellow
- Salt
- Pepper
- 60 grams butter
- For the green mash:
- 500 grams broccoli
- 140 grams butter
- 40 grams parmesan cheese
- For the lemon butter:
- 120 grams butter
- 30 ml. lemon juice
- Pepper
- Salt

Directions:

1. Pre heat your oven at 100°C.
2. Cut the salmon into small pieces. Combine all the burger ingredients with the fish in a blender. Pulse for thirty seconds. Make 8 patties.
3. Warm-up butter in an iron pan. Fry the burgers for five minutes.
4. Boil water, along with some salt in a pot, put the broccoli florets. Cook for 3 to 4 minutes. Drain. Add parmesan cheese and

butter. Blend the ingredients using an immersion blender. Add pepper and salt.
5. Combine lemon juice with butter, pepper, and salt. Beat using an electric beater.
6. Put a dollop of lemon butter on the top and green mash by the side. Serve.

Nutrition:
Calories: 1025.3 **Fat:** 90.1g **Carbohydrates:** 6.8g
Protein: 44.5g

122. Egg Salad Recipe

 Preparation Time: 15 minutes

 Cooking Time: 20 minutes

 Servings: 6

Ingredients:

- 3 tablespoons mayonnaise
- 3 tablespoons Greek yogurt
- 2 tablespoons red wine vinegar
- Kosher salt
- Ground black pepper
- 8 hard-boiled eggs
- 8 strips bacon
- 1 avocado
- 500 grams crumbled blue cheese
- 500 grams cherry tomatoes
- 2 tablespoons chives

Directions:

7. Stir mayonnaise, cream, and the red wine vinegar in a small bowl. Add pepper and salt.
8. Mix the eggs, bacon, avocado, blue cheese, and cherry tomatoes in a large bowl. Fold in the mayonnaise dressing, add salt and pepper. Garnish with the chives and serve.

Nutrition:
Calories: 200 **Fat:** 18g **Carbohydrates:** 3g **Protein:** 10g

123. Taco Stuffed Avocados

 Preparation Time: 10 minutes

Cooking Time: 25 minutes

Servings: 8

Ingredients:

- 4 ripe avocados
- Lime juice
- Olive oil
- One onion
- 450 grams ground beef
- One packet taco seasoning
- Kosher salt
- Ground black pepper
- 85 grams Mexican cheese
- 500 grams lettuce
- 500 grams quartered grape tomatoes
- Sour cream

Directions:

1. Scoop a bit of avocado flesh. Put. Squeeze lime juice over all the avocados.
2. Warm-up oil in a pan over a medium heat. Put onion and cook for 5 minutes. Put minced beef and taco seasoning. Add salt and pepper and cook for 6 minutes. Remove and drain.

3. Fill every half of the avocado with beef, then top with reserved avocado, cheese, lettuce, tomato, and a dollop of sour cream. Serve.

 Nutrition:
Calories: 324 **Fat:** 24g **Carbohydrates:** 16g **Protein:** 15g

124. Buffalo Shrimp Lettuce Wraps

 Preparation Time: 15 minutes | **Cooking Time:** 20 minutes | **Servings:** 4

Ingredients:

- ¼ tablespoon butter
- 2 garlic cloves
- 20 ml. hot sauce
- Olive oil
- 450 grams shrimp tails removed
- Kosher salt
- Ground black pepper
- 1 head romaine leaf
- 1/4 red onion
- 1 rib celery
- 500 grams blue cheese

Directions:

Make buffalo sauce:
1. Melt the butter over a medium heat in a small saucepan. Add the garlic and cook for 1 minute. Add hot sauce and stir. Adjust to low.

Make shrimp:
1. Warm-up oil in a large pan over a medium heat. Put shrimp, salt, and pepper to season. Cook, around 2 minutes per side. Remove then put buffalo sauce, toss.

Assemble wraps:
1. Put a small scoop of shrimp in the centre of a roman leaf, then top with red onion, celery, and blue cheese. Serve.

 Nutrition:
Calories: 242 **Fat:** 12g **Carbohydrates:** 7g **Protein:** 25g

125. Broccoli Bacon Salad

 Preparation Time: 15 minutes | **Cooking Time:** 15 minutes | **Servings:** 6

Ingredients:

- For the salad:
- Kosher salt
- 3 heads broccoli
- 2 carrots
- 1/2 red onion
- 500 grams cranberries
- 500 grams almonds
- Six slices bacon
- For the dressing:
- 500 grams mayonnaise
- 3 tablespoons apple cider vinegar
- Kosher salt
- Ground black pepper

Directions:

1. Boil 250 grams of salted water. Prepare a large bowl of ice water.
2. Put broccoli florets in the heated water and cook for 1 to 2 minutes. Cool the broccoli in cold water. Drain.

3. Combine broccoli, red onion, carrots, cranberries, nuts, and bacon in a large bowl.
4. Mix vinegar and mayonnaise in a bowl and add salt and pepper.
5. Pour the broccoli mixture over the dressing. Mix and serve.

 Nutrition:
Calories: 280 **Fat:** 25g **Carbohydrates:** 9g **Protein:** 6g

126. Keto Egg Salad

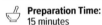 **Preparation Time:** 15 minutes | **Cooking Time:** 15 minutes | **Servings:** 4

Ingredients:

- 3 tablespoons mayonnaise
- 2 teaspoons lemon juice
- 1 teaspoon chives
- Ground black pepper
- Kosher salt
- Six hard-boiled eggs
- 1 avocado
- Lettuce
- Cooked bacon

Directions:

1. Mix the mayonnaise, lemon juice, and chives, and then add pepper and salt.
2. Add the eggs and the avocado to mix. Serve with the bacon and lettuce.

 Nutrition:
Calories: 408 **Fat:** 39g **Carbohydrates:** 5g **Protein:** 13g

127. Loaded Cauliflower Salad

 Preparation Time: 15 minutes | **Cooking Time:** 30 minutes | **Servings:** 4

Ingredients:

- 1 large head cauliflower
- 6 slices bacon
- 60 grams sour cream
- 30 grams mayonnaise
- 1 tablespoon lemon juice
- ½ teaspoon garlic powder
- Kosher salt
- Ground black pepper
- 60 grams cheddar
- 60 grams chives

Directions:

1. Boil ¼ water, put cauliflower, cover pan, and steam for 4 minutes. Drain and cool.
2. Cook the pork for around 3 minutes per side. Drain then cut.
3. Mix the sour cream, mayonnaise, lemon juice, and garlic powder in a big bowl. Toss the cauliflower florets. Add salt pepper, bacon, cheddar, and chives. Serve.

 Nutrition:
Calories: 440 **Fat:** 35g **Carbohydrates:** 13g **Protein:** 19g

128. Caprese Zoodles

 Preparation Time: 15 minutes | **Cooking Time:** 0 minutes | **Servings:** 4

Ingredients:

- 4 courgettes
- 28 grams. extra-virgin olive oil
- Kosher salt
- Ground black pepper
- 300 grams cherry tomatoes halved
- 130 grams mozzarella balls
- 60 grams basil leaves
- 2 tablespoons balsamic vinegar

Directions:

1. Create zoodles out of courgette using a spiralizer.
2. Mix the zoodles, olive oil, salt, and pepper. Marinate for 15 minutes.
3. Put the tomatoes, mozzarella, and basil and toss.
4. Serve with balsamic vinegar on top.

 Nutrition:
Calories: 417 **Fat:** 24g **Carbohydrates:** 11g **Protein:** 36g

129. Courgette Sushi

Preparation Time: 20 minutes	**Cooking Time:** 0 minutes	**Servings:** 6

Ingredients:

- 2 courgettes
- 130 ml. cream cheese
- 1 teaspoon Sriracha hot sauce
- 1 teaspoon lime juice
- 130 grams crab meat
- 60 grams carrot
- 60 grams avocado
- 60 grams cucumber
- 1 teaspoon toasted sesame seeds

Directions:

1. Slice each courgette into thin flat strips. Put aside.
2. Combine cream cheese, sriracha, and lime juice in a medium-sized bowl.
3. Place 2 slices of courgette horizontally flat on a cutting board. Place a thin layer of cream cheese over it, then top with the left with the crab, carrot, avocado, and cucumber.
4. Roll up courgette. Serve with sesame seeds.

 Nutrition:
Calories: 450 **Fat:** 25g **Carbohydrates:** 23g **Protein:** 35g

130. Asian Chicken Lettuce Wraps

Preparation Time: 15 minutes	**Cooking Time:** 15 minutes	**Servings:** 4

Ingredients:

- 3 tablespoon hoisin sauce
- 2 tablespoon low-sodium soy sauce
- 2 tablespoon rice wine vinegar
- 1 tablespoon Sriracha
- 1 teaspoon sesame oil
- 1 tablespoon extra-virgin olive oil
- 2 cloves garlic
- 1 tablespoon grated ginger
- 450 grams minced chicken
- 60 grams chestnuts
- 2 spring onions

- Kosher salt
- Ground black pepper
- Large leafy lettuce
- Cooked white rice

Directions:

Make the sauce:

1. Mix the hoisin sauce, soy sauce, rice wine vinegar, sriracha, and sesame oil in a small bowl.
2. Mix the olive oil in a large pan, put the onions and cook for 5 minutes, then stir in garlic and ginger and cook for 1-minute. Add the minced chicken and cook.
3. Add the sauce and cook for 1 to 2 minutes. Turn off the heat and put in the spring onions and chestnuts. Season with pepper and salt.
4. Add a tablespoon of rice to the chicken mixture in the center of a lettuce leaf. Serve.

 Nutrition:
Calories: 315 **Fat:** 12g **Carbohydrates:** 5g **Protein:** 34g

131. California Burger Bowls

Preparation Time: 15 minutes	**Cooking Time:** 20 minutes	**Servings:** 4

Ingredients:

- For the dressing:
- 60 grams extra-virgin olive oil
- 40 ml balsamic vinegar
- 3 tablespoons Dijon mustard
- 2 teaspoons honey
- 1 clove garlic
- Kosher salt
- Ground black pepper
- For the burger:
- 450 grams grass-fed organic minced beef
- 1 teaspoon Worcestershire sauce
- ½ teaspoon chili powder
- ½ teaspoon onion powder
- Kosher salt
- Ground black pepper
- 1 package of butterhead/round lettuce
- 1 medium red onion
- 1 avocado
- 2 tomatoes

Directions:

Make the dressing:

1. Mix the dressing ingredients in a medium bowl. Set aside.

Make burgers:

1. Combine beef and Worcestershire sauce, chili powder, and onion powder in another large bowl. Add pepper and salt, mix. Form into four patties.
2. Grill the onions for 3 minutes each. Remove and detach burgers from the grill pan. Cook for 4 minutes per side.

Assemble:

1. Put lettuce in a large bowl and add the dressing. Finish with a patty burger, grilled onions, 60 grams slices of avocado, and tomatoes. Serve.

 Nutrition:
Calories: 407 **Fat:** 19g **Carbohydrates:** 33g **Protein:** 26g

132. Parmesan Brussels Sprouts Salad

Preparation Time: 15 minutes	Cooking Time: 25 minutes	Servings: 6

Ingredients:

- Olive oil
- 2 tablespoons lemon juice
- 60 grams parsley
- Salt
- Pepper
- 1kg Brussels sprouts
- 60 grams toasted almonds
- 60 grams pomegranate seeds
- Shaved Parmesan

Directions:

1. Mix olive oil, lemon juice, parsley, 2 teaspoons of salt, and one teaspoon of pepper.
2. Add the sprouts and toss.
3. Let it sit for 20 minutes and up to 4 hours before serving.
4. Fold in almonds and pomegranate seeds and garnish with a rasped parmesan. Serve.

Nutrition:
Calories: 130 **Fat:** 9g **Carbohydrates:** 8g **Protein:** 4g

133. Chicken Taco Avocados

Preparation Time: 15 minutes	Cooking Time: 20 minutes	Servings: 6

Ingredients:

- For the filling:
- 130 grams black beans
- 130 grams canned sweetcorn
- 120 grams green chilies
- 130 grams rotisserie chicken
- 130 grams Cheddar
- 1 package taco seasoning
- 30 grams coriander
- 3 ripe avocados
- For the dressing:
- 130 ml. ranch dressing
- 64 ml. lime juice
- 1 tablespoon coriander
- 1 teaspoon Kosher salt
- 1 teaspoon Ground black pepper

Directions:

1. Warm up the grill.

For the filling:

1. Mix black beans, corn, 60 grams can of green chilies, shredded chicken, cheddar, taco seasoning, and fresh coriander in a bowl. Halve three avocados and split, eliminating pit. Mash the flesh in a small bowl and set aside. Fill the avocado boats with 43 grams of filling. Put cheddar and fresh coriander, then grill for 2 minutes.

For the dressing:

1. Mix ranch dressing, lime juice, the remaining green chilies, coriander, salt, and pepper. Fold in mashed avocados. Serve with dressing and coriander.

Nutrition:
Calories: 324 **Fat:** 24g **Carbohydrates:** 16g **Protein:** 15g

134. Keto Quesadillas

Preparation Time: 15 minutes	Cooking Time: 25 minutes	Servings: 4

Ingredients:

- 15 grams. extra-virgin olive oil
- 1 pepper
- 60 grams onion
- 25 grams chili powder
- Kosher salt
- Ground black pepper
- 400 grams grams Monterey Jack
- 400 grams cheddar
- 500 grams chicken
- 1 avocado
- 1 onion
- Sour cream

Directions:

1. Preheat the oven to 200°C, fan 180°C, gas 6, and line 2 medium baking trays with parchment paper.
2. Heat oil in a medium pan. Put the onion and pepper, chili powder, salt, and pepper. Cook for 5 minutes.
3. Stir cheeses in a medium-sized dish. Put 60 grams of mixed cheese on prepared baking sheets. Form a circle, the size of a tortilla flour.
4. Bake the cheeses for 8 to 10 minutes. Put a batter of onion, pepper, shredded chicken, and slices of avocado to one half of each of the cheese circles. Cool and fold one side of the "tortilla" cheese over the other side with the fillings. Bake for 3 to 4 more minutes.
5. Serve with onion and sour cream.

Nutrition:
Calories: 473 **Fat:** 41g **Carbohydrates:** 5g **Protein:** 21g

135. No-Bread Italian Subs

Preparation Time: 15 minutes	Cooking Time: 15 minutes	Servings: 6

Ingredients:

- 60 grams mayonnaise
- 2 tablespoons red wine vinegar
- Olive oil
- 1 small garlic clove, grated
- 1 teaspoon Italian seasoning
- 6 slices ham
- 12 salami slices
- 12 pepperoni slices
- 6 provolone/edam slices
- 130 grams romaine
- 60 grams roasted red peppers

Directions:

1. Make creamy Italian dressing by mixing together the mayo, vinegar, butter, garlic, and Italian seasoning.
2. Assemble the sandwiches by stacking a slice of ham, 2 salami pieces, 2 pepperoni slices, and a slice of provolone.
3. Add a handful of romaine and a couple of the roasted red peppers. Put creamy Italian sauce, then roll it up and eat.

Nutrition:
Calories: 390 **Fat:** 34g **Carbohydrates:** 3g **Protein:** 16g

136. Basil Avocado Frail Salad Wraps & Sweet Potato Chips

 Preparation Time: 15 minutes   **Cooking Time:** 30 minutes   **Servings:** 4

Ingredients:

- For the sweet potato chips:
- Kosher salt
- Ground black pepper
- cooking spray
- 2 -3 medium potatoes
- For the shrimp salad:
- 60 grams small red onion
- 20 large shrimp
- 100 grams halved baby plum tomatoes
- Cooking spray
- 2 avocados
- 4 fresh basil leaves
- 2 large heads of butterhead/round lettuce
- For the marinade:
- 2 lemon juice
- 2 cloves garlic
- 3 basil leaves
- 2 tablespoons white wine vinegar
- 3 tablespoons extra-virgin olive oil
- ½ teaspoon paprika
- Salt
- Pepper

Directions:

For sweet potato chips:

1. Preheat the oven to 220°C, fan 200°C, gas 8, then grease a large baking tray. Put the sweet potatoes wedge with salt and pepper on the tray.
2. Roast for 15 minutes, then turn over and roast for a further15 minutes. Cool and put aside.

For shrimp salad:

1. Grease a large pan, cook the shrimp, occasionally stirring, for 2 minutes per side. Set aside.

For marinade:

1. Mix the lemon juice, garlic, basil, vinegar, butter, and paprika, put salt and pepper.
2. Stir the tomatoes, onion, avocados, and basil. Fold in the shrimps. Mix.
3. Serve with lettuce cups.

 Nutrition: **Calories:** 351 **Fat:** 6g **Carbohydrates:** 14g **Protein:** 10g

137. Cauliflower Leek Soup

 Preparation Time: 15 minutes   **Cooking Time:** 45 minutes   **Servings:** 2

Ingredients:

- ½ tablespoons olive oil
- ½ tablespoon garlic
- ½ tablespoons butter
- 250 grams vegetable broth
- 1 leek
- Salt
- 120 grams cauliflower
- black pepper
- 30 grams double cream

Directions:

1. Put the oil and butter in the pan to heat. Add garlic, cauliflower, and leek pieces and cook for 5 minutes on low.
2. Add vegetable broth and boil. Cover the pan and cook on low for 45 minutes.
3. Remove from the heat then blend the soup in a mixer. Add double cream, salt, pepper, and blend more, until smooth.
4. Serve with salt and pepper.

 Nutrition: **Calories:** 165 **Fat:** 13.1g **Carbohydrates:** 8g **Proteins:** 2.4g

138. Sugar-Free Blueberry Cottage Cheese Parfaits

 Preparation Time: 5 minutes   **Cooking Time:** 5 minutes   **Servings:** 2

Ingredients:

- 225 g cheese, low fat
- 1/8 tablespoon cinnamon
- 60 grams vanilla extract
- 6 drops stevia, liquid
- 150 grams berries

Directions:

1. Blend cheese, vanilla extract, cinnamon, and stevia into the blender.
2. Remove and pour these into bowls.
3. Put the berries on top of the cheese parfaits. Serve.

 Nutrition: **Calories:** 240 **Fat:** 2.2 g **Carbohydrates:** 12.5g **Proteins:** 14.8g

139. Low-Calorie Cheesy Broccoli Quiche

 Preparation Time: 25 minutes   **Cooking Time:** 30 minutes   **Servings:** 2

Ingredients:

- 1/3 tablespoon butter
- Black pepper
- 120 grams broccoli
- ¼ teaspoon garlic powder
- 2 tablespoons full-fat cream
- 30 grams spring onions
- Kosher salt
- 30 grams cheddar cheese
- 2 eggs

Directions:

1. Preheat the oven to 220°C, fan 200°C, gas 8., then grease the baking dish with butter.
2. Add broccoli and 4 to 8 tablespoons of water and place the bowl in the microwave for 3 minutes. Mix and put back in the microwave for a further 3 minutes.
3. Beat the eggs in a bowl. Pour all leftover ingredients (including the eggs) in with broccoli.
4. Then put the mixture in the baking dish. Bake in the oven for 30 minutes. Slice and serve.

Nutrition:
Calories: 196 **Fat:** 14g **Carbohydrates:** 5g Proteins: 12g

140. Low-Carb Broccoli Leek Soup

Preparation Time: 15 minutes	Cooking Time: 15 minutes	Servings: 2

Ingredients:

- 60 grams leek
- 100 grams cream cheese
- 50 grams broccoli
- 60 grams double cream
- 120 ml. water
- 60 grams black pepper
- 60 grams vegetable bouillon cube
- 30 grams basil
- 5 grams garlic
- Salt

Directions:
1. Put water into a pan and put in chopped broccoli, chopped leek, and salt. Boil on high.
2. Then simmer on low. Add in the remaining ingredients, simmer for 1 minute. Remove from the heat.
3. Blend the soup mixture into a blender. Serve.

 Nutrition:
Calories: 545 **Fat:** 50g **Carbohydrates:** 10g **Proteins:** 15g

141. Low-Carb Chicken Taco Soup

Preparation Time: 10 minutes	Cooking Time: 12 minutes	Servings: 2

Ingredients:
- 120 ml. chicken broth
- 60 grams tomatoes
- 60 grams boneless chicken
- 4 green chilies
- 60 grams package cream cheese
- 1 tablespoon seasoning

Directions:
1. Put chicken broth, boneless chicken, cheese, tomatoes, and green chilies in a pressure cooker.
2. Cook for 10 minutes. Remove. Shred the chicken.
3. Put shredded chicken in the soup and stir. Then add Italian seasoning. Serve.

Nutrition:
Calories: 239 **Fat:** 12g **Carbohydrates:** 3g **Proteins:** 26g

142. Keto Chicken & Veggies Soup

Preparation Time: 5 minutes	Cooking Time: 30 minutes	Servings: 2

Ingredients:
- 1 tablespoon olive oil
- 130 ml. chicken broth
- 60 grams onion
- ¼ tablespoon Italian seasoning
- 2 peppers

- 1 Bay leaves
- ½ tablespoon garlic
- Sea salt
- 30 grams green beans
- Black pepper
- 60 grams tomatoes
- 2 chicken breast pieces

Directions:
1. Massage the chicken with salt and pepper and grill for 10 minutes.
2. Put onions and pepper into heated oil and simmer for 5-6 minutes on low.
3. Add all leftover ingredients and simmer for 15 minutes on a low heat. Remove. Serve.

 Nutrition:
Calories: 256 **Fat:** 2g **Carbohydrates:** 11g **Proteins:** 2g

143. Low-Carb Seafood Soup with Mayo

Preparation Time: 15 minutes	Cooking Time: 40 minutes	Servings: 2

Ingredients:
- ¼ tablespoon olive oil
- ½ chopped onion
- ¼ tablespoon garlic
- 250 ml. fish broth
- 1 tomato
- Thyme
- Salt
- Garlic Mayo
- 90 grams white fish
- Olive oil
- 30 grams shrimps
- Garlic clove
- 30 grams mussels
- 1 egg
- 30 grams scallops
- ½ tablespoon lemon juice
- 1to 3 bay leaves
- Salt
- 1/2 lime

Directions:
1. Cook onions and garlic in heated olive oil. Add broth, bay leaf, tomatoes, and salt. After boiling, cover for 20 minutes on a low flame.
2. Add all the ingredients and cook for 4 minutes.
3. Blend garlic mayo in the blender and add olive oil.
4. Put the mayo and serve with thyme and lime.

 Nutrition:
Calories: 592 **Fat:** 47g **Carbohydrates:** 8g **Proteins:** 27g

144. Keto Tortilla Chips

Preparation Time: 10 minutes	Cooking Time: 40 minutes	Servings: 2

Ingredients:
- 60 grams cube of mozzarella cheese
- ¼ teaspoon cumin powder
- 20 grams almond flour
- 1 teaspoon coriander
- 1 tablespoon cream cheese
- Chili powder
- 1 egg
- Salt

Directions:

1. Microwave the mozzarella cheese, cream cheese, and flour for 30 seconds. Stir and allow to set for 30 seconds more.
2. Put spices and egg into the cheese mixture to make the dough.
3. Divide the dough into 2 pieces and place on a large rectangle of parchment paper.
4. Remove the parchment paper. Bake in the oven for 15 minutes at 200°C, fan 180°C, gas 6.
5. Bake the other side of the dough in the same way.
6. Remove and cut into rectangular chips. Bake again for 2 minutes and serve.

 Nutrition:
Calories: 236   **Fat:** 16g   **Carbohydrates:** 4g   **Proteins:** 11g

145. Chicken Courgette Alfredo

Preparation Time: 15 minutes	**Cooking Time:** 30 minutes	**Servings:** 2

Ingredients:

- 100 grams chicken breast
- Basil
- 100 grams courgette
- 90 grams cauliflower
- 40 grams cream cheese
- Mayo
- Black pepper
- 1 teaspoon olive oil
- 1 teaspoon garlic

Directions:

1. Marinate chicken with basil, salt, and pepper. Grill the chicken and set it aside.
2. Add oil, garlic, and courgette and cook for 8 to 10 minutes.
3. Put cream cheese in with the courgette with salt and pepper.
4. Let the cauliflower steam in water. Mash the steamed cauliflower and add salt, pepper, and herbs.
5. Serve the cheesy courgette with mashed cauliflower and enjoy an excellent lunch.

 Nutrition:
Calories: 262   **Fat:** 9.8g   **Carbohydrates:** 13g   **Proteins:** 30g

146. Low Carbohydrates: Chicken Cheese

Preparation Time: 10 minutes	**Cooking Time:** 20 minutes	**Servings:** 2

Ingredients:

- 150 grams chicken breast
- Salt
- ½ tablespoon Italian seasoning
- Pepper
- ½ teaspoon paprika
- ½ onion
- ¼ teaspoon onion powder
- 1 teaspoon garlic
- ½ tablespoon olive oil
- ½ fire-roasted pepper
- 425 grams tomato
- Red pepper flakes
- ½ tablespoon parsley
- 30 grams mozzarella cheese

Directions:

1. Marinate the chicken with salt, pepper, onion powder, and seasoning. Cook the chicken on low for 15 minutes.
2. Put the onion and all the other ingredients, except the cheese and into a pan and simmer for 7 minutes.
3. Put this sauce into a dish and place the cheese on the top of the chicken pieces. Warm-up for 1 to 2 minutes. Garnish with parsley and serve.

 Nutrition:
Calories: 309   **Fat:** 9g   **Carbohydrates:** 9g   **Proteins:** 37g

147. Lemon Chicken Spaghetti Squash Boats

Preparation Time: 10 minutes	**Cooking Time:** 1 hour and 10 minutes	**Servings:** 2

Ingredients:

- 60 grams spaghetti squash
- 60 grams onion
- 1 tablespoon olive oil
- 1 tablespoon garlic
- 500 grams chicken breast
- 300 g cherry tomatoes
- Sea Salt
- 60 grams chicken broth
- Black pepper
- ½ tablespoon lime
- 130 grams spinach

Directions:

1. Combine the olive oil, salt, and pepper with half of the squash. Bake for 40 minutes at 180°C.
2. Stir fry the chicken pieces in olive oil.
3. Remove the chicken and pour 11 teaspoons olive oil in with the onions. Add garlic and stir. Then add salt, pepper, and tomatoes, and simmer.
4. Put in the lemon juice and chicken broth, cook for 15 minutes.
5. Then add the chicken and spinach and cook for a further 3 to 4 minutes.
6. Shred the baked squash. Pour the sauce on the top of the shredded squash and serve.

 Nutrition:
Calories: 234   **Fat:** 10g   **Carbohydrates:** 10g   **Proteins:** 26g

148. Stuffed Portobello Mushrooms

Preparation Time: 5 minutes	**Cooking Time:** 10 minutes	**Servings:** 2

Ingredients:

- ¼ tablespoon butter
- Balsamic glaze
- 1 clove garlic
- 100 g mozzarella cheese
- 1 teaspoon parsley
- 30 grams tomatoes
- 2 large Portobello mushrooms

Directions:

1. Preheat the oven to 220°C, fan 200°C, gas 8. Warm up the butter and stir in the garlic.
2. Grease the bottoms of the mushrooms with butter and place them butter side down on the baking dish/tray.
3. Fill the mushrooms with cheese slices and tomato slices. Grill in the microwave.
4. Top the mushrooms with salt, basil, and balsamic glaze. Serve.

 Nutrition:
Calories: 260 **Fat:** 5g **Carbohydrates:** 12g **Proteins:** 20g

149. Low Carbohydrates: Mexican Stuffed Peppers

Preparation Time: 10 minutes	Cooking Time: 20 minutes	Servings: 2

Ingredients:

- 1 large pepper
- ¼ teaspoon chipotle chili
- 1 teaspoon coconut oil
- Cinnamon
- 250 g minced beef
- 40 grams Tomato puree
- 1 large onion
- 30 grams cheddar cheese
- 1 teaspoon grounded cumin
- Coriander leaves
- ½ tablespoon chili powder

Directions:

5. Bake the whole pepper in a baking dish for 5 minutes at 180°C.
6. Cook the minced beef for 10 minutes.
7. Then add in the onions and mushrooms and cook for a further 10 minutes.
8. Put the cumin, chili powder, cinnamon, chipotle, and salt into the beef, then cook again for a further 10 minutes. Remove from the heat and add tomato puree, then stir.
9. Fill the peppers with the beef mixture and with cheese plus coriander.
10. Microwave for 1 minute then serve.

 Nutrition:
Calories: 247 **Fat:** 15 g **Carbohydrates:** 9g **Proteins:** 22g

150. Low-Carb Broccoli Mash

Preparation Time: 10 minutes	Cooking Time: 5 minutes	Servings: 2

Ingredients:

- 325 grams broccoli
- 60 grams clove garlic
- 60 grams parsley
- Salt
- ½ teaspoon dried thyme
- 40 grams butter
- Pepper

Directions:

1. Add salt into the water in a pan and boil. Put broccoli florets into the pan and cook for a few minutes. Remove the water and separate the soft broccoli.
2. Place all the ingredients in a blender and pulse. Serve.

 Nutrition:
Calories: 210 **Fat:** 18g **Carbohydrates:** 7g **Proteins:** 5g

151. Roasted Tri-Color Vegetables

Preparation Time: 10 minutes	Cooking Time: 30 minutes	Servings: 2

Ingredients:

- 150 grams Brussels sprouts
- Black pepper grounded
- 75 grams cherry tomatoes
- 1 teaspoon dried thyme
- 75 grams mushrooms, chopped
- 3 tablespoons olive oil
- Salt

Directions:

1. Preheat the oven to 220°C, fan 200°C, gas 8. Put all vegetables in a baking dish.
2. Mix in salt, pepper, and oil. Bake for 20 minutes. Serve.

 Nutrition:
Calories: 208 **Fat:** 18g **Carbohydrates:** 6g **Proteins:** 4 g

152. Easy Keto Smoked Salmon Lunch Bowl

Preparation Time: 15 minutes	Cooking Time: 10 minutes	Servings: 2

Ingredients:

- 340 grams smoked salmon
- 4 tablespoons mayonnaise
- 56 grams spinach
- 1 teaspoon olive oil
- 1 medium lime
- Pepper
- Salt

Directions:

1. Arrange the mayonnaise, salmon, spinach on a plate. Sprinkle olive oil over the spinach.
2. Serve with lime wedges and add salt and pepper.

 Nutrition:
Calories: 457 **Fat:** 34.8g **Carbohydrates:** 1.9g **Protein:** 32.3g

153. Easy One-Pan Minced Beef and Green Beans

 Preparation Time: 15 minutes	Cooking Time: 15 minutes	Servings: 2

Ingredients:

- 300 grams minced beef
- 200 grams green beans
- Pepper
- Salt

- 2 tablespoons sour cream
- 200 grams butter

Directions:

1. Heat the butter in a pan over a high heat.
2. Put the minced beef plus the pepper and salt. Cook.
3. Reduce heat to medium. Add the remaining butter and the green beans then cook for 5 minutes. Put pepper and salt, then transfer onto plates. Serve with a dollop of sour cream.

Nutrition:
Calories: 787   **Fat:** 71.75g   **Carbohydrates:** 6.65g   **Protein:** 27.5g

154. Easy Spinach and Bacon Salad

Preparation Time: 15 minutes	Cooking Time: 15 minutes	Servings: 4

Ingredients:

- 250 grams spinach
- 4 large, hard-boiled eggs
- 150 grams bacon
- 2 medium red onions
- 250 grams of mayonnaise
- Pepper
- Salt

Directions:

1. Cook the bacon, then chop it into pieces, set aside.
2. Slice the hard-boiled eggs, and then rinse the spinach.
3. Combine the lettuce, mayonnaise, and bacon fat into a large cup, put pepper and salt.
4. Add the red onion, sliced eggs, and bacon into the salad, then toss. Serve.

Nutrition:
Calories: 509.15   **Fat:** 45.9g   **Carbohydrates:** 2.5g   **Protein:** 19.75g

155. Easy Keto Italian Plate

Preparation Time: 10-15 minutes	Cooking Time: 0 minutes	Servings: 2

Ingredients:

- 200 grams mozzarella cheese
- 200 grams prosciutto
- 2 tomatoes
- Olive oil
- 10 whole green olives
- Pepper
- Salt

Directions:

1. Arrange the tomato, olives, mozzarella, and prosciutto on a plate.
2. Season the tomato and cheese with pepper and salt. Serve with olive oil.

Nutrition:
Calories: 780.98   **Fat:** 60.74g   **Carbohydrates:** 5.9g   **Protein:** 50.87g

156. Fresh Broccoli and Dill Keto Salad

Preparation Time: 15 minutes	Cooking Time: 7 minutes	Servings: 3

Ingredients:

- 500 grams broccoli
- 60 grams mayonnaise
- 60 grams dill, chopped
- Salt
- Pepper

Directions:

1. Boil salted water in a saucepan. Put the chopped broccoli in the pan and boil for 3-5 minutes. Drain and set aside. Once cooled, mix the rest of the ingredients together. Season with pepper and salt, then serve.

Nutrition:
Calories: 303.33   **Fat:** 28.1g   **Carbohydrates:** 6.2g   **Protein:** 4.03g

157. Keto Smoked Salmon Filled Avocados

Preparation Time: 10-15 minutes	Cooking Time: 0 minutes	Servings: 1

Ingredients:

- 1 avocado
- 40 grams smoked salmon
- 4 tablespoons sour cream
- 1 tablespoon lemon juice
- Pepper
- Salt

Directions:

1. Cut the avocado into two equal pieces.
2. Place the sour cream in the hollow parts of the avocado with smoked salmon.
3. Put pepper and salt, squeeze lemon juice over the top.
4. Serve.

Nutrition:
Calories: 517   **Carbohydrates:** 6.7g   **Fat:** 42.6g   **Protein:** 20.6g

158. Low-Carb Broccoli Lemon Parmesan Soup

Preparation Time: 15 minutes	Cooking Time: 15 minutes	Servings: 4

Ingredients:

- 380 ml. of water
- 120 ml. unsweetened almond milk
- 356 grams broccoli florets
- 120 ml. double cream
- 40 grams Parmesan cheese
- Salt
- Pepper
- 2 tablespoons lemon juice

Directions:

1. Add broccoli to water and cook over a medium-high heat.
2. Take out 120 grams of the cooking liquid and remove the rest.

3. Blend half the broccoli, reserved cooking oil, unsweetened almond milk, cream, plus salt and pepper in a blender.
4. Add the blended ingredients to the remaining broccoli and stir with Parmesan cheese and lemon juice. Cook until heated through. Serve with Parmesan cheese on the top.

 Nutrition:
Calories: 371 **Fat:** 28.38g **Carbohydrates:** 11.67g **Protein:** 14.63g

159. Prosciutto and Mozzarella Bomb

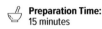 **Preparation Time:** 15 minutes | **Cooking Time:** 10 minutes | **Servings:** 4

Ingredients:
- 120 grams sliced prosciutto
- 230 grams mozzarella balls
- Olive oil

Directions:
1. Layer half of the prosciutto vertically. Lay the remaining slices horizontally across the first set of slices. Place mozzarella balls, upside down, onto the crisscrossed prosciutto slices.
2. Wrap the mozzarella ball with the prosciutto slices. Warm up the olive oil in a skillet, crisp the prosciutto, then serve.

 Nutrition:
Calories: 253 **Fat:** 19.35g **Carbohydrates:** 1.08g **Protein:** 18g

160. Summer Tuna Avocado Salad

 **Preparation Time:** 15 minutes | **Cooking Time:** 0 minutes | **Servings:** 2

Ingredients:
- 1 can tuna flakes
- 1 medium avocado
- 1 medium cucumber
- 30 grams coriander
- 1 tablespoon lemon juice
- 1 tablespoon olive oil
- Olive oil
- Pepper
- Salt

Directions:
1. Chop the tuna flakes, avocado, cucumber, and coriander, and transfer it into a salad bowl. Toss well to combine.
2. Sprinkle with the lemon and olive oil. Serve.

 Nutrition:
Calories 303 **Fat:** 22.6g **Carbohydrates:** 5.2g **Protein:** 16.7g

161. Mushrooms & Goat Cheese Salad

 Preparation Time: 15 minutes | **Cooking Time:** 10 minutes | **Servings:** 1

Ingredients:
- 1 tablespoon butter
- 56 grams portobello mushrooms
- Pepper
- Salt
- 120 grams spring mix (kale, cabbage etc.)
- 30 grams cooked bacon
- 30 grams goat cheese
- 1 tablespoon olive oil
- 1 tablespoon balsamic vinegar

Directions:
1. Sautee the mushrooms, season with pepper and salt.
2. Place the salad greens in a bowl. Top with goat cheese and crumbled bacon and mix together.
3. Whisk the olive oil in a small bowl with the balsamic vinegar. Place the salad on top of the mushrooms and serve.

 Nutrition:
Calories: 243 **Fat:** 21g **Carbohydrates:** 8g **Protein:** 20g

162. Keto Bacon Sushi

 **Preparation Time:** 15 minutes | **Cooking Time:** 13 minutes | **Servings:** 4

Ingredients:
- 6 slices bacon
- 1 avocado
- 2 cucumbers
- 2 medium carrots
- 120 grams cream cheese

Directions:
1. Preheat the oven to 200°C, fan 180°C, gas 6. Line a baking sheet. Place bacon slices in an even layer and bake, for 11 to 13 minutes.
2. Meanwhile, slice cucumbers, avocado, and carrots into parts roughly the width of the bacon.
3. Spread an even layer of cream cheese in the cooled-down bacon. Divide vegetables evenly and place them on one end. Roll up vegetables tightly. Garnish and serve.

 Nutrition:
Calories: 345 **Fat:** 30g **Carbohydrates:** 11g **Protein:** 28g

163. Coleslaw Keto Wrap

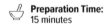 **Preparation Time:** 15 minutes | **Cooking Time:** 0 minutes | **Servings:** 2

Ingredients:
- 300 grams Red Cabbage
- 150 grams Green Onions
- 50 grams Mayonnaise
- 6 ml. Apple Cider Vinegar
- Salt
- 16 spring greens (large leaves - kale, spinach etc.)
- 500 grams Minced Meat, cooked
- Alfalfa Sprouts
- Toothpicks

Directions:

1. Mix slaw ingredients with a spoon in a large-sized bowl.
2. Place a green leaf on a plate and scoop a tablespoon of cole-slaw on the edge of the leaf. Top it with a scoop of meat and sprouts. Roll and tuck the sides.
3. Insert the toothpicks to seal the leaf. Serve.

 Nutrition:
Calories: 409   **Fat:** 42g   **Carbohydrates:** 4g   **Protein:** 2g

164. Keto Chicken Club Lettuce Wrap

Preparation Time: 15 minutes	Cooking Time: 15 minutes	Servings: 1

Ingredients:

- 1 head iceberg lettuce
- 1 tablespoon mayonnaise
- 6 slices of organic chicken
- Bacon
- Tomato

Directions:

1. Layer 6-8 large leaves of lettuce in the center of the parchment paper, around 9-10 inches.
2. Spread the mayo in the center and lay with chicken, bacon, and tomato.
3. Roll the wrap up halfway, then roll tuck in the ends of the wrap.
4. Cut it in half. Serve.

 Nutrition:
Calories: 837   **Fat:** 78g   **Carbohydrates:** 15g   **Protein:** 28g

165. Keto Broccoli Salad

Preparation Time: 10 minutes	Cooking Time: 0 minutes	Servings: 4-6

Ingredients:

- For salad:
- 2 broccoli
- 2 red cabbage
- 5 sliced almonds
- 1 onion
- 20 grams raisins
- For the orange almond dressing
- 33 c orange juice
- 25 c almond butter
- 1 tablespoon coconut aminos
- 1 shallot
- Salt

Directions:

1. Pulse the salt, shallot, amino, nut butter, and orange juice using a blender.
2. Combine the other ingredients in a bowl. Toss it with dressing and serve.

 Nutrition:
Calories: 1022   **Fat:** 94g   **Carbohydrates:** 13g   **Protein:** 22g

166. Keto Sheet Pan Chicken and Rainbow Veggies

Preparation Time: 15 minutes	Cooking Time: 25 minutes	Servings: 4

Ingredients:

- Nonstick spray
- 500 grams Chicken Breasts
- Sesame oil
- Soy sauce
- 30 grams Honey
- 2 Red Peppers
- 2 Yellow Peppers
- 3 Carrots
- 60 grams broccoli
- 2 Red Onions
- 1 tablespoon Extra Virgin Olive Oil
- Pepper & salt
- Parsley

Directions:

1. Grease the baking tray, preheat the oven to 200°C, fan 180°C, gas 6.
2. Put the chicken in the middle of the sheet. Separately, combine the oil and the soy sauce. Brush over the chicken.
3. Separate veggies across the plate. Sprinkle with oil and then toss. Season with pepper & salt.
4. Set tray into the oven and cook for 25 minutes. Garnish using parsley. Serve.

 Nutrition:
Calories: 437   **Carbohydrates:** 9g   **Fat:** 30g   **Protein:** 30g

167. Skinny Bang-Bang Courgette Noodles

 Preparation Time: 15 minutes	Cooking Time: 15 minutes	Servings: 4

Ingredients:

- For the noodles:
- 4 medium courgettes, spiraled
- 1 tablespoon olive oil
- For the sauce:
- 2 tablespoons plain Greek yogurt
- 2 tablespoons mayo
- 2 tablespoons Thai sweet chili sauce
- 1.5 teaspoons Honey
- 1.5 teaspoons Sriracha
- 2 teaspoons Lime Juice

Directions:

1. Pour the oil into a large pan at a medium temperature. Stir in the spiraled courgetti noodles.
2. Cook well until they get soft.
3. Remove then drain, and let it rest for 10 minutes. Combine sauce ingredients into a bowl.
4. Mix in the noodles to the sauce. Serve.

 Nutrition:
Calories: 189   **Fat:** 1g   **Carbohydrates:** 18g   **Protein:** 9g

168. Keto Caesar Salad

Preparation Time: 15 minutes	Cooking Time: 0 minutes	Servings: 4

Ingredients:

- 5 grams Mayonnaise
- 3 tablespoons Apple Cider Vinegar
- 1 teaspoon Dijon Mustard
- 4 Anchovy Fillets
- 24 Romaine Heart Leaves
- 200 grams Pork Rinds
- Parmesan

Directions:

1. Process the mayo with vinegar, mustard, and anchovies into a blender.
2. Prepare romaine leaves and pour the dressing.
3. Top with pork rinds and serve.

Nutrition:
Calories: 993 **Fat:** 86g **Carbohydrates:** 4g **Protein:** 47g

169. Keto Buffalo Chicken Empanadas

Preparation Time: 20 minutes	Cooking Time: 30 minutes	Servings: 6

Ingredients:

- For the empanada dough:
- 150 grams mozzarella cheese
- 90 grams cream cheese
- 1 whisked egg
- 250 grams almond flour
- For the buffalo chicken filling:
- 250 grams shredded chicken
- 2 tablespoons butter
- 20 grams Hot Sauce

Directions:

1. Preheat the oven to 220°C, fan 200°C, gas 8.
2. Microwave the cheese & cream cheese for 1-minute. Stir the flour and egg into the dish.
3. With another bowl, combine the chicken with sauce and set aside.
4. Cover a flat surface with plastic wrap and sprinkle with almond flour.
5. Grease a rolling pin, press the dough flat.
6. Make the circle shapes out of this dough with a lid.
7. Portion out spoonful's of filling into these dough circles.
8. Fold the other half over to close up into half-moon shapes.
9. Bake for 9 minutes. Serve.

Nutrition:
Calories: 1217 **Fat:** 96g **Carbohydrates:** 20g **Protein:** 74g

170. Pepperoni and Cheddar Stromboli

Preparation Time: 15 minutes	Cooking Time: 20 minutes	Servings: 3

Ingredients:

- 150 grams Mozzarella Cheese
- 50 grams Almond Flour
- 3 tablespoons Coconut Flour
- 1 teaspoon Italian Seasoning
- 1 Egg
- 150 grams Deli Ham
- 90 grams Pepperoni
- 190 grams Cheddar Cheese
- 1 tablespoon butter
- 600 grams Salad Greens

Directions:

1. Preheat the oven to 200°C, fan 180°C, gas 6.
2. Melt the mozzarella. Mix flours & Italian seasoning in a separate bowl.
3. Dump in the melty cheese and mix with pepper and salt.
4. Stir in the egg and process the dough. Pour it onto that prepared baking tray.
5. Roll out the dough. Cut slits that mark out 4 equal rectangles.
6. Put the ham and cheese, then brush with butter and close up.
7. Bake for 17 minutes. Slice and serve.

Nutrition:
Calories: 240 **Fat:** 13g **Carbohydrates:** 20g **Protein:** 11g

171. Tuna Casserole

Preparation Time: 15 minutes	Cooking Time: 10 minutes	Servings: 4

Ingredients:

- 1 can tuna
- 50 grams butter
- Salt
- Black pepper
- 1 teaspoon chili powder
- 6 stalks celery
- 1 pepper, green
- 1 onion
- 115 grams parmesan cheese
- 130 grams mayonnaise

Directions:

1. Preheat the oven to 200°C, fan 180°C, gas 6.
2. Fry the chopped onion, pepper, and celery in the melted butter for 5 minutes.
3. Mix with chili powder, parmesan cheese, tuna, and mayonnaise.
4. Grease a baking tray. Add the tuna mixture to the fried vegetables.
5. Bake for 20 minutes. Serve.

Nutrition:
Calories 953 **Fat:** 83g **Carbohydrates:** 5g **Protein:** 43g

172. Brussels Sprout and Hamburger Gratin

Preparation Time: 15 minutes	Cooking Time: 20 minutes	Servings: 4

Ingredients:

- 500 grams minced beef
- 150 grams bacon
- 150 grams brussels sprouts
- Salt

- Black pepper
- ½ teaspoon thyme
- 130 grams cheese, cheddar
- 1 tablespoon Italian seasoning
- 2 tablespoons butter
- 4 tablespoons sour cream

Directions:

1. Preheat the oven to 200°C, fan 180°C, gas 6.
2. Fry bacon and brussel sprouts in butter for 5 minutes.
3. Stir in the sour cream and put it into a greased baking tray/dish.
4. Cook the minced beef and season with salt and pepper, then add this mix to the baking tray/dish.
5. Top with the herbs and the shredded cheese. Bake for a further 20 minutes. Serve.

 Nutrition:
Calories: 770   **Fat:** 62g   **Carbohydrates:** 8g   **Protein:** 42g

173. Carpaccio

Preparation Time: 15 minutes	**Cooking Time:** 5 minutes	**Servings:** 4

Ingredients:

- 100 grams smoked prime rib
- 30 grams rocket
- 20 grams Parmesan cheese
- 10 grams pine nuts
- 7 grams of butter
- 3 tablespoons olive oil with orange
- 1 tablespoon lemon juice
- Pepper
- Salt

Directions:

1. Arrange the meat slices on a plate. Place the rocket on top of the meat.
2. Spread Parmesan cheese over the rocket.
3. Put the butter in a frying pan. Add the pine nuts, bake for a few minutes over a medium heat and then sprinkle them over the carpaccio.
4. For the vinaigrette, mix the lemon juice into the olive oil, season with pepper and salt, and drizzle over the carpaccio. Serve.

 Nutrition:
Calories: 350   **Fat:** 24g   **Carbohydrates:** 2g   **Protein:** 31g

174. Keto Croque Monsieur

Preparation Time: 15 minutes	**Cooking Time:** 7 minutes	**Servings:** 4

Ingredients:

- 2 eggs
- 25 grams grated cheese
- 25 grams ham
- 40 ml of cream
- 40 grams mascarpone
- 30 grams of butter
- Pepper
- Salt
- Basil leaves

Directions:

1. Beat eggs in a bowl, season with salt and pepper.
2. Add the cream, mascarpone, and grated cheese and mix.
3. Melt the butter over a medium heat. Adjust the heat to low.
4. Add half of the omelette mixture to the frying pan and then place a slice of ham on top. Put the rest of the omelette mixture over the ham. Fry for 2-3 minutes over a low heat.
5. Then put the omelette back in the frying pan to fry for another 1-2 minutes.
6. Garnish with a few basil leaves. Serve.

 Nutrition:
Calories: 350   **Fat:** 24g   **Carbohydrates:** 2g   **Protein:** 31g

175. Keto Wraps with Cream Cheese and Salmon

Preparation Time: 15 minutes	**Cooking Time:** 10 minutes	**Servings:** 4

Ingredients:

- 80 grams of cream cheese
- 1 tablespoon dill
- 30 grams smoked salmon
- 1 egg
- 15 grams of butter
- Pinch cayenne pepper
- Pepper
- Salt

Directions:

1. Beat the egg well in a bowl.
2. Melt the butter over a medium heat in a small frying pan. Put half of the beaten egg into the pan.
3. Carefully loosen the egg on the edges with a silicone spatula and turn the wafer-thin omelette, about 45 seconds each side. Remove.
4. Cut the dill into small pieces and put them in a bowl.
5. Add the cream cheese and the salmon, that has been cut into small pieces. Mix.
6. Stir in cayenne pepper and season with salt and pepper.
7. Spread a layer on the wrap and roll it up. Cut the wrap in half and serve.

 Nutrition:
Calories: 479   **Fat:** 45g   **Carbohydrates:** 4g   **Protein:** 16 g

176. Savory Keto Broccoli Cheese Muffins

Preparation Time: 15 minutes	**Cooking Time:** 10 minutes	**Servings:** 4

Ingredients:

- 4 eggs
- 75 grams Parmesan cheese
- 125 grams young cheese (ricotta, goat cheese, feta)
- 125 grams mozzarella
- 75 grams broccoli
- 1.5 teaspoon baking powder
- 0.25 teaspoon garlic powder
- 0.25 teaspoon mustard

Directions:

1. Preheat the oven to 160°C, fan 140°C, gas 2.
2. Boil water in saucepan, add the broccoli pieces, for 1 minute. Drain.
3. Grate the Parmesan cheese and the young cheese. Cut the mozzarella into small pieces.
4. Beat the eggs, add the broccoli, cheese, and mustard.
5. Then add the garlic powder and baking powder and mix.
6. Add baking powder and garlic powder.
7. Fill a silicone muffin tray with the broccoli-cheese egg batter and bake for 10 minutes. Serve.

 Nutrition:
Calories: 349 **Fat:** 25g **Carbohydrates:** 3g **Protein:** 28g

177. Keto Rusk

Preparation Time: 15 minutes	**Cooking Time:** 9 minutes	**Servings:** 6

Ingredients:

- 35 grams of almond flour
- 1 egg
- 1 tablespoon butter
- 0.5 teaspoon baking powder
- 1/8 teaspoon salt

 Directions:

1. Preheat the oven to 200°C, fan 180°C, gas 6. Put all the ingredients in a cup and mix.
2. Microwave for 90 seconds.
3. Cool down and cut the dough into 5 equal slices and place on a sheet with baking paper.
4. Bake for 5-6 minutes then serve.

 Nutrition:
Calories: 256 **Fat:** 4g **Protein:** 22g **Carbohydrates:** 25g

178. Flaxseed Hemp Flour Bun

Preparation Time: 15 minutes	**Cooking Time:** 8 minutes	**Servings:** 4

Ingredients:

- 1 teaspoon hemp flour
- 1 teaspoon linseed flour
- 1 teaspoon psyllium
- 1 teaspoon baking powder
- 1 egg
- 0.5 teaspoon butter

Directions:

1. Preheat the oven to 180°C, fan 160°C, gas 4. Put all dry ingredients in a large bowl, and mix.
2. Add the egg and the butter then mix it again. Microwave for 1 minute.
3. Remove the sandwich and cut it into three slices. Bake those slices for 5 minutes.
4. Serve.

 Nutrition:
Calories: 182 **Fat:** 15g **Carbohydrates:** 14g **Protein:** 11g

179. Keto Muffins with Roquefort

Preparation Time: 15 minutes	**Cooking Time:** 18 minutes	**Servings:** 4

Ingredients:

- 150 grams courgette
- 50 ml extra virgin olive oil
- Pepper
- 100 grams red pepper
- 75 grams Roquefort
- 100 grams mascarpone
- 6 eggs
- 5 grams baking powder

Directions:

1. Preheat the oven to 175°C.
2. Fry the courgette and pepper for 5 minutes. Beat the eggs with the baking powder.
3. Mix the vegetables, butter, mascarpone, and cheese and put into the muffin tins.
4. Bake for 15 minutes. Serve.

 Nutrition:
Calories: 160 **Fat:** 14g **Carbohydrates:** 1g **Protein:** 6g

180. Keto Wrap

Preparation Time: 15 minutes	**Cooking Time:** 5 minutes	**Servings:** 2

Ingredients:

- 1 egg
- 0.5 teaspoon coconut fat
- 0.5 teaspoon curry powder

Directions:

1. Warm-up coconut fat in a small frying pan over a high heat.
2. Beat the egg plus the curry powder with salt in a bowl.
3. Put the batter into the frying pan. Bake this wafer-thin omelette for 10-20 seconds.
4. Turn the wrap over and bake for a few seconds. Serve.

 Nutrition:
Calories: 128 **Protein:** 6g **Fat:** 12g **Carbohydrates:** 1 g

181. Savory Keto Muffins

Preparation Time: 15 minutes	**Cooking Time:** 20 minutes	**Servings:** 5

Ingredients:

- 4 eggs
- 1 forest outing
- 100 grams chorizo
- 75 grams mascarpone
- 100 grams grated cheese
- Salt
- Pepper

Directions:

1. Preheat the oven to 175°C.
2. Beat the eggs with the mascarpone.
3. Add the spring onion, cheese, and chorizo to the egg batter. Season with salt and pepper. Mix.
4. Bake for 9 - 14 minutes. Cooldown and serve.

 Nutrition:
Calories: 315   **Protein:** 17g   **Fat:** 26g   **Carbohydrates:** 4g

DINNER

182. Quick Pumpkin Soup

Preparation Time: 10 minutes	Cooking Time: 20 minutes	Servings: 4–6

Ingredients:

- 120 ml. coconut milk
- 250 ml. chicken broth
- 600 grams baked pumpkin
- 1 teaspoon garlic powder
- 1 teaspoon ground cinnamon
- 1 teaspoon dried ginger
- 1 teaspoon nutmeg
- 1 teaspoon paprika
- Salt and pepper (to taste)
- Sour cream or coconut yogurt (for topping)
- Pumpkin seeds (toasted, for topping)

Directions:

1. Combine the coconut milk, broth, baked pumpkin, and spices in a pan (use a medium heat).
2. Stir occasionally and simmer for 15 minutes.
3. With an immersion blender, blend the soup mixture for 1 minute.
4. Top with sour cream or coconut yogurt and pumpkin seeds.

Nutrition:
Calories: 569   **Fat:** 9.8g   **Carbohydrates:** 8.1g   **Protein:** 3.1g

183. Fresh Avocado Soup

Preparation Time: 5 minutes	Cooking Time: 10 minutes	Servings: 2

Ingredients:

- 1 ripe avocado
- 2 romaine lettuce leaves (washed and chopped)
- 130 ml. of coconut milk (chilled)
- 1 tablespoon lime juice
- 20 fresh mint leaves
- Salt (to taste)

Directions:

1. Mix all your ingredients thoroughly in a blender.
2. Chill in the fridge for 5–10 minutes. Then serve.

Nutrition:
Calories: 280   **Fat:** 26g   **Carbohydrates:** 12g   **Protein:** 4g

184. Creamy Garlic Chicken

Preparation Time: 5 minutes	Cooking Time: 15 minutes	Servings: 4

Ingredients:

- 4 chicken breasts (finely sliced)
- 1 teaspoon garlic powder
- 1 teaspoon paprika
- 2 tablespoon butter
- 1 teaspoon salt
- 130 grams of double cream
- 60 grams of sun-dried tomatoes
- 2 cloves garlic (minced)
- 130 grams of spinach (chopped)

Directions:

1. Blend the paprika, garlic powder, and salt and sprinkle over both sides of the chicken.
2. Melt the butter in a frying pan (choose a medium heat).
3. Add the chicken breast and fry for 5 minutes on each side. Set aside.
4. Add the double cream, sun-dried tomatoes, and garlic to the pan and whisk well to combine.
5. Cook for 2 minutes.
6. Add spinach and sauté for an additional 3 minutes. Return the chicken to the pan and cover it with the sauce.

Nutrition:
Calories: 330   **Fat:** 26g   **Carbohydrates:** 12g   **Protein:** 36g

185. Shrimp Scampi with Garlic

Preparation Time: 5 minutes	Cooking Time: 10 minutes	Servings: 4

Ingredients:

- 500 grams of shrimp
- 3 tablespoons olive oil
- 1 bulb of shallot (sliced)
- 4 cloves of garlic (minced)
- 64 ml. pinot grigio
- 4 tablespoon salted butter
- 1 tablespoon lemon juice
- ½ teaspoon sea salt
- ¼ teaspoon black pepper
- ¼ teaspoon red pepper flakes
- 30 grams of parsley (chopped)

Directions:

1. Pour the olive oil into the heated frying pan.
2. Add the garlic and shallots and fry for about 2 minutes.
3. Combine the Pinot Grigio, salted butter, and lemon juice.
4. Pour this mixture into the pan and cook for 5 minutes.
5. Put the parsley, black pepper, red pepper flakes, and sea salt into the pan and whisk well.
6. Add the shrimp and fry until they are pink (about 3 minutes).

 Nutrition:
Calories: 344　**Fat:** 7g　**Carbohydrates:** 7g　**Protein:** 32g

186. Chinese Pork Bowl

Preparation Time: 5 minutes	**Cooking Time:** 15 minutes	**Servings:** 4

Ingredients:

- 160 grams pounds of pork belly (cut into bite-size pieces)
- 2 tablespoons tamari soy sauce
- 1 tablespoon rice vinegar
- 2 cloves of garlic (smashed)
- 60 grams butter
- 500 grams of brussels sprouts (rinsed, trimmed, halved, or quartered)
- 60 grams leek (chopped)
- Salt
- Pepper

Directions:

1. Fry the pork over a medium-high heat until it is starting to turn golden brown.
2. Combine the garlic cloves, butter, and brussels sprouts.
3. Add to a pan, whisk well and cook until the sprouts turn golden brown.
4. Stir the soy sauce and rice vinegar together and pour the sauce into the pan.
5. Sprinkle with salt and pepper.
6. Top with chopped leek.

 Nutrition:
Calories: 993　**Fat:** 97g　**Carbohydrates:** 7g　**Protein:** 19g

187. Chicken Pan with Veggies and Pesto

Preparation Time: 10 minutes	**Cooking Time:** 20 minutes	**Servings:** 4

Ingredients:

- 2 tablespoons olive oil
- 500 grams of chicken thighs (skinless, boneless, sliced into strips)
- 90 grams of oil-packed sun-dried tomatoes (chopped)
- 500 grams of asparagus ends
- 30 grams of basil pesto
- 120 grams of cherry tomatoes (red and yellow, halved)
- Salt (to taste)

Directions:

1. Heat olive oil in a frying pan over medium-high heat.
2. Put salt on the chicken slices and then put it into a pan, add the sun-dried tomatoes and fry for 5–10 minutes.
3. Remove the chicken slices and season with salt.
4. Add asparagus to the pan.
5. Cook for additional 5–10 minutes.
6. Place the chicken back in the pan, pour in the pesto, and whisk.
7. Fry for 1–2 minutes. Remove from the heat.
8. Add the halved cherry tomatoes and pesto. Stir well and serve.

 Nutrition:
Calories: 423　**Fat:** 32g　**Carbohydrates:** 12g　**Protein:** 2g

188. Cabbage Soup with Beef

Preparation Time: 15 minutes	**Cooking Time:** 20 minutes	**Servings:** 4

Ingredients:

- 2 tablespoons olive oil
- 1 medium onion (chopped)
- 500 grams of fillet steak (cut into pieces)
- 60 grams stalk celery (chopped)
- 1 carrot (peeled and chopped)
- 60 grams head small green cabbage (cut into pieces)
- 2 cloves of garlic (minced)
- 500 ml. of beef broth
- 2 tablespoons of fresh parsley (chopped)
- 1 teaspoon dried thyme
- 1 teaspoon dried rosemary
- 1 teaspoon garlic powder
- Salt and black pepper (to taste)

Directions:

1. Heat oil in a pan (use a medium heat).
2. Add the beef and cook until it is browned.
3. Put the onion into the pan and boil for 3–4 minutes.
4. Add the celery and carrot.
5. Stir well and cook for about 3–4 minutes.
6. Add the cabbage and boil until it starts softening.
7. Add garlic and simmer for about 1 minute.
8. Pour the broth into the pan.
9. Add the parsley and garlic powder.
10. Mix thoroughly and reduce heat to a medium-low.
11. Cook for 10–15 minutes.

 Nutrition:
Calories: 541　**Fat:** 11g　**Carbohydrates:** 44g　**Protein:** 12g

189. Cauliflower Rice Soup with Chicken

Preparation Time: 10 minutes	**Cooking Time:** 1 hour	**Servings:** 5

Ingredients:

- 300 grams of chicken breasts (boneless and skinless)
- 8 tablespoons butter
- 30 grams celery (chopped)
- 70 grams onion (chopped)
- 4 cloves garlic (minced)
- 200 grams cauliflower rice
- 1 tablespoon parsley (chopped)
- 2 teaspoons of poultry seasoning
- 70 grams carrots, grated
- ¾ teaspoon rosemary
- Salt
- ¾ teaspoon pepper
- 150 grams of cream cheese
- 200 ml. chicken broth

Directions:

1. Put shredded chicken breasts into a saucepan and pour in the chicken broth.
2. Add salt and pepper. Cook for 1 hour.
3. In another pot, melt the butter.
4. Add the onion, garlic, and celery.
5. Sauté until the mix is translucent.
6. Add the riced cauliflower, rosemary, and carrot.
7. Mix and cook for 7 minutes.
8. Add the chicken breasts and broth to the cauliflower mix.
9. Put the lid on & simmer for 15 minutes.

 Nutrition:
Calories: 415 **Fat:** 30g **Carbohydrates:** 6g **Protein:** 27g

190. Baked Courgette Noodles with Feta

Preparation Time: 15 minutes	Cooking Time: 15 minutes	Servings: 1

Ingredients:

- 1 plum tomato
- 2 courgettes
- 8 cubes Feta cheese
- 1 teaspoon pepper
- 1 tablespoon olive oil

Directions:

1. Preheat the oven to 170°C.
2. Slice the noodles with a spiralizer and add the olive oil, tomatoes, pepper, and salt.
3. Bake for 10 to 15 minutes. Transfer then add cheese cubes, toss. Serve.

 Nutrition:
Calories: 447 **Carbohydrates:** 44g **Protein:** 4g **Fat:** 8g

191. Brussels Sprouts With Bacon

Preparation Time: 15 minutes	Cooking Time: 40 minutes	Servings: 6

Ingredients:

- 450 grams Bacon
- 450 grams Brussels sprouts
- Black pepper

Directions:

1. Preheat the oven to 200°C, fan 180°C, gas 6.
2. Slice the bacon into small lengthwise pieces. Put the sprouts and bacon with pepper.
3. Bake for 35 to 40 minutes. Serve.

 Nutrition:
Calories: 258 **Carbohydrates:** 12g **Protein:** 6g **Fat:** 4g

192. Bunless Burger - Keto Style

Preparation Time: 15 minutes	Cooking Time: 25 minutes	Servings: 6

Ingredients:

- 0,5 kg. Minced beef
- 1 tablespoon Worcestershire sauce
- 1 tablespoon steak seasoning
- 2 tablespoons olive oil
- 115 grams onion

Directions:

1. Mix the beef, olive oil, Worcestershire sauce, and seasonings.
2. Grill the burger. Prepare the onions by adding one tablespoon of oil in a pan to a medium-low heat. Sauté. Serve.

 Nutrition:
Calories: 479 **Carbohydrates:** 2g **Protein:** 26g **Fat:** 40g

193. Coffee BBQ Pork Belly

Preparation Time: 15 minutes	Cooking Time: 60 minutes	Servings: 4

Ingredients:

- 300 ml. Beef stock
- 1 kg. Pork belly
- 4 tablespoons Olive oil
- Low-carb barbecue dry rub
- 2 tablespoons Instant Espresso Powder

Directions:

1. Preheat the oven to 190°C, fan 170°C, gas 5.
2. Heat up the beef stock in a small saucepan.
3. Mix in the dry barbecue rub and espresso powder.
4. Put the pork belly, skin side up in a shallow dish and drizzle half of the oil over the top.
5. Put the hot stock around the pork belly. Bake for 45 minutes.
6. Sear each slice for three minutes per side. Serve.

 Nutrition:
Calories: 644 **Carbohydrates:** 2.6g **Protein:** 2 g **Fat:** 68g

194. Garlic & Thyme Lamb Chops

Preparation Time: 15 minutes	Cooking Time: 10 minutes	Servings: 6

Ingredients:

- 400 grams Lamb chops
- 4 garlic cloves
- 2 thyme sprigs
- 1 teaspoon ground thyme
- 3 tablespoons olive oil

Directions:

1. Preheat a pan. Add the olive oil. Rub the chops with the spices.
2. Put the chops in the pan with the garlic and sprigs of thyme.
3. Sauté for 3 to 4 minutes and serve.

 Nutrition:
Calories: 252   **Carbohydrates:** 33g   **Protein:** 14g   **Fat:** 21g

195. Jamaican Jerk Pork Roast

Preparation Time: 15 minutes	**Cooking Time:** 4 hours	🍴 **Servings:** 12

Ingredients:

- 1 tablespoon Olive oil
- 2 kg. Pork shoulder
- 250 ml. Beef Broth
- 30 grams Jamaican Jerk spice blend

Directions:

1. Rub the roast well with the oil and the jerk spice blend. Sear the roast on all sides. Add the beef broth.
2. Simmer for four hours on low. Shred and serve.

 Nutrition:
Calories: 282   **Carbohydrates:** 17g   **Protein:** 23g   **Fat:** 20g

196. Keto Meatballs

Preparation Time: 15 minutes	**Cooking Time:** 20 minutes	**Servings:** 10

Ingredients:

- 1 egg
- 150 grams Grated parmesan
- 150 grams Shredded mozzarella
- 450 grams minced beef
- 15 grams garlic

Directions:

1. Preheat the oven to 200°C, fan 180°C, gas 6. Combine all of the ingredients.
2. Shape into meatballs. Bake for 18-20 minutes. Cool and serve.

 Nutrition:
Calories: 223   **Carbohydrates:** 4g   **Protein:** 12.2g   **Fat:** 10.9g

197. Mixed Vegetable Patties - Instant Pot

Preparation Time: 15 minutes	**Cooking Time:** 10 minutes	**Servings:** 4

Ingredients:

- 120 grams cauliflower florets
- 1 bag vegetables
- 200 ml. Water
- 120 grams Flax meal
- Olive oil

Directions:

1. Steam the veggies in a steamer basket for 4 to 5 minutes.
2. Mash in the flax meal. Shape into 4 patties.
3. Cook the patties for 3 minutes per side.
4. Serve.

 Nutrition:
Calories: 220   **Carbohydrates:** 3 grams   **Protein:** 4 grams
Fat: 10 grams

198. Roasted Leg of Lamb

Preparation Time: 15 minutes	**Cooking Time:** 1 hour & 30 minutes	🍴 **Servings:** 6

Ingredients:

- 50 ml. Reduced-sodium beef broth
- 2 kg. lamb leg
- 6 garlic cloves
- 1 tablespoon rosemary leaves
- 1 teaspoon black pepper

Directions:

5. Preheat the oven to 200°C, fan 180°C, gas 6.
6. Put the lamb in a pan and add the broth and seasonings.
7. Roast for 30 minutes and lower the heat to 220° C Cook for one hour.
8. Cool and serve.

 Nutrition:
Calories: 223   **Carbohydrates:** 15g   **Protein:** 22g   **Fat:** 13g

199. Salmon Pasta

Preparation Time: 15 minutes	**Cooking Time:** 1 hour & 30 minutes	**Servings:** 2

Ingredients:

- 2 tablespoons coconut oil
- 2 courgettes
- 230 grams Smoked salmon
- 30 grams Keto-friendly mayo

Directions:

1. Make noodle-like strands from the courgettes.
2. Heat up the oil, in a pan, add the salmon and sauté for 2 to 3 minutes.
3. Stir in the noodles and sauté for 1 to 2 more minutes.
4. Stir in the mayo and serve.

 Nutrition:
Calories: 470   **Carbohydrates:** 3g   **Protein:** 21g   **Fat:** 42g

200. Pan Fried Cod

 Preparation Time: 15 minutes | **Cooking Time:** 30 minutes | **Servings:** 4

Ingredients:

- 6 garlic cloves
- 3 tablespoons ghee
- 4 cod fillets
- Optional: garlic powder

Directions:

1. Toss half of the garlic into a pan with the ghee.
2. Put the fillets in the pan, add the garlic, pepper, and salt.
3. Turn it over and add the remainder of the garlic. Cook.
4. Serve with garlic.

Nutrition:
Calories: 446 **Carbohydrates:** 15g **Protein:** 21g **Fat:** 7g

201. Slow-Cooked Kalua Pork & Cabbage

 Preparation Time: 15 minutes | **Cooking Time:** 11 hours | **Servings:** 12

Ingredients:

- 1,5 kg. pork shoulder butt
- 1 medium cabbage
- 7 strips bacon
- Sea salt

Directions:

1. Trim the fat from the roast.
2. Layer most of the bacon in the slow cooker. Put salt over the roast and add to the slow cooker on top of the bacon. Cook on low for 8 to 10 hours. Put in the cabbage and cook for an hour.
3. Shred the roast. Serve with cabbage and juice from the slow cooker.

Nutrition:
Calories: 369 **Carbohydrates:** 16g **Protein:** 22g **Fat:** 13g

202. Steak Pinwheels

 Preparation Time: 15 minutes | **Cooking Time:** 25 minutes | **Servings:** 6

Ingredients:

- 1 kg. Flank steak
- 230 grams Mozzarella cheese
- 1 bunch Spinach

Directions:

1. Preheat the oven to 220°C, fan 200°C, gas 8.
2. Slice the steak into six portions. Beat until thin with a mallet.
3. Shred the cheese using a food processor and sprinkle on the steak. Roll it up and tie it with cooking twine.

4. Line the pan with the pinwheels and place it on a layer of spinach. Bake in the oven for 25 minutes.

Nutrition:
Calories: 414 **Carbohydrates:** 11g **Protein:** 55g **Fat:** 22g

203. Tangy Shrimp

 Preparation Time: 15 minutes | **Cooking Time:** 15 minutes | **Servings:** 2

Ingredients:

- 3 garlic cloves
- Olive oil
- 250 grams Jumbo shrimp/ prawns
- 1 lemon
- Cayenne pepper

Directions:

1. Sauté the garlic and cayenne with olive oil.
2. Peel and devein the shrimp.
3. Cook for 2 to 3 minutes per side.
4. Season with pepper and salt and add lemon wedges. Use the rest of the garlic oil for a dipping sauce.
5. Serve.

Nutrition:
Calories: 335 **Carbohydrates:** 3g **Protein:** 23g **Fat:** 27g

204. Chicken Salad with Champagne Vinegar

Preparation Time: 15 minutes | **Cooking Time:** 10 minutes | **Servings:** 3

Ingredients:

- 60 grams sliced red onion
- 64 ml. champagne vinegar
- 1 package of Chipotle paste (or smoked paprika)
- 250 grams mixed greens (kale, cabbage etc.)
- 250 grams of sweet butter lettuce
- 60 grams of cooked; then crumbled bacon
- 120 grams of halved cherry tomatoes
- 60 grams of almond flour
- 60 grams sliced avocado
- 120 ml Green Goddess Dressing
- 2 sliced hard-boiled eggs

Directions:

1. Put the red onion and the vinegar in a bowl.
2. Open the bag of the chipotle adobo flavor, then toss the almond flour in the bag; then add in the chicken and shake it very well.
3. Toss the chicken in your Air Fryer basket and lock the lid. Set the timer to about 8 to 10 minutes at a temperature of about 220° C. When the timer beeps; turn off your Air Fryer.
4. Transfer the chicken to a bowl and add in the lettuce, the bacon, the greens, the tomatoes, and the avocado. Toss your ingredients very well with the dressing.

5. Top your salad with the pickled onion, the hard-boiled eggs, and the baked chicken shakers!

 Nutrition:
Calories: 565 **Carbohydrates:** 11g **Protein:** 8.9g **Fat:** 4.6g

205. Mexican Beef Salad

 **Preparation Time:** 15 minutes | **Cooking Time:** 12 minutes | **Servings:** 6

Ingredients:
- 0,5 kg minced beef
- 1 tablespoon taco seasoning
- 220 grams cherry tomatoes, halved
- 60 grams chives or spring onions, chopped
- 43 ml. salsa
- Olive oil
- 230 grams lettuce, chopped
- 1 large cucumber, chopped
- 30 grams cheddar cheese, shredded
- 43 grams sour cream

Directions:
1. Heat-up oil over a high heat in a pan and stir fry the beef for about 8-10 minutes, breaking up the pieces with a spatula.
2. Stir in the taco seasoning and remove from the heat. Set aside to cool slightly.
3. Meanwhile, in a large bowl, add the remaining ingredients and mix well.
4. Add the minced beef and toss to coat well.
5. Serve immediately.

 Nutrition:
Calories: 263 **Carbohydrates:** 7g **Protein:** 28.1g **Fat:** 13.1g

206. Cherry Tomatoes Tilapia Salad

Preparation Time: 15 minutes | **Cooking Time:** 18 minutes | **Servings:** 3

Ingredients:
- 400 grams mixed greens (cabbage, kale etc.)
- 120 grams of cherry tomatoes
- 1 red onion, chopped
- 1 medium avocado
- 2 to 3 Tortilla Crusted Tilapia fillet

Directions:
1. Spray the tilapia fillet with a little bit of cooking spray.
2. Put the fillets in your Air Fryer basket. Lock the lid of your Air Fryer and set the timer to about 18 minutes and the temperature to about 220° C.
3. When the timer beeps; turn off your Air Fryer and transfer the fillet to a bowl.
4. Add about half of the fillets in a large bowl, then toss it with the tomatoes, the greens, and the red onion.
5. Add the lime dressing and mix again.
6. When the timer beeps, turn off your Air Fryer and transfer the fish to the veggie salad. Serve and enjoy your salad!

 Nutrition:
Calories: 271 **Carbohydrates:** 10.1g **Protein:** 18.5g **Fat:** 8g

207. Crunchy Chicken Milanese

 Preparation Time: 15 minutes | **Cooking Time:** 10 minutes | **Servings:** 2

Ingredients:
- Chicken breasts (2, skinless, boneless)
- 60 grams coconut flour
- 1 egg, lightly beaten
- 60 grams crushed pork rinds
- Olive oil

Directions:
1. Pound the chicken breasts using a heavy mallet.
2. Prepare 2 separate prep plates and one small, shallow bowl.
3. On plate 1, put the coconut flour, cayenne pepper, pink salt, and pepper. Mix together. 4. On plate 2, put the crushed pork rinds.
5. Warm up the olive oil, then dredge chicken breasts in flour mixture, then egg and finish with pork rinds.
6. Set a pan with oil over a medium heat and add your coated chicken.
7. Cook the chicken for 10 minutes and serve.

 Nutrition:
Calories: 604 **Carbohydrates:** 17g **Protein:** 65g **Fat:** 29g

208. Parmesan Baked Chicken

Preparation Time: 15 minutes | **Cooking Time:** 20 minutes | **Servings:** 2

Ingredients:
- 2 tablespoons ghee
- 2 boneless skinless chicken breasts
- 60 grams mayonnaise
- 30 grams grated Parmesan cheese
- 30 grams crushed pork rinds

Directions:
1. Preheat the oven to 200° C, fan 180°C, gas 6.
2. Put both chicken breasts in a large baking dish and coat it with ghee.
3. Pat dry the chicken breasts with a paper towel, season with pink salt and pepper, and place in the prepared baking dish.
4. In a small bowl, mix to combine the mayonnaise, Parmesan cheese, and Italian seasoning.
5. Slather the mayonnaise mixture evenly over the chicken breasts and sprinkle the crushed pork rinds on top of the mayonnaise mixture.
6. Bake until the topping is browned, about 20 minutes, and serve.

 Nutrition:
Calories: 850 **Carbohydrates:** 2g **Protein:** 60g **Fat:** 67g

209. Cheesy Bacon and Broccoli Chicken

 Preparation Time: 15 minutes | **Cooking Time:** 1 hour | **Servings:** 2

Ingredients:

- 2 boneless skinless chicken breasts
- 4 bacon slices
- 180 grams cream cheese, room temp.
- 250 grams frozen broccoli florets thawed
- 90 grams grated Cheddar cheese

Directions:

1. Warm up the oven to 220° Celsius, fan 200°C, gas 8, then choose a baking dish that is large enough to hold both chicken breasts and coat the inside with the ghee. Pat dry the chicken breasts with a paper towel and season with pink salt and pepper. Place the chicken breasts and the bacon slices in the baking dish and bake in the oven for 25 minutes.
2. Shred the chicken. Season it again with pink salt and pepper. Place the bacon on a kitchen paper–lined plate to crisp up and then crumble it.
3. In a medium bowl, combine the cream cheese, shredded chicken, broccoli, and half of the bacon crumbles. Transfer the chicken mixture, and top with the cheddar and the remaining half of the bacon crumbles.
4. Bake for about 35 minutes and serve.

 Nutrition:
Calories: 935 **Carbohydrates:** 10g **Protein:** 75g **Fat:** 66g

210. Buttery Garlic Chicken

Preparation Time: 15 minutes	Cooking Time: 40 minutes	Servings: 2

Ingredients:

- 2 tablespoons ghee, melted
- 2 boneless skinless chicken breasts
- 4 tablespoons butter
- 2 garlic garlic cloves, crushed
- 30 grams grated Parmesan cheese

Directions:

1. Warm up the oven to 220° Celsius, fan 200°C, gas 8 then choose a baking dish that is large enough to hold both chicken breasts and coat the inside with the ghee.
2. Pat dry the chicken breasts and season with pink salt, pepper, and Italian seasoning.
3. Place the chicken in the baking dish. Melt the butter in a pan.
4. Put the crushed garlic in the pan and cook for 5 minutes, then remove the butter-garlic mixture from the heat and pour it over the chicken breasts.
5. Roast the chicken in the oven for 30 to 35 minutes, until cooked through.
6. Sprinkle some of the Parmesan cheese on top of each chicken breast.
7. Let it rest in the baking dish for 5 minutes, then spoon the butter sauce over the chicken, and serve.

 Nutrition:
Calories: 642 **Carbohydrates:** 2g **Protein:** 57g **Fat:** 45g

211. Creamy Slow Cooker Chicken

Preparation Time: 15 minutes	Cooking Time: 4 hours & 15 minutes	Servings: 2

Ingredients:

- 2 boneless skinless chicken breasts
- 120 ml. Alfredo Sauce
- 30 grams chopped sun-dried tomatoes
- 30 grams Parmesan cheese, grated
- 250 grams fresh spinach

Directions:

1. Melt the ghee in a pan, then add the chicken and cook for about 4 minutes on each side.
2. With the crock insert in place, transfer the chicken to your slow cooker. Set your slow cooker to low.
3. In a small bowl, mix the Alfredo sauce, sun-dried tomatoes, Parmesan cheese, salt, and pepper.
4. Pour the sauce over the chicken. Cover and cook on low for 4 hours.
5. Then add the fresh spinach.
6. Cover and cook for 5 minutes more, until the spinach is slightly wilted, and serve.

Nutrition:
Calories: 900 **Carbohydrates:** 9g **Protein:** 70g **Fat:** 66g

212. Braised Chicken Thighs with Kalamata Olives

 Preparation Time: 15 minutes	Cooking Time: 40 minutes	Servings: 2

Ingredients:

- 4 chicken thighs, skin on
- 70 ml. chicken broth
- 1 lemon, sliced
- 50 ml. lemon juice
- 70 grams pitted Kalamata olives
- 2 tablespoons butter

Directions:

1. Warm up the oven to 220° C, fan 200°C, gas 8, then dry the chicken, and season to taste.
2. In a medium oven-safe pan or high-sided baking dish over a medium-high heat, melt butter on the hob.
3. When the butter has melted and is hot, add the chicken thighs, skin-side down, and leave them for about 8 minutes, or until the skin is brown and crispy. Turn the chicken over and cook for 2 minutes on the second side.
4. Around the chicken thighs, pour in the chicken broth, and add the lemon slices, lemon juice, and olives.
5. Bake in the oven for about 30 minutes, until the chicken is cooked through.
6. Add the butter to the broth mixture.
7. . Divide the chicken and olives between 2 plates and serve.

Nutrition:
Calories: 567 **Carbohydrates:** 4g **Protein:** 33g **Fat:** 47g

213. Baked Garlic and Paprika Chicken Legs

 Preparation Time: 15 minutes | **Cooking Time:** 55 minutes | **Servings:** 2

Ingredients:

- 450 grams chicken drumsticks, skin on
- 2 tablespoons paprika
- 2 garlic cloves, crushed
- 60 grams fresh green beans
- 1 tablespoon olive oil

Directions:

1. Preheat your oven to 220° Celsius, fan 200°C, gas 8.
2. Combine all the ingredients in a large bowl, mix, together and transfer to a baking dish.
3. Bake for 60 minutes until crisp and thoroughly cooked.

 Nutrition:
Calories: 700 **Carbohydrates:** 10g **Protein:** 63g **Fat:** 45g

214. Chicken Curry with Masala

 Preparation Time: 15 minutes | **Cooking Time:** 30 minutes | **Servings:** 4

Ingredients:

- 2 tablespoons olive oil
- 4 tablespoons crushed jalapeno
- 500 grams of chopped boneless skinless chicken thighs
- 1 teaspoon garam masala
- 30 grams of chopped coriander
- 2 tablespoons diced ginger
- 120 grams of chopped tomatoes
- 1 teaspoon turmeric
- 2 tablespoons lemon juice
- 28 ml. of lemon juice

Directions:

4. Heat your Air Fryer to a temperature of about 200° C. Grease the Air Fryer pan with the cooking spray. Add the jalapenos and the ginger. Add in the chicken and the tomatoes and stir.
5. Add the spices and 15 grams. of oil and 15 ml. of water.
6. Now, set the timer to 30 minutes. When the timer beeps, turn off your Air Fryer. Serve and enjoy your lunch!

 Nutrition:
Calories: 254 **Carbohydrates:** 9g **Protein:** 27.8g **Fat:** 14g

215. Chicken Quesadilla

 Preparation Time: 15 minutes | **Cooking Time:** 5 minutes | **Servings:** 2

Ingredients:

- 1 tablespoon olive oil
- 2 low-carbohydrate tortillas
- 60 grams grated Mexican blend cheese
- 56 grams shredded chicken
- 2 tablespoons sour cream

Directions:

1. Heat the olive oil in a large pan, then put a tortilla in the pan.
2. Top the tortilla with 30 grams of cheese, the chicken, the Tajin seasoning, and the remaining 30 grams of cheese.
3. Then top with the second tortilla.
4. Once the bottom tortilla gets golden, and the cheese begins to melt, after about 2 minutes, flip the quesadilla over.
5. The second side will cook faster, about 1 minute.
6. Once the second tortilla is crispy and golden, transfer the quesadilla to a cutting board and let sit for 2 minutes.
7. Cut the quesadilla into 4 wedges using a pizza cutter or chef's knife.
8. Transfer half the quesadilla to each of the 2 plates.
9. Add 15 grams of sour cream (on the side or on top) and serve hot.

 Nutrition:
Calories: 414 **Carbohydrates:** 24g **Protein:** 26g **Fat:** 28g

216. Slow Cooker Barbecue Ribs

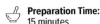 **Preparation Time:** 15 minutes | **Cooking Time:** 4 hours | **Servings:** 2

Ingredients:

- 1 kg. pork ribs
- Salt
- Freshly ground black pepper
- 10 grams package dry rib-seasoning rub
- 11 teaspoon sugar-free barbecue sauce

Directions:

1. With the crock insert in place, preheat your slow cooker to high.
2. Generously season the pork ribs with pink salt, pepper, and dry rib-seasoning rub.
3. Stand the ribs up along the walls of the slow-cooker insert, with the bonier side facing inward.
4. Pour the barbecue sauce on both sides of the ribs, using just enough to coat.
5. Cover, cook for 4 hours and serve.

 Nutrition:
Calories: 956 **Carbohydrates:** 5g **Protein:** 68g **Fat:** 72g

217. Barbacoa Beef Roast

Preparation Time: 15 minutes | **Cooking Time:** 8 hours | **Servings:** 4

Ingredients:

- 450 grams beef chuck roast
- 4 chipotle peppers in adobo sauce
- 1 can green jalapeño chilis
- 2 tablespoons apple cider vinegar
- 70 ml. beef broth

Directions:

1. With the crock insert in place, preheat your slow cooker to low.
2. Massage the beef chuck roast on both sides with pink salt and pepper. Put the roast in the slow cooker.
3. Pulse the chipotle peppers and their adobo sauce, jalapeños, and apple cider vinegar in a blender.
4. Add the beef broth and pulse a few more times. Pour the chili mixture over the top of the roast.
5. Cover and cook on low for 8 hours, then shred the meat. Serve hot.

 Nutrition:
Calories: 723 **Carbohydrates:** 7g **Protein:** 66g **Fat:** 46g

218. Beef & Broccoli Roast

Preparation Time: 15 minutes	Cooking Time: 4 hours & 30 minutes	Servings: 2

Ingredients:

- 450 grams beef chuck roast
- 60 grams beef broth
- 32 ml. soy sauce
- 1 teaspoon toasted sesame oil
- 500 grams broccoli, frozen

Directions:

1. With the crock insert in place, preheat your slow cooker to low.
2. On a cutting board, season the chuck roast with pink salt and pepper, and slice the roast thin. Put the sliced beef in your slow cooker.
3. Combine sesame oil and beef broth in a small bowl then pour over the beef. Cover and cook on low for 4 hours.
4. Add the frozen broccoli and cook for 30 minutes more. If you need more liquid, add additional beef broth.
5. Serve hot.

 Nutrition:
Calories: 803 **Carbohydrates:** 18g **Protein:** 74g **Fat:** 49g

219. Cauliflower and Pumpkin Casserole

Preparation Time: 15 minutes	Cooking Time: 1 hour & 30 minutes	Servings: 4

Ingredients:

- 2 tablespoons Olive oil
- 1 onion, chopped
- 150 grams kale
- 1 little clove garlic, chopped
- Salt
- Pepper
- 200 ml. low sodium/salt chicken broth
- 250 grams pumpkin
- 250 grams courgette
- 2 tablespoons mayonnaise
- 380 grams frozen, thawed brown rice
- 120 grams grated Swiss cheese
- 43 grams grated Parmesan
- 120 grams panko flour
- 1 large beaten egg
- Cooking spray

Directions:

1. Preheat oven to 200° C, fan 180°C, gas 6 .
2. Heat the oil in a large non-stick pan over a medium heat. Add onions and cook, occasionally stirring, until browned and tender (about 5 minutes).
3. Add the cabbage, garlic, 60 grams teaspoon salt, and 60 grams teaspoon pepper and cook until the cabbage is light (about 2 minutes).
4. Add the stock and cook for 5 minutes, then put the pumpkin, courgette, and 60 grams teaspoon salt and mix well. Continuously cooking for 8 minutes. Remove from heat and add mayonnaise.
5. In a bowl, combine cooked vegetables, brown rice, cheese, 60 grams flour, and a large egg and mix well.
6. Spray a 2-litre casserole dish with cooking spray. Put the mixture in the dish and cover with the remaining flour, 1.21 teaspoon salt, and a few pinches of pepper. Bake until the pumpkin and courgette are tender and the top golden and crispy (about 35 minutes). Serve hot.

 Advanced Preparation Tip: Freeze the casserole for up to 2 weeks. Cover with aluminum foil and heat at 180 ° C until warm (35 to 45 minutes).

 Nutrition:
Calories: 966 **Carbohydrates:** 11g **Fat:** 3g **Protein:** 5g

220. Thai Beef Salad

Preparation Time: 15 minutes	Cooking Time: 30 minutes	Servings: 4

Ingredients:

- 800 grams beef tenderloin
- For the marinade:
- 2 tablespoons soy sauce
- 1 tablespoon honey
- 1 pinch of the ground pepper
- For the sauce:
- 1 small bunch of fresh coriander
- 1 small bouquet of mint
- 3 tablespoons fish sauce
- 1 lime
- 1 clove of garlic
- 2 tablespoons sugar palm
- 10 drops tabasco sauce
- 1 small glass of raw Thai rice to make grilled rice powder
- 200 grams of arugula or young shoots of salad

Directions:

1. Cut the beef tenderloin into strips and put in a container. Sprinkle with 2 tablespoons soy sauce, 15 grams honey, and pepper. Cover thoroughly and let marinate for 1 hour at room temperature.
2. Meanwhile, prepare the roasted rice powder. Pour a glass of Thai rice into a non-stick pan. Dry fry the rice, constantly stirring to avoid burning. When it has a lovely color, serve on a plate and let it cool.
3. When it has cooled, reduce it to powder with a blender.
4. Wash and finely chop mint and coriander. Put in a container and add lime juice, chopped garlic clove, 50 grams mam, 50 grams brown sugar, 50 ml. water, 11 teaspoon sauce soy, and a dozen

drop of Tabasco. Mix well and let stand the time that the sugar melts and the flavors mix.

5. Place a bed of salad on a dish. Cook the beef strips then place them on the salad.
6. Sprinkle with a spoonful of sauce and roasted rice powder. To be served as is or with Thai cooked white rice scented.

 Nutrition:
Calories: 687   **Carbohydrates:** 33g   **Fat:** 22g   **Protein:** 30g

221. Stuffed Apples with Shrimp

Preparation Time: 15 minutes	**Cooking Time:** 30 minutes	**Servings:** 4

Ingredients:

- 6 medium apples
- 1 lemon juice
- 60 grams butter
- Filling:
- 300 grams of shrimp/prawns
- 1 onion, chopped
- 60 grams chopped parsley
- 2 tablespoons flour
- 1 can of cream
- 100 grams of curd cheese or cream cheese
- 1 tablespoon butter
- 1 tablespoon pepper sauce
- Salt

Directions:

1. Remove the core from the centre of the apple and leaving a cavity.
2. Pass a little lemon and some butter on the apples, bake them in the oven 30 minutes at 180°C.
3. Remove from oven, let cool and bring to freeze.
4. Prepare the shrimp sauce in a pan by mixing the butter with the flour, onion, parsley, and pepper sauce.
5. Then add the prawn/shrimp to the sauce. When boiling, mix the cream cheese or sour cream.
6. Stuff each apple. Serve hot or cold, as you prefer.

 Nutrition:
Calories: 741   **Carbohydrates:** 44g   **Fat:** 15g   **Protein:** 36g

222. Grilled Chicken Salad with Oranges

Preparation Time: 15 minutes	**Cooking Time:** 15 minutes	**Servings:** 4

Ingredients:

- 75 ml. orange juice
- 30 ml. lemon juice
- 3 tablespoons extra virgin olive oil
- 1 tablespoon Dijon mustard
- 2 cloves of garlic, chopped
- Salt
- Pepper
- 450 grams skinless chicken breast, trimmed
- 25 grams pistachio or flaked almonds, toasted
- 600 grams of mesclun, rinsed and dried (or watercress)
- 75 grams chopped red onion
- 2 medium oranges, peeled, quartered, and sliced

Directions:

1. Place the orange juice, lemon juice, oil, mustard, garlic, salt, and pepper in a small bowl or jar with an airtight lid; shake to mix. Reserve 75 milliliters of this salad vinaigrette and 45 milliliters for basting.
2. Place the rest of the vinaigrette in a shallow glass dish or resealable plastic bag. Add the chicken and turn it over to coat. Cover or close and marinate in the refrigerator for at least 20 minutes or up to 2 hours.
3. Preheat the barbecue on a medium heat. Lightly oil the grill by rubbing it with a crumpled kitchen towel soaked in oil. Grill the chicken 10 to 15 centimeters (four to six inches) from the heat source, basting the cooked sides with the basting vinaigrette until it is no longer pink in the center, and an instant-read thermometer inserted in the thickest part records reads 175° C, 4 to 6 minutes on each side. Transfer then let it rest for 5 minutes.
4. Meanwhile, grill almonds in a small, dry pan on a medium-low heat, stirring constantly, until lightly browned, about 2 to 3 minutes. Transfer them to a bowl and let them cool.
5. Place the salad and onion mixture in a large bowl then mix with the vinaigrette reserved for the salad.
6. Slice chicken and spread on salads. Place orange slices on top and sprinkle with pistachios.

 Nutrition:
Calories: 654   **Carbohydrates:** 21g   **Fat:** 14g   **Protein:** 25g

223. Red Curry with Vegetables

 **Preparation Time:** 15 minutes	**Cooking Time:** 30 minutes	**Servings:** 4

Ingredients:

- 600 grams sweet potatoes
- 200 grams canned chickpeas
- 2 leeks (white part)
- 2 tomatoes
- 100 grams of spinach shoots
- 40 ml. of coconut milk
- 1 can of Greek yogurt
- 1 lime
- 3 cm fresh ginger
- 1 small bunch of coriander
- 60 grams red onion
- 2 cloves garlic
- 4 tablespoons red curry paste
- Salt

Directions:

1. Chop the sweet potatoes into pieces. Clean the leek whites and cut them into slices. Peel and seed the tomatoes.
2. Mix the Greek yogurt with a drizzle of lime juice, chopped onion, salt, and half of the coriander leaves.
3. In a frying pan, heat 11 teaspoon of coconut milk until it reduces and forms many small bubbles. Brown curry paste with chopped ginger and garlic.
4. Add vegetables, drained chickpeas, remaining coconut milk, and salt. Cook for 20 min covered, then 5 min without lid for the sauce to thicken.
5. When serving, add spinach sprouts and remaining coriander. Serve with the yogurt sauce.

Nutrition:
Calories: 254 **Carbohydrates:** 13g **Fat:** 4g **Protein:** 3g

224. Baked Turkey Breast with Cranberry Sauce

 | Preparation Time: 15 minutes | Cooking Time: 1 hour & 30 minutes | Servings: 3 |

Ingredients:

- 2 kg. of whole turkey breast
- 1 tablespoon olive oil
- 40 grams onion
- 3 cloves of garlic
- 5 grams dried thyme
- 5 grams poultry seasonings
- Salt
- 30 grams butter
- 30 grams chopped shallot
- 30 grams chopped onion
- 1 clove garlic
- 2 tablespoons flour
- 100 grams blueberries
- 250 grams apple cider
- 2 tablespoons maple honey
- Pepper

Directions:

1. Grind in the blender 30 grams onion and 2 garlic cloves with herbs.
2. Grease the turkey breast with oil. Place in a baking tray, add half a lemon, and bake at 190° C, fan 170°C, gas 5 .
3. Bring the lemon to the boil, add the blueberries, and leave a few minutes.
4. In a separate pan add in the butter (2 tablespoons) and fry the onion (60 grams), shallot, and garlic (1 clove).
5. Add the flour to the onion and shallot and leave a few minutes.
6. Then add the lemon, blueberries, and honey and leave on low heat. Season with salt and pepper, let the blueberries get soft. It can be strained if required.
7. Let it thicken slightly.
8. Slice the thin turkey breast and serve with the blueberry sauce.

 Nutrition:
Calories: 1258 **Carbohydrates:** 77g **Fat:** 17g **Protein:** 23g

225. Italian Keto Casserole

 | Preparation Time: 15 minutes | Cooking Time: 1 hour | Servings: 4 |

Ingredients:

- 200 grams Shirataki noodles
- 2 tablespoons olive oil
- 1 small onion, chopped
- 2 garlic cloves, finely chopped
- 1 teaspoon dried marjoram
- 450 grams minced beef
- Salt
- Pepper
- 2 chopped tomatoes
- 120 grams full fat cream
- 340 grams ricotta cheese
- 100 grams grated parmesan
- 1 egg
- 30 grams parsley, roughly chopped

Directions:

1. Preheat the oven to 190° Celsius, fan 170°C, gas 5.
2. Prepare the shirataki noodles as indicated on the packaging, strain well, and set aside.
3. Fry oil, onion, garlic, marjoram for 2-3 minutes, until the onion is soft.
4. Add minced beef, salt, and pepper, and simmer, stirring, while the mixture is browned.
5. Add tomatoes and full fat cream and cook for 5 minutes.
6. Remove from the heat and mix with noodles. Transfer the mixture to a baking dish.
7. Mix ricotta, parmesan, egg, and parsley. Spoon over the casserole.
8. Bake for about 35-45 minutes until golden brown.

 Nutrition:
Calories: 369 **Carbohydrates:** 44g **Fat:** 10g **Protein:** 20g

226. Salmon Keto Cutlets

 | Preparation Time: 15 minutes | Cooking Time: 10 minutes | Servings: 4 |

Ingredients:

- 450 g canned salmon
- 60 grams almond flour
- 30 grams shallots, finely chopped
- 2 tablespoons parsley, finely chopped
- 1 tablespoon dried chopped onions
- 2 large eggs
- Zest of 1 lemon
- 1 clove garlic, finely chopped
- ½ teaspoon salt
- ½ teaspoon ground white pepper
- 3 tablespoons olive oil

Directions:

1. Put all the ingredients, except the oil, in a large bowl and mix well.
2. Form 8, identical cutlets.
3. Fry salmon cutlets in portions, adding more oil as needed, for 2-3 minutes on each side.
4. Serve the cutlets warm or cold with lemon wedges and low carbohydrate mayonnaise.

Nutrition:
Calories: 456 **Carbohydrates:** 55g **Fat:** 19g **Protein:** 35g

227. Baked Cauliflower

| Preparation Time: 15 minutes | Cooking Time: 60 minutes | Servings: 2 |

Ingredients:

- 1 medium cauliflower
- 113 grams of salted butter
- 100 grams finely grated parmesan
- 3 tablespoons Dijon mustard
- 2 minced garlic cloves
- Zest of 1 lemon
- Salt

- Pepper
- 40 grams fresh Parmesan
- 1 tablespoon chopped parsley

Directions:

1. Preheat the oven to 190° Celsius, fan 170°C, gas 5.
2. Put the cauliflower in a small baking dish.
3. Put the remaining ingredients in a small saucepan, except for fresh parmesan and parsley, and put on a low heat until they melt. Whip together.
4. Cover the cauliflower in a quarter of the oil mixture.
5. Bake for 20 minutes, then remove from the oven and pour over another quarter of the oil mixture.
6. Bake for another 20 minutes and pour over the remaining oil mixture.
7. Cook for another 20-30 minutes until the core is soft.
8. Put on a plate, sprinkle a drop of oil, grate fresh parmesan and sprinkle with parsley.

 Nutrition:
Calories: 420 **Carbohydrates:** 41g **Fat:** 11g **Protein:** 19g

228. Risotto with Mushrooms

 Preparation Time: 15 minutes | **Cooking Time:** 25 minutes | **Servings:** 2

Ingredients:

- 2 tablespoons olive oil
- 2 chopped garlic cloves
- 1 small onion, finely chopped
- Salt
- White Pepper
- 200 grams chopped mushrooms
- 30 grams chopped oregano leaves
- 255 grams cauliflower rice
- 40 grams vegetable broth/ stock
- 2 tablespoons butter
- 100 grams grated parmesan

Directions:

1. Sauté oil, garlic, onions, salt and pepper for 5-7 minutes. until the onions become transparent.
2. Add mushrooms and oregano and cook for 5 minutes.
3. Add cauliflower rice and vegetable broth, then reduce the heat to medium. Cook the risotto, frequently stirring, for 10-15 minutes, until the cauliflower is soft.
4. Remove from heat and mix with butter and parmesan.
5. Taste and add more seasoning if you want.

 Nutrition:
Calories: 362 **Carbohydrates:** 31g **Fat:** 7g **Protein:** 4g

229. Low Carb Green Bean Casserole

 **Preparation Time:** 15 minutes | **Cooking Time:** 60 minutes | **Servings:** 4

Ingredients:

- 2 tablespoons butter
- 1 small, chopped onion
- 2 chopped garlic cloves
- 230 grams chopped mushrooms
- Salt
- Pepper
- 90 ml. chicken stock
- 50 grams full fat cream
- ½ teaspoon xanthan gum
- 450 grams green beans (trimmed)
- 60 grams crushed crackling

Directions:

1. Preheat the oven to 190° degrees, fan 170°C, gas 5.
2. Add oil, onion, and garlic to a non-stick pan over a high heat. Fry until the onion is transparent.
3. Add mushrooms, salt, and pepper. Cook for 7 minutes until the mushrooms are tender.
4. Add chicken stock and cream and bring to a boil. Sprinkle with xanthan gum, mix and cook for 5 minutes.
5. Add the green beans to the creamy mixture and pour into the baking dish.
6. Cover with foil and bake for 20 minutes.
7. Remove the foil, sprinkle with crackling and bake for another 10-15 minutes.

 Nutrition:
Calories: 554 **Carbohydrates:** 6g **Fat:** 18g **Protein:** 8g

230. Avocado Low Carb Burger

 Preparation Time: 15 minutes | **Cooking Time:** 25 minutes | **Servings:** 4

Ingredients:

- 1 avocado
- 1 leaf of lettuce
- 2 slices of prosciutto or any ham
- 1 slice of tomato
- 1 egg
- Olive oil
- For the sauce:
- 1 tablespoon low carb mayonnaise
- ¼ teaspoon low carb hot sauce
- ¼ teaspoon mustard
- ¼ teaspoon Italian seasoning
- ½ teaspoon sesame seeds

Directions:

1. In a small bowl, combine keto-friendly mayonnaise, mustard, hot sauce, and Italian seasoning.
2. Heat 60 grams tablespoon of olive oil in a pan and cook an egg. The yolk must be soft.
3. Cut the avocado in half, remove the peel and stone. Cut the narrowest part of the avocado so that the fruit can stand on a plate.
4. Fill the hole in one-half of the avocado with the prepared sauce.
5. Top with lettuce, prosciutto strips, a slice of tomato, and a fried egg.
6. Cover with the other half of the avocado and sprinkle with sesame seeds (optional).

Nutrition:
Calories: 416 **Carbohydrates:** 15g **Fat:** 55g **Protein:** 35g

231. Protein Gnocchi with Basil Pesto

Preparation Time: 15 minutes	**Cooking Time:** 30 minutes	**Servings:** 4

Ingredients:

- 400 grams potatoes
- 60 grams protein powder, neutral
- 50 grams wheat flour
- Salt
- 20 grams nutmeg
- 2 tablespoons flour for the work surface
- 1 bunch basil
- 30 grams pine nuts
- 1 clove of garlic
- 100 ml olive oil
- Salt
- Pepper

Directions:

1. The recipe is a bit tricky. So, take your time.
2. Slice the potatoes into small pieces and cook for 20-25 minutes. Let the potatoes cool.
3. Put the pieces of potato, the protein powder, the flour, and the spices together in a blender and mix everything properly.
4. Put flour on the work surface and divide the dough into four parts.
5. Form long, round snakes out of the dough.
6. Slice the snakes every 1.5-2 cm, press briefly with a fork and you're done with the raw gnocchi.
7. Now put the gnocchi together in lightly boiling water for 3-4 minutes and wait until they float up. Serve.

 Nutrition:
Calories: 347 **Carbohydrates:** 33g **Fat:** 11g **Protein:** 7g

232. Summery Bowls with Fresh Vegetables and Protein Quark

Preparation Time: 15 minutes	**Cooking Time:** 10 minutes	**Servings:** 4

Ingredients:

- 100 grams green salad
- 100 grams radish
- 200 grams turnip or celeriac
- 70 grams carrots
- 70 grams red lenses
- 50 gras tomatoes
- 2 spring onions
- 20 grams Nuts/seeds
- 150 grams soy yogurt
- 2 tablespoons mixed herbs
- 1 teaspoon lemon juice
- 20 grams Nutri-Plus Shape & Shake, neutral
- Salt
- Pepper

Directions:

1. Wash the salad and the vegetables and peel the turnip.
2. Simmer the red lentils for about 7 minutes.
3. During that time, grate the vegetables.

4. Mix the soy yogurt with lemon juice, protein powder, salt, and herbs.
5. Arrange all the ingredients together in a deep plate or bowl and top with the spring onions and nuts.

 Nutrition:
Calories: 357 **Carbohydrates:** 10g **Fat:** 16g **Protein:** 80g

233. Beef and Kale Pan

Preparation Time: 10 minutes	**Cooking Time:** 20 minutes	**Servings:** 4

Ingredients:

- 500 grams beef stew meat, cubed
- 1 red onion, chopped
- 1 tablespoon olive oil
- 2 garlic cloves, chopped
- 120 grams kale, torn
- 120 ml. beef stock
- 1 teaspoon chili powder
- ½ teaspoon sweet paprika
- 1 teaspoon rosemary, dried
- 1 tablespoon coriander, chopped

Directions:

6. Ensure that you heat the pan; add the onion and the garlic, stir and sauté for 2 minutes.
7. Add the meat and brown it for 5 minutes.
8. Add the rest of the ingredients, simmer, then cook over a medium heat for 13 minutes more.
9. Divide the mix between plates and serve for lunch.

 Nutrition:
Calories: 477g **Fat:** 10g **Fiber:** 3g **Carbohydrates:** 1g
Protein: 12g

234. Salmon and Lemon Relish

Preparation Time: 10 minutes	**Cooking Time:** 1 hour	**Servings:** 2

Ingredients:

- 2 medium salmon fillets
- Salt
- Black pepper
- A drizzle of olive oil
- 1 shallot, chopped
- 11 teaspoons of lemon juice
- 1 big lemon
- 30 ml. olive oil
- 2 tablespoons of parsley

Directions:

1. Grease salmon fillets with olive oil, season with salt and pepper, place on a lined baking sheet, place in the oven at 200° C, fan 180°C, gas 6 , and bake for 1 hour.
2. Stir 11 teaspoons of lemon juice, salt, and pepper in a bowl, and leave aside for 10 minutes.
3. Cut the whole lemon in wedges and then very thinly.
4. Add the lemons to shallots, parsley, and 32 ml. olive oil and stir.
5. Break the salmon into medium pieces and serve with the lemon relish on the side.

Nutrition:
Calories: 500   **Fat:** 10g   **Carbohydrates:** 5g   **Protein:** 20g

235. Mustard Glazed Salmon

 Preparation Time: 10 minutes   **Cooking Time:** 20 minutes   **Servings:** 1

Ingredients:

- 1 big salmon fillet
- Salt
- Black Pepper
- 60 grams mustard
- 1 tablespoon coconut oil
- 1 tablespoon maple extract

Directions:

1. Mix maple extract with mustard in a bowl.
2. Massage salmon with salt and pepper and half of the mustard mix
3. Heat up a pan to a high heat, place salmon flesh side down and cook for 5 minutes.
4. Rub salmon with the rest of the mixture, transfer to a baking dish, place in the oven at 200° C, fan 180°C, gas 6 and bake for 15 minutes.
5. Serve with a tasty side salad.
6. Enjoy!

Nutrition:
Calories: 666   **Fat:** 7g   **Carbohydrates:** 35g   **Protein:** 23g

236. Turkey and Tomatoes

 Preparation Time: 10 minutes   **Cooking Time:** 30 minutes   **Servings:** 4

Ingredients:

- 2 shallots, chopped
- 1 tablespoon ghee, melted
- 120 ml. chicken stock
- 500 grams turkey breast, skinless, boneless, and cubed
- 120 grams cherry tomatoes, halved
- 1 tablespoon rosemary, chopped

Directions:

1. Ensure that the pan containing ghee is heated, add the shallots and the meat, and brown for 5 minutes.
2. Add the rest of the ingredients, simmer, and cook over a medium heat for 25 minutes, stirring often.
3. Divide into bowls and serve.

Nutrition:
Calories: 411   **Fat:** 44g   **Carbohydrates:** 33g   **Protein:** 10g

237. Grilled Squid and Tasty Guacamole

 Preparation Time: 10 minutes   **Cooking Time:** 10 minutes   **Servings:** 2

Ingredients:

- 2 medium squid, tentacles separated and tubes scored lengthwise
- A drizzle of olive oil
- Juice from 1 lime
- Black Pepper
- Salt
- For the guacamole:
- 2 avocados, pitted, peeled, and chopped
- Some coriander springs, chopped
- 2 red chilies, chopped
- 1 tomato, chopped
- 1 red onion, chopped
- Juice from 2 limes

Directions:

1. Season squid and squid tentacles with salt, pepper, drizzle some olive oil, and massage generously. Grill for 2 minutes on a medium-high heat. Cook for 2 minutes more.
2. Add juice from 1 lime, toss to coat, and keep warm. Put the avocado in a bowl and mash using a fork.
3. Add coriander, chilies, tomato, onion, and juice from 2 limes and stir well everything.
4. Divide squid on plates, top with guacamole and serve.

Nutrition:
Calories: 500   **Fat:** 43g   **Carbohydrates:** 7g   **Protein:** 20g

238. Salmon Bowls

 Preparation Time: 10 minutes   **Cooking Time:** 15 minutes   **Servings:** 4

Ingredients:

- 500 kg. salmon fillets, boneless, skinless, and roughly cubed
- 130 ml. chicken stock
- 2 spring onions, chopped
- 1 tablespoon olive oil
- 120 grams kalamata olives, pitted and halved
- 1 avocado, pitted, peeled, and roughly cubed
- 120 grams baby spinach
- 30 grams coriander, chopped
- 1 tablespoon basil, chopped
- 1 teaspoon lime juice

Directions:

1. Ensure that you heat the pan, add the spring onions and the salmon, toss gently, then cook for 5 minutes.
2. Add the olives and the other ingredients, and then cook over a medium heat for 10 minutes more.
3. Divide the mix into bowls and serve for lunch.

Nutrition:
Calories: 254   **Fat:** 17g   **Carbohydrates:** 6g   **Protein:** 20g

239. Shrimp and Cauliflower Delight

 Preparation Time: 10 minutes   **Cooking Time:** 15 minutes   **Servings:** 2

Ingredients:

- 1 tablespoon ghee
- 1 tablespoon parsley
- 1 cauliflower head, florets separated
- 500 grams shrimp/prawns, peeled and deveined
- 32 ml. of coconut milk
- 250 grams mushrooms, roughly chopped
- A pinch of red pepper flakes
- Black pepper
- Salt
- 2 garlic cloves, minced
- 4 bacon slices
- 70 ml. beef stock
- 1 tablespoon chives, chopped
- 11 teaspoons of bacon fat

Directions:

1. Heat a pan, add bacon, cook until it's crispy, transfer to kitchen towels, and leave aside.
2. Heat up 11 teaspoons of bacon fat on another pan over medium-high heat, add shrimp, cook for 2 minutes on each side and transfer to a bowl.
3. Cook mushrooms, stir and cook for 3-4 minutes. Add in garlic, pepper flakes, cook for 1 minute.
4. Put beef stock, salt, pepper, and return shrimp to pan. Stir. Mince cauliflower in the food processor. Cook for 5 minutes.
5. Add ghee and butter, stir and blend using an immersion blender. Season with salt and pepper, stir.
6. Top with shrimp mixture and serve with parsley and chives sprinkled all over. Enjoy!

 Nutrition:
Calories: 432 **Fat:** 8g **Carbohydrates:** 6g **Protein:** 20g

240. Scallops and Fennel Sauce

Preparation Time: 10 minutes	**Cooking Time:** 10 minutes	**Servings:** 2

Ingredients:

- 6 scallops
- 1 fennel, trimmed, leaves chopped, and bulbs cut in wedges
- Lime juice
- 1 lime, cut in wedges
- Zest from 1 lime
- 1 egg yolk
- 3 tablespoons ghee, melted and heated up
- ½ tablespoons olive oil
- Pepper
- Salt

Directions:

1. Season scallops with salt and pepper put in a bowl and mix with half of the lime juice and half of the zest and toss to coat.
2. In a bowl, mix the egg yolk with some salt and pepper, the rest of the lime juice, and the rest of the lime zest, and whisk well.
3. Add melted ghee and stir very well. Also, add fennel leaves and stir.
4. Brush fennel wedges with oil, place on heated grill over medium-high heat, cook for 2 minutes, turn over and cook for 2 minutes more.
5. Add scallops on the grill, cook for 2 minutes, turn over and cook for 2 minutes more.

6. Divide fennel and scallops on plates, drizzle fennel, and ghee mix, and serve with lime wedges on the side. Enjoy!

 Nutrition:
Calories: 340 **Fat:** 24g **Carbohydrates:** 12g **Protein:** 25g

241. Salmon Stuffed with Shrimp

Preparation Time: 10 minutes	**Cooking Time:** 25 minutes	**Servings:** 2

Ingredients:

- 2 salmon fillets
- A drizzle of olive oil
- 150 grams tiger shrimp/ prawns, peeled, deveined, and chopped
- 6 mushrooms, chopped
- 3 onions, chopped
- 250 grams spinach
- 35 grams macadamia nuts, toasted and chopped
- Black pepper and salt to taste
- A pinch of nutmeg
- 30 grams mayonnaise

Directions:

1. Heat a pan add mushrooms, onions, salt, and pepper, stir and cook for 4 minutes.
2. Add macadamia nuts, stir and cook for 2 minutes.
3. Add spinach, stir and cook for 1 minute.
4. Add shrimp, stir and cook for 1 minute.
5. Take off heat, leave aside for a few minutes, add mayo and nutmeg and stir well.
6. Make an incision lengthwise in each salmon fillet, sprinkle salt and pepper, divide spinach and shrimp mix into incisions, and place on a working surface.
7. Grease the pan with oil over a medium-high heat, add stuffed salmon, skin side down, cook for 1 minute, reduce temperature, cover pan and cook for 8 minutes.
8. Grill for 3 minutes, divide among plates and serve.
9. Enjoy!

 Nutrition:
Calories: 430 **Fat:** 30g **Carbohydrates:** 7g **Protein:** 50g

242. Pork Casserole

Preparation Time: 10 minutes	**Cooking Time:** 40 minutes	**Servings:** 4

Ingredients:

- 130 grams cheddar cheese, grated
- 2 eggs, whisked
- 500 grams pork loin, cubed
- 60 ml. avocado oil
- 2 shallots, chopped
- 3 garlic cloves, chopped
- 120 grams red peppers
- 60 grams double cream
- 1 tablespoon chives, chopped
- ½ teaspoon cumin, ground

Directions:

1. Ensure that you heat the pan; add the shallots and the garlic and sauté for 2 minutes.

2. Add the peppers and the meat, toss, then cook for 5 minutes more.
3. Add the cumin, salt, pepper, toss, and take off the heat.
4. In a bowl, mix the eggs with the cream and the cheese, whisk, and pour over the pork mix.
5. Cook with chives on top at 180 degrees F for 30 minutes.
6. Divide the mix between plates and serve for lunch.

 Nutrition:
Calories: 455 **Fat:** 34g **Carbohydrates:** 13g **Protein:** 33g

243. **Incredible Salmon Dish**

Preparation Time: 10 minutes	**Cooking Time:** 15 minutes	**Servings:** 4

Ingredients:

- 380 ml. of ice water
- 2 teaspoons sriracha sauce
- 4 teaspoons stevia
- 3 spring onions, chopped
- Salt
- Black Pepper
- 2 teaspoons flaxseed oil
- 4 teaspoons apple cider vinegar
- 3 teaspoons avocado oil
- 4 medium salmon fillets
- 250 grams baby rocket
- 250 grams cabbage, finely chopped
- 1 and ½ teaspoon Jamaican jerk seasoning
- 30 grams pumpkin seeds, toasted
- 250 grams watermelon radish, julienned

Directions:

7. Put ice water in a bowl, add spring onions, and leave aside.
8. In another bowl, mix sriracha sauce with stevia and stir well.
9. Transfer 2 tablespoons of this mix to a bowl and mix with half of the avocado oil, flaxseed oil, vinegar, salt, and pepper, and whisk.
10. Sprinkle jerk seasoning over salmon, rub with sriracha and stevia mix, and season with salt and pepper.
11. Heat up a pan with the rest of the avocado oil over medium-high heat, add salmon, flesh side down, cook for 4 minutes, flip and cook for 4 minutes more and divide among plates.
12. In a bowl, mix radishes with cabbage and rocket.
13. Add salt, pepper, sriracha, and vinegar mix and toss well.
14. Add this to salmon fillets, drizzle the remaining sriracha, and stevia sauce all over and top with pumpkin seeds and drained scallions.
15. Enjoy!

 Nutrition:

Calories: 570 **Fat:** 6g **Fiber:** 19g **Carbohydrates:** 1g

244. **Green Chicken Curry**

Preparation Time: 15 minutes	**Cooking Time:** 30 minutes	**Servings:** 4

Ingredients:

- 500 grams chicken breasts, chopped into cubes
- 1 tablespoon olive oil
- 2 tablespoons green curry paste
- 130 ml. unsweetened coconut milk
- 130 ml. chicken broth/stock
- 130 grams asparagus spears
- 130 grams green beans
- Salt
- Black pepper
- 70 grams basil leaves

Directions:

1. Sauté the curry paste for 1–2 minutes. Add the chicken and cook for 8–10 minutes.
2. Add coconut milk and broth, boil. Cook on low for 8–10 minutes.
3. Add the asparagus, green beans, salt, and black pepper, and cook for a further 4–5 minutes.
4. Serve.

 Nutrition:
Calories: 294 **Carbohydrates:** 4.3 g **Fat:** 16.2 g **Protein:** 28.6 g

245. **Creamy Pork Stew**

Preparation Time: 15 minutes	**Cooking Time:** 1 hour 35 minutes	**Servings:** 8

Ingredients:

- 120 grams butter
- 250 grams pounds boneless pork ribs
- 1 onion
- 4 garlic cloves
- 164 ml. chicken broth/stock
- 2 cans sugar-free chopped tomatoes
- 2 teaspoons dried oregano
- 1 teaspoon ground cumin
- Salt
- 2 tablespoons lime juice
- 60 grams sour cream

Directions:

1. Cook the pork, onions, and garlic for 4–5 minutes.
2. Add the broth, tomatoes, oregano, cumin, and salt, and mix. Simmer to low.
3. Combine in the sour cream plus lime juice and serve.

 Nutrition:
Calories: 304 **Carbohydrates:** 4.7 g **Fat:** 12.4 g **Protein:** 39.5 g

246. **Salmon & Shrimp Stew**

Preparation Time: 20 minutes	**Cooking Time:** 25 minutes	**Servings:** 6

Ingredients:

- 2 tablespoons coconut oil
- 70 grams onion
- 2 garlic cloves
- 1 Serrano or Jalapeño pepper
- 1 teaspoon smoked paprika
- 250 grams tomatoes
- 250 ml. chicken broth
- 500 grams salmon fillets
- 500 grams shrimp/prawns
- 2 tablespoons lime juice
- Salt
- Ground black pepper
- 3 tablespoons parsley

Directions:

4. Sauté the onion for 5–6 minutes.
5. Add the garlic, Serrano pepper, and paprika.
6. Add the tomatoes and broth then boil. Simmer for 5 minutes.
7. Add the salmon and simmer again 3–4 minutes.
8. Put in the shrimp then cook for 4–5 minutes.
9. Mix in lemon juice, salt plus black pepper, and serve with parsley.

 Nutrition:
Calories: 247 **Carbohydrates:** 3.9 g **Fat:** 17g **Protein:** 32.7 g

247. Chicken Casserole

Preparation Time: 15 minutes	Cooking Time: 1 hour 10 minutes	Servings: 6

Ingredients:

Chicken Layer:
- 6 grass-fed chicken breasts
- Salt
- Pepper
- Bacon Layer:
- 5 bacon slices
- 40 grams onion
- 40 grams jalapeno pepper
- 60 grams mayonnaise
- 1 packet cream cheese
- 90 grams Parmesan cheese
- 120 grams cheddar cheese

Topping:
- 1 package pork skins
- 30 grams butter
- 60 grams Parmesan cheese

Directions:

1. Warm-up oven to 200° C, fan 180°C, gas 6 .
2. Put the chicken breasts in the greased casserole dish then season with salt and black pepper.
3. Bake for 30–40 minutes.

For the bacon layer:
1. Cook the bacon for 8–10 minutes. Transfer.
2. Sauté onion for 4–5 minutes. Remove, stir in bacon and remaining ingredients.
3. Remove the casserole dish then add the bacon mixture.
4. Mix all topping ingredients. Place the topping over the bacon mixture. Bake for 15 minutes. Serve.

 Nutrition:
Calories: 826 **Carbohydrates:** 2.5 g **Fat:** 62.9 g
Protein: 60.6 g

248. Creamy Chicken Bake

Preparation Time: 15 minutes	Cooking Time: 1 hour 10 minutes	Servings: 6

Ingredients:

- 2 onions
- 3 garlic cloves
- 1 teaspoon tarragon
- 250 grams cream cheese
- 120 ml. chicken broth/stock
- 2 tablespoons lemon juice
- 70 grams double cream

- 160 grams Herbs de Provence
- Salt
- Pepper
- 4 grass-fed chicken breasts

Directions:

1. Preheat the oven to 200°C, fan 180°C, gas 6.
2. Cook the onion, garlic, and tarragon for 4–5 minutes in a pan. Transfer to an oven proof dish.
3. Cook the cream cheese, 60 ml. of broth, and lemon juice for 3–4 minutes.
4. Stir in the cream, herbs de Provence, salt, and black pepper, remove from the heat.
5. Pour remaining broth and chicken breast plus the cream mixture into the oven proof dish. Bake for 45–60 minutes.
6. Serve.

 Nutrition:
Calories: 729 **Carbohydrates:** 5.6 g **Fat:** 52.8 g
Protein: 55.8 g

249. Beef & Veggie Casserole

Preparation Time: 20 minutes	Cooking Time: 55 minutes	Servings: 6

Ingredients:

- 3 tablespoons butter
- 500 grams grass-fed minced beef
- 1 onion
- 2 garlic cloves
- 120 grams pumpkin
- 120 grams broccoli
- 250 grams cheddar cheese
- 1 tablespoon Dijon mustard
- 6 organic eggs
- 70 grams double cream
- Salt
- Black pepper

Directions:

1. Cook the beef for 8–10 minutes. Transfer it to a mixing bowl.
2. Next, cook the onion and garlic for 10 minutes. Add the pumpkin and cook for additional 6 minutes.
3. Add the broccoli and cook for another 4 minutes. Transfer to the mixing bowl with the cooked beef and stir well to combine.
4. Preheat the oven to 190°C, fan 170°C, gas 5.
5. Put 2/3 of cheese and mustard in the beef mixture and mix well.
6. In another mixing bowl, add cream, eggs, salt, and black pepper, and beat.
7. In a baking dish, place the beef mixture and top with egg mixture, plus the remaining cheese.
8. Bake for 25 minutes. Serve.

 Nutrition:
Calories: 472 **Carbohydrates:** 5.5 g **Fat:** 34.6 g
Protein: 32.6 g

250. Beef with Peppers

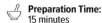 Preparation Time: 15 minutes	Cooking Time: 10 minutes	Servings: 4

Ingredients:

- 1 tablespoon Olive oil
- 500 grams grass-fed flank steak
- 1 red pepper
- 1 green pepper
- 1 tablespoon ginger
- 3 tablespoons low-sodium soy sauce
- 1 ½ tablespoons balsamic vinegar
- 2 teaspoons Sriracha

Directions:

1. Cook the steak slices for 2 minutes. Add the peppers and cook for additional 2–3 minutes.
2. Transfer the beef mixture to a plate. Grill the remaining ingredients for 1 minute. Add the beef mixture and cook for a further 1–2 minutes. Serve.

Nutrition:
Calories: 274 **Carbohydrates:** 3.8 g **Fat:** 13.1 g **Protein:** 32.9 g

251. Braised Lamb shanks

Preparation Time: 15 minutes	Cooking Time: 2 hours 35 minutes	Servings: 4

Ingredients:

- 4 grass-fed lamb shanks
- 2 tablespoons butter
- Salt
- ground black pepper
- 6 garlic cloves
- 6 rosemary sprigs
- 120 ml. chicken broth/stock

Directions:

1. Preheat the oven to 220°C, fan 200°C, gas 8.
2. Coat the shanks with butter and season with salt and pepper. Roast for 20 minutes.
3. Remove, the shanks and then reduce the heat to 190° C, fan 170° C, gas 5.
4. Place the garlic cloves and rosemary over and around the lamb.
5. Roast for 2 hours. Put the broth into a roasting pan.
6. Increase the temperature of the oven to 200° C, fan 180° C, gas 6. Roast 15 minutes more.
7. Serve.

Nutrition:
Calories: 1093 **Carbohydrates:** 2 g **Fat:** 44.2 g **Protein:** 161.4 g

252. Shrimp & Pepper Stir-Fry

Preparation Time: 20 minutes	Cooking Time: 10 minutes	Servings: 6

Ingredients:

- 70 ml. low-sodium soy sauce
- 2 tablespoons balsamic vinegar
- 2 tablespoons Erythritol
- 1 tablespoon arrowroot starch/ground arrowroot or cornstarch
- 1 tablespoon ginger
- ½ teaspoon red pepper flakes
- 3 tablespoons olive oil
- ½ red pepper
- ½ yellow pepper
- ½ green pepper
- 1 onion
- 1 red chili
- 150 grams shrimp
- 2 spring onions

Directions:

1. Mix soy sauce, vinegar, erythritol, arrowroot starch, ginger, and red pepper flakes. Set aside.
2. Stir-fry the peppers, onion, and red chili for 1–2 minutes.
3. In the center of the wok, place the shrimp and cook for 1–2 minutes.
4. Stir the shrimp with the pepper mixture and cook for 2 minutes.
5. Stir in the sauce and cook for a further 2–3 minutes.
6. Stir in the spring onions and remove from the heat. Serve hot.

Nutrition:
Calories: 355 **Carbohydrates:** 6.5 g **Fat:** 9 g **Protein:** 27.6 g

253. Veggies & Walnut Loaf

Preparation Time: 15 minutes	Cooking Time: 1 hour 10 minutes	Servings: 10

Ingredients:

- 1 tablespoon olive oil
- 2 onions
- 2 garlic cloves
- 1 teaspoon dried rosemary
- 120 grams walnuts
- 2 carrots
- 1 celery stalk
- 1 green pepper
- 120 grams button mushrooms
- 5 organic eggs
- 160 grams almond flour
- Salt
- Ground black pepper

Directions:

1. Preheat the oven to 190°C, fan 170°C, gas 5. Sauté the onion for 4–5 minutes.
2. Add the garlic and rosemary and sauté for 1 minute.
3. Add the walnuts and vegetables for 3–4 minutes. Put aside.
4. Beat the eggs, flour, sea salt, and black pepper.
5. Mix the egg mixture with the vegetable mixture.
6. Bake for 50–60 minutes. Serve.

Nutrition:
Calories: 611 **Carbohydrates:** 4.6 g **Fat:** 19.5 g **Protein:** 5.9 g

254. Keto Sloppy Joes

Preparation Time: 15 minutes	Cooking Time: 1 hour 10 minutes	Servings: 3

Ingredients:

- 160 grams almond flour
- 5 tablespoons ground psyllium husk powder (or flaxseed or linseed powder)
- 1teaspoon sea salt
- 2 teaspoons baking powder
- 2 teaspoons cider vinegar
- 60 ml. boiling water

- 3 egg whites
- Olive oil
- 500 grams minced beef
- 1 onion
- 4 garlic cloves
- 250 grams crushed tomatoes
- 1 tablespoon chili powder
- 1 tablespoon Dijon powder
- 1 tablespoon red wine vinegar
- 4 tablespoons tomato paste
- 2 teaspoons salt
- ¼ teaspoon ground black pepper
- 50 grams mayonnaise
- 6oz. cheese

Directions:

1. Preheat the oven to 220°C, fan 200°C, gas 8 and then mix all the dry ingredients.
2. Add some vinegar, egg whites, and boiled water. Whisk for 30 seconds.
3. Form the dough into 5 or 8 pieces of bread. Bake it for 55 minutes.
4. Cook the onion and garlic. Add the minced beef and cook for additional 5 minutes. Add the rest of the ingredients and continue cooking the mixture for an additional 10 minutes.
5. Let it simmer for 5 more minutes.
6. Serve.

 Nutrition:
Calories: 456   **Carbohydrates:** 19g   **Fat:** 10g   **Protein:** 30g

255. Low Carb Crack Slaw Egg Roll in a Bowl Recipe

Preparation Time: 15 minutes	**Cooking Time:** 20 minutes	**Servings:** 2

Ingredients:

- 500 ground beef
- 250 grams shredded coleslaw mix
- 1 tablespoon avocado oil
- Salt
- Pepper
- 4 cloves garlic
- 3 tablespoons ginger
- 30 grams coconut aminos
- 2 tablespoons toasted sesame oil
- 30 grams green onions

Directions:

1. Warm-up avocado oil in a large pan put in the garlic and cook.
2. Add the mined beef and cook for 10 minutes, season with salt and black pepper.
3. Lower the heat and add the coleslaw mix and the coconut aminos. Stir to cook for 5 minutes.
4. Remove from the heat and add in the onions and the toasted sesame oil. Serve.

 Nutrition:
Calories: 336   **Carbohydrates:** 2g   **Fat:** 13g   **Protein:** 8g

256. Low Carb Beef Stir Fry

Preparation Time: 15 minutes	**Cooking Time:** 20 minutes	**Servings:** 4

Ingredients:

- 60 grams courgette
- 30 grams organic broccoli florets
- 1 baby Bok Choy
- 2 tablespoons avocado oil
- 2 teaspoons coconut aminos
- 1 ginger
- 250 grams skirt steak

Directions:

1. Cook the steak on high heat for 10 minutes. Then, adjust to medium heat and put in the broccoli, ginger, ghee, and coconut aminos.
2. Add in the book choy and cook for two to three minutes.
3. Put the courgette into the mix and cook it for 5 more minutes.
4. Serve.

 Nutrition:
Calories: 658   **Carbohydrates:** 12g   **Fat:** 25g   **Protein:** 40g

257. One Pan Pesto Chicken and Veggies

 **Preparation Time:** 15 minutes	**Cooking Time:** 25 minutes	**Servings:** 4

Ingredients:

- 2 tablespoons olive oil
- 120 grams cherry chopped tomatoes
- 30 grams basil pesto
- 43 grams sun-dried tomatoes
- 500 grams chicken thigh
- 500 grams asparagus

Directions:

1. Warm up a large pan. Put olive oil and the sliced chicken on medium heat.
2. Add salt, stir well and then add the sun-dried tomatoes. Cook for 10 minutes and then transfer the chicken and tomatoes onto a plate.
3. Put the asparagus in the pan and pour on the pesto. Add in the remaining sun-dried tomatoes. Cook for 5 to 10 minutes. Transfer.
4. Place the chicken back in the pan and pour in the pesto. Stir for 2 minutes.
5. Serve with the asparagus.

 Nutrition:
Calories: 540   **Carbohydrates:** 9g   **Fat:** 24g   **Protein:** 23g

258. Crispy Peanut Tofu and Cauliflower Rice Stir-Fry

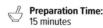 **Preparation Time:** 15 minutes	**Cooking Time:** 1 hour	**Servings:** 4

Ingredients:

- 250 grams tofu
- 1 tablespoon toasted sesame oil
- 2 cloves chopped garlic
- 1 cauliflower head

Sauce:

- 1 ½ tablespoon toasted sesame oil
- ½ teaspoon chilli garlic sauce
- 2 ½ tablespoons peanut butter
- 32 ml. low sodium soy sauce
- 60 grams light brown sugar

Directions:

1. Preheat the oven to 200°C, fan 180°C, gas 6. Cube the tofu.
2. Bake the tofu for 25 minutes and cool.
3. Combine the sauce ingredients. Put the tofu in the sauce and stir. Leave for 15 minutes.
4. Cook the veggies in a bit of sesame oil and soy sauce. Set aside.
5. Grab the tofu and put it on the pan. Stir then set aside.
6. Steam the cauliflower rice for 5 to 8 minutes. Add some sauce and stir.
7. Add up the rest of the ingredients. Put the cauliflower rice with the veggies and tofu. Serve.

 Nutrition:
Calories: 524   **Carbohydrates:** 39g   **Fat:** 34g   **Protein:** 25g

259. Simple Keto Fried Chicken

 **Preparation Time:** 15 minutes | **Cooking Time:** 45 minutes | **Servings:** 4

Ingredients:

- 4 boneless chicken thighs
- Frying oil
- 2 eggs
- 2 tablespoons double cream
- Breading
- 150 grams grated parmesan cheese
- 150 grams blanched almond flour
- Salt
- ½ teaspoon black pepper
- ½ teaspoon cayenne
- ½ teaspoon paprika

Directions:

1. Beat the eggs and cream. Separately, mix all the breading ingredients. Set aside.
2. Cut the chicken thigh into 3 even pieces.
3. Dip the chicken in the bread first, before dipping it in the egg wash and then finally, dipping it in the breading again. Fry chicken for 5 minutes. Pat dry the chicken. Serve.

 Nutrition:
Calories: 455   **Carbohydrates:** 12g   **Fat:** 15g   **Protein:** 30g

260. Keto Butter Chicken

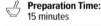 **Preparation Time:** 15 minutes | **Cooking Time:** 20 minutes | **Servings:** 4

Ingredients:

- 500 grams chicken breast
- 1 tablespoon coconut oil
- 2 teaspoons garam masala
- 3 teaspoons grated ginger
- 3 teaspoons garlic
- 115 grams plain yogurt
- Sauce:
- 50 grams butter

- 1 tablespoon ground coriander
- 60 grams double cream
- ½ tablespoon garam masala
- 2 teaspoon ginger
- 2 teaspoons chopped garlic
- 2 teaspoon cumin
- 1 teaspoon chili powder
- 1 onion
- 250 grams crushed tomatoes
- Salt

Directions:

1. Mix chicken pieces, gram masala, garlic, and grated ginger. Stir and add the yogurt. Chill for 30 minutes.
2. For the sauce, blend the ginger, garlic, onion, tomatoes, and spices. Put aside.
3. Cook the chicken pieces. Once cooked, pour in the sauce, and simmer for 5 minutes. Serve.

 Nutrition:
Calories: 459   **Carbohydrates:** 7g   **Fat:** 22g   **Protein:** 36g

261. Keto Squash Shrimps Recipe

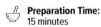 **Preparation Time:** 15 minutes | **Cooking Time:** 25 minutes | **Servings:** 2

Ingredients:

- 2 summer squashes (courgette)
- 500 grams shrimp/prawns
- 2 tablespoons butter unsalted
- 2 tablespoons lemon juice
- 2 tablespoons parsley
- 120 ml. chicken broth/stock
- 1/8 teaspoons red chili flakes
- 1 clove garlic
- Salt
- Pepper

Directions:

1. Put salt in the squash noodles on top. Set aside for 30 minutes.
2. Pat dry. Fry the garlic. Add some chicken broth, red chili flakes, and lemon juice.
3. Once it boils, add the shrimp, and cook. Lower the heat.
4. Add salt and pepper, put the summer squash noodles and parsley into the mix. Serve.

 Nutrition:
Calories: 366   **Carbohydrates:** 7g   **Fat:** 15g   **Protein:** 49g

262. Keto Lasagna

 **Preparation Time:** 15 minutes | **Cooking Time:** 1 hour | **Servings:** 2

Ingredients:

- 250 grams cream cheese
- 3 eggs
- Kosher salt
- Ground black pepper
- 250 grams mozzarella
- 50 grams parmesan
- Pinch red pepper flakes
- Parsley
- Sauce:
- 100 ml. marinara
- 1 tablespoon tomato paste
- 500 grams minced beef
- 100 grams parmesan
- 220 grams mozzarella

- Olive oil
- 1 tablespoon extra virgin olive oil
- 1 teaspoon dried oregano
- 50 grams onion
- 220 grams ricotta

Directions:

1. Preheat the oven to 220°C, fan 200°C, gas 8.
2. Melt the cream cheese, mozzarella, and parmesan on a hob. Transfer to an oven proof dish.
3. Add the eggs, salt, and pepper.
4. Bake for 15 to 20 minutes.
5. Cook the onion for 5 minutes, then the garlic. Add in the tomato paste. Then the minced beef, season with salt and pepper. Cook, then put aside.
6. Cook marinara sauce, add pepper, red pepper flakes, and ground pepper. Stir.
7. Take out the noodles, cut in half widthwise and then cut them again into 3 pieces.
8. Put 2 noodles at the bottom of the dish, then layer the parmesan and mozzarella shreds alternately.
9. Bake for 30 minutes. Garnish and serve.

Nutrition:
Calories: 508 **Carbohydrates:** 8g **Fat:** 39g **Protein:** 33g

263. Creamy Tuscan Garlic Chicken

Preparation Time: 15 minutes	Cooking Time: 30 minutes	Servings: 4

Ingredients:

- 500 grams chicken breast
- 100 ml. chicken broth/stock
- 100 grams parmesan cheese
- 100 grams sun-dried tomatoes
- 130 grams double cream
- 150 grams spinach
- 1 tablespoons olive oil
- 1 teaspoon garlic powder
- 1 teaspoon Italian seasoning

Directions:

1. Cook the chicken using olive oil, on a medium heat for 5 minutes, put aside.
2. Combine the cream, garlic powder, Italian seasoning, parmesan cheese, and chicken broth.
3. Add the sundried tomatoes and spinach and simmer.
4. Add the chicken back into the other ingredients and serve.

Nutrition:
Calories: 368 **Carbohydrates:** 7g **Fat:** 24g **Protein:** 30g

264. Ancho Macho Chili

Preparation Time: 20 minutes	Cooking Time: 1 hour and 30 minutes	Servings: 4

Ingredients:

- 1 kg. lean sirloin
- Salt
- Pepper
- 1,5 tablespoon Olive oil
- 1 Onion, chopped
- 10 grams Chili Powder

- 200 grams tomato with green chillies
- 70 ml. chicken broth/stock
- 2 cloves garlic

Directions:

1. Preheat the oven to 220°C, fan 200°C, gas 8.
2. Coat beef with pepper and salt.
3. Cook the onion for a few minutes.
4. Put in the last four ingredients and simmer. Add in the beef with all its juices and cook for 2 hours. Stir and serve.

Nutrition:
Calories: 644 **Carbohydrates:** 6g **Fat:** 40g **Protein:** 58g

265. Chicken Supreme Pizza

Preparation Time: 25 minutes	Cooking Time: 30 minutes	Servings: 4-8

Ingredients:

- 150 grams cooked chicken breast
- 130 grams almond flour
- 1 teaspoon baking Powder
- Salt
- 60 ml. water
- 1 red onion
- 1 red pepper
- 1 green pepper
- 120 grams Mozzarella cheese

Directions:

1. Preheat the oven to 200°C, fan 180°C, gas 6.
2. Blend the flour, the salt and baking powder. Add the water and the oil to the flour mixture to make the dough. Flatten the dough. Dump out the dough. Press it out and coat the pan with oil.
3. Bake for 12 minutes. Remove then sprinkle with cheese and then add chicken, pepper, and onion.
4. Bake again for 15 minutes, slice, and serve.

Nutrition:
Calories: 654 **Carbohydrates:** 44g **Fiber:** 10g **Fat:** 12g
Protein: 16g

266. Baked Jerked Chicken

Preparation Time: 20 minutes	Cooking Time: 1 hour and 30 minutes	Servings: 4

Ingredients:

- 1 kg. chicken thighs
- Olive oil
- Apple Cider Vinegar
- Salt
- 1 teaspoon powdered onion
- ½ teaspoon garlic
- ½ teaspoon nutmeg
- ½ teaspoon pepper
- ½ teaspoon powdered ginger
- ½ teaspoon powdered cayenne
- ½ teaspoon cinnamon
- ½ teaspoon dried thyme

Directions:

1. Mix all ingredients, excluding the chicken. Leave it for 5 minutes.

2. Then, add in the prepared chicken pieces. Stir well.
3. Marinade for 4 hours.
4. Preheat the oven to 220°C, fan 200°C, gas 8.
5. Cook for 1 hour and 25 minutes.
6. Serve

 Nutrition:
Calories: 459 **Carbohydrates:** 4g **Fat:** 12g **Protein:** 16g

267. Chicken Schnitzel

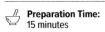 **Preparation Time:** 15 minutes | **Cooking Time:** 15 minutes | **Servings:** 3

Ingredients:
- 500 grams chicken breast
- 60 grams almond flour
- 1 egg
- ½ tablespoon garlic powder
- ½ tablespoon onion powder
- Keto-Safe Oil

Directions:
1. Combine the garlic power flour and onion in a bowl. Separately, beat the egg.
2. With a mallet, pound out the chicken. Put the chicken in the egg mixture. Then roll well through the flour.
3. Take a deep-frying pan and warm-up the oil to medium-high temperature.
4. Add chicken in batches. Fry. Pat dry and serve.

 Nutrition:
Calories: 541 **Carbohydrates:** 32g **Fat:** 17g **Protein:** 61g

268. Broccoli and Chicken Casserole v

 **Preparation Time:** 15 minutes | **Cooking Time:** 35 minutes | **Servings:** 4

Ingredients:
- 500 grams chicken breast
- 250 grams softened cream cheese
- 80 grams double cream
- 1 teaspoon garlic powder
- 1 teaspoon onion powder
- Salt
- Pepper
- 250 grams, broccoli florets
- 120 grams mozzarella
- 120 grams parmesan

Directions:
1. Preheat the oven to 200°C, fan 180°C, gas 6.
2. Combine the cream cheese with pepper and salt. Stir in the cubed chicken.
3. Put in the baking dish. Put the broccoli into the chicken-cheese mixture.
4. Top the dish with cheese, bake for about 26 minutes and remove. Take off the foil and bake again for 10 minutes. Serve.

 Nutrition:
Calories: 393 **Carbohydrates:** 20g **Fat:** 25g **Protein:** 21g

269. Baked Fish with Lemon Butter

 Preparation Time: 15 minutes | **Cooking Time:** 15 minutes | **Servings:** 2

Ingredients:
- 250 grams white fish fillets
- Olive oil
- Pepper
- Salt
- 1 medium-sized broccoli
- 60 grams butter
- 1 teaspoon garlic paste
- 1 medium-sized lemon

Directions:
1. Preheat the oven to 220°C, fan 200°C, gas 8
2. Set the fish out onto some parchment paper and season with pepper and salt. Pour over olive oil and lemon slices. Bake for 15 minutes.
3. Steam the broccoli for five minutes. Put aside.
4. Warm-up the butter, then stir in lemon zest, garlic, remaining lemon slices, and broccoli. Cook for 2 minutes before serving.

 Nutrition:
Calories: 357 **Carbohydrates:** 14g **Fat:** 15g **Protein:** 34g

270. Chicken Broccoli Alfredo

 Preparation Time: 15 minutes | **Cooking Time:** 10 minutes | **Servings:** 4

Ingredients:
- 500 grams chicken breast
- 250 grams spinach
- 120 grams broccoli
- 1 tablespoon butter
- 50 ml. double cream
- 1 clove garlic
- 2 tablespoons onion, chopped
- Salt
- Pepper

Directions:
1. Boil broccoli for 10 minutes.
2. Melt the butter with the onion and garlic, add in the chicken. Sauté for 5 minutes.
3. Then add the spinach and broccoli. stir in the cream with seasonings. Cook for 5 more minutes and serve.

 Nutrition:
Calories: 523 **Carbohydrates:** 34g **Fat:** 19g **Protein:** 34g

271. Grilled Cheesy Buffalo Chicken

 Preparation Time: 15 minutes | **Cooking Time:** 10 minutes | **Servings:** 2

Ingredients:
- 300 grams chicken breast
- 2 garlic cloves
- 90 grams mozzarella cheese
- 1 tablespoon butter
- 50 grams hot sauce
- 1 tablespoon lemon juice
- ½ teaspoon celery salt
- Pepper
- Salt

Directions:

1. Mix the chopped garlic, hot sauce, celery salt, melted butter, lemon juice, pepper, and salt, and then add the chicken into the mixture.
2. Fill each chicken breast with cheese. Roll up, then secure with a toothpick to close the pocket.
3. Grease the grill. Cook for 5 minutes, flipping, and do another 5 minutes. Cooldown and serve.

 Nutrition:
Calories: 499 **Carbohydrates:** 22g **Fat:** 5g **Protein:** 24g

272. Middle Eastern Shawarma

 Preparation Time: 15 minutes   **Cooking Time:** 10 minutes   **Servings:** 3

Ingredients:

- 500 grams lamb shoulder
- 2 tablespoons yogurt
- 1 tablespoon water
- 1 teaspoon white vinegar
- 2 teaspoons lemon juice
- 1 teaspoon olive oil
- 60 grams chopped onion
- 1 clove garlic
- ½ teaspoon black pepper
- ½ teaspoon cumin
- ½ teaspoon nutmeg
- ½ teaspoon cloves
- ½ teaspoon mace
- ½ teaspoon powdered cayenne

Directions:

1. Mix the yogurt with the garlic, and add all the other ingredients, except the lamb.
2. Whisk it.
3. Marinade the lamb strips with this mixture, for a full day.
4. Set a large pan to a high temperature. Add the lamb pieces and cook for 5 minutes.
5. Serve.

 Nutrition:
Calories: 677 **Carbohydrates:** 45g **Fat:** 16g **Protein:** 32g

273. Tex Mex Casserole

 Preparation Time: 15 minutes   **Cooking Time:** 25 minutes   **Servings:** 4

Ingredients:

- 120 grams sour cream
- 1 spring onion
- 120 grams guacamole
- 120 grams leafy greens
- 1 kg. minced beef
- 3 tablespoons tex-mex seasoning
- 120 grams Monterey Jack cheese
- 56 grams Jalapenos pickled
- 200 grams crushed tomatoes
- 56 grams butter

Directions:

1. Preheat the oven to 200°C, fan 180°C, gas 6. Cook the minced beef entirely in the melted butter. Add in the Tex Mex seasoning and the tomatoes and mix well.
2. Put the meat batter in a greased baking dish. Scatter the cheese, and the jalapenos on top, then bake for 25 minutes.
3. Chop up the scallion then mix it with the sour cream. Serve the meat mix with a spoon of the sour cream, a scoop of guacamole, and some leafy greens.

 Nutrition:
Calories: 860 **Carbohydrates:** 8g **Fat:** 69g **Protein:** 49g

274. Baked Fish Fillets with Vegetables in Foil

 Preparation Time: 15 minutes   **Cooking Time:** 40 minutes   **Servings:** 3

Ingredients:

- 450 grams cod
- 1 red pepper
- 6 cherry tomatoes
- 1 leek
- 60 grams onion
- 60 grams courgette
- 1 clove garlic
- 2 tablespoons olives
- 30 grams butter
- Olive oil
- 1 lemon, sliced
- Coriander leaves
- Salt
- Pepper

Directions:

1. Preheat the oven to 200°C, fan 180°C, gas 6. Transfer all the vegetables to a baking tray lined with foil.
2. Cut the fish into bite-sized pieces and add to the vegetables.
3. Add salt and pepper, olive oil, and add pieces of butter. Bake for 35 – 40 minutes.
4. Serve.

 Nutrition:
Calories: 339 **Fat:** 19g **Protein:** 35g **Carbohydrates:** 5g

275. Fish & Chips

 Preparation Time: 15 minutes   **Cooking Time:** 30 minutes   **Servings:** 2

Ingredients:

- For chips:
- ½ tablespoons olive oil
- 1 medium courgette
- Salt
- Pepper
- For fish:
- 100 grams cod
- Oil
- 70 grams almond flour
- ¼ teaspoon onion powder
- For Sauce:
- 2 tablespoons dill pickle relish
- 1 tablespoon curry powder
- 10 grams mayonnaise
- ½ teaspoon paprika powder
- 10 grams parmesan cheese
- 1 egg
- Salt
- Pepper

Directions:

1. Mix all the sauce ingredients in a bowl. Set aside.
2. Preheat the oven to 200°C, fan 180°C, gas 6. Make thin courgette rods, brush with oil, and spread on the baking tray. Put salt and pepper then bake for 30 minutes.
3. Beat the egg in a bowl. On a separate plate, combine the parmesan cheese, almond flour, and the remaining spices.
4. Slice the fish into 1 inch by 1-inch pieces. Roll them on the flour mixture. Dip in the beaten egg and then in the flour again. Fry the fish for three minutes. Serve.

 Nutrition:
Calories: 463   **Fat:** 26.2 g   **Protein:** 49g   **Carbohydrates:** 6g

276. Baked Salmon with Almonds and Cream Sauce

 **Preparation Time:** 10 minutes   **Cooking Time:** 20 minutes   **Servings:** 2

Ingredients:

- Almond Crumbs Creamy Sauce
- 3 tablespoons almonds
- 2 tablespoons almond milk
- 100 grams cream cheese
- Salt
- 1 salmon fillet
- 1 teaspoon coconut oil
- 2 tablespoons lemon zest
- Salt
- Pepper

Directions:

5. Cut the salmon in half. Rub the salmon with the lemon zest, salt, and pepper. Marinade for 20 minutes.
6. Fry the fish on both sides. Top with almond crumbs and bake for 10 to 15 minutes.
7. Remove and put aside.
8. Place the baking dish on the heat and add the cream cheese. Combine the fish baking juices and the cheese. Mix, then pour the sauce on the fish. Serve.

 Nutrition:
Calories: 522   **Fat:** 44g   **Protein:** 28g   **Carbohydrates:** 2.4g

277. Shrimp and Sausage Bake

 Preparation Time: 15 minutes   **Cooking Time:** 20 minutes   **Servings:** 4

Ingredients:

- 2 tablespoons Olive oil
- 180 grams chorizo sausage
- 60 grams pound shrimp/prawn
- 1 small onion, chopped
- 10 grams garlic powder
- 40ml. Herbed Chicken Stock
- Pinch red pepper flakes
- 1 red pepper

Directions:

1. Sauté the sausage for 6 minutes. Add the shrimp and sauté for 4 minutes.
2. Remove both and set aside. Cook the red pepper, onion, and garlic to a pan for 4 minutes.
3. Combine together the chicken stock along with the cooked sausage and shrimp. Simmer for 3 minutes.
4. Stir in the red pepper flake and serve.

 Nutrition:
Calories: 588   **Fat:** 24g   **Protein:** 20g   **Carbohydrates:** 6g

278. Herb Butter Scallops

 Preparation Time: 10 minutes   **Cooking Time:** 10 minutes   **Servings:** 4

Ingredients:

- 500 grams sea scallops
- Black pepper
- Salt
- 8 teaspoons butter
- 2 teaspoons garlic
- Lemon juice of 1 lemon
- 2 teaspoons basil
- 1 teaspoon thyme

Directions:

1. Pat dry the scallops then put pepper. Sear each side for 2 minutes per side.
2. Remove then set aside. Sauté the garlic for 3 minutes. Stir in the lemon juice, basil, and thyme and return the scallops to the pan, mix.
3. Serve.

 Nutrition:
Calories: 512   **Fat:** 24g   **Protein:** 19g   **Carbohydrates:** 4g

279. Pan-Seared Halibut with Citrus Butter Sauce

 Preparation Time: 10 minutes   **Cooking Time:** 15 minutes   **Servings:** 4

Ingredients:

- 4 halibut fillets
- Salt
- Ground pepper
- 30 grams butter
- 1 tablespoon garlic
- 1 shallot
- 3 tablespoons dry white wine
- 1 tablespoon orange juice
- 1 tablespoon lemon juice
- 2 teaspoons parsley
- 2 teaspoons olive oil

Directions:

1. Pat dry the fish and season with salt and pepper. Set aside.
2. Sauté the garlic and shallot for 3 minutes.
3. Whisk in the white wine, lemon juice, and orange juice and simmer for 2 minutes.

4. Remove the sauce and stir in the parsley; set aside.
5. Pan fry the fish for 10 minutes. Serve with sauce.

 Nutrition:
Calories: 741   **Fat:** 26g   **Protein:** 22g   **Carbohydrates:** 2g

280. Baked Coconut Haddock

 **Preparation Time:** 10 minutes	**Cooking Time:** 12 minutes	**Servings:** 4

Ingredients:

- 4 boneless haddock fillets
- Salt
- Freshly ground pepper
- 120 grams shredded unsweetened coconut
- 60 grams ground hazelnuts
- 2 tablespoons coconut oil

Directions:

6. Preheat the oven to 200°C, fan 180°C, gas 6.
7. Pat dry fillets and lightly season them with salt and pepper.
8. Stir together the shredded coconut and hazelnut in a small bowl.
9. Cover the fish fillets in the coconut mixture so that both sides of each piece are thickly coated.
10. Put the fish on the baking tray and lightly brush both sides of each piece with the coconut oil.
11. Bake the haddock until the topping is golden and the fish flakes easily with a fork, about 12 minutes. Serve.

 Nutrition:
Calories: 447   **Fat:** 24g   **Protein:** 20g   **Carbohydrates:** 13g

281. Spicy Steak Curry

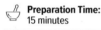 **Preparation Time:** 15 minutes	**Cooking Time:** 40 minutes	**Servings:** 6

Ingredients:

- 120 grams plain yogurt
- ½ teaspoon garlic paste
- ½ teaspoon ginger paste
- ½ teaspoon ground cloves
- ½ teaspoon ground cumin
- 2 teaspoons red pepper flakes
- ¼ teaspoon ground turmeric
- Salt
- 2 pounds grass-fed round steak
- Olive oil
- 1 medium onion
- 2 tablespoons lemon juice
- 40 grams coriander

Directions:

1. Mix yogurt, garlic paste, ginger paste, and spices. Add the steak pieces. Set aside.
2. Sauté the onion for 4-5 minutes. Add the steak pieces with marinade and mix.
3. Simmer for 25 minutes. Stir in the lemon juice and simmer 10 minutes.
4. Garnish with coriander and serve.

 Nutrition:
Calories: 440   **Carbohydrates:** 47g   **Fat:** 23g   **Protein:** 48.3g

282. Beef Stew

 **Preparation Time:** 15 minutes	 **Cooking Time:** 1 hour 40 minutes	**Servings:** 4

Ingredients:

- 500 grams grass-fed beef chuck
- Salt
- Black Pepper
- 60 grams butter
- 1 onion
- 2 garlic cloves
- 120 ml. beef broth
- 1 bay leaf
- 1 teaspoon dried thyme
- ½ teaspoon dried rosemary
- 1 carrot
- 120 grams celery stalks
- 1 tablespoon lemon juice

Directions:

1. Season the beef cubes with salt and black pepper.
2. Sear the beef cubes for 4-5 minutes. Add the onion and garlic, then adjust the heat to medium and cook for 4-5 minutes. Add the broth, bay leaf, and dried herbs and boil.
3. Simmer for 45 minutes. Stir in the carrot and celery and simmer for 30-45 minutes.
4. Stir in lemon juice, salt, and black pepper. Serve.

 Nutrition:
Calories: 413   **Carbohydrate:** 5.9g   **Fat:** 32g   **Protein:** 52g

283. Beef & Cabbage Stew

Preparation Time: 15 minutes	**Cooking Time:** 2 hours 50 minutes	**Servings:** 8

Ingredients:

- 1kg. grass-fed beef stew meat
- 200 ml. hot chicken broth/ stock
- 2 onions
- 2 bay leaves
- 1 teaspoon Greek seasoning
- Salt
- Black Pepper
- 3 celery stalks
- 1 package cabbage
- 1 can sugar-free tomato sauce
- 1 can sugar-free whole plum tomatoes

Directions:

1. Sear the beef for 4-5 minutes.
2. Stir in the broth, onion, bay leaves, Greek seasoning, salt, and black pepper and boil. Adjust the heat to low and cook for 2 hours.
3. Stir in the celery and cabbage and cook for 30 minutes. Stir in the tomato sauce and chopped plum tomatoes and cook, uncovered for 15-20 minutes. Stir in the salt, discard bay leaves and serve.

 Nutrition:
Calories: 478   **Carbohydrate:** 7g   **Fat:** 23g   **Protein:** 36.5g

284. Cheese steak soup

Preparation Time: 15 minutes	Cooking Time: 20 minutes	Servings: 10

Ingredients

- 3 tablespoons butter
- 55 grams red onion
- 140 grams green pepper
- 110 grams mushrooms
- Salt
- Pepper
- 950 ml. beef broth/stock
- 110 grams cream cheese
- 170 grams grated white cheddar cheese
- 85 grams edam cheese, sliced

Directions

1. In a large saucepan over medium heat, melt the butter. Once hot, add the onions and sauté until tender but not browned, about 5 minutes.
2. Stir in the peppers and mushrooms and sprinkle with salt and pepper. Cook another 3 to 4 minutes, until tender.
3. Add the roast beef and toss to mix well. Stir in the broth and bring to a simmer. Cook 10 minutes.
4. Place the cream cheese in a blender and add about ¼ of the hot broth from the pan. Blend until smooth and the cream cheese is melted. Pour the mixture back into the pan and stir in the grated cheese until melted.
5. Preheat the grill. Ladle the soup into oven-proof bowls or ramekins and top with a piece of edam. Set on a baking tray and place under the grill until the cheese is melted and bubbly, 2 to 4 minutes.
6. Serve immediately.

Nutrition:
Calories: 567 **Carbohydrates:** 33g **Fat:** 25 g **Protein:** 29 g

285. Keto Fajitas

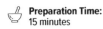 Preparation Time: 15 minutes	Cooking Time: 20 minutes	Servings: 4

Ingredients

- 1 tablespoon chili powder
- 1 tablespoon paprika powder
- 2 teaspoon dried oregano
- 2 teaspoons ground cumin
- Salt
- 650 grams chicken breasts
- 120 grams red pepper
- 110 grams onion
- 2 garlic cloves
- 60 ml olive oil
- 2 tablespoons lime juice
- 30 grams coriander

Directions

1. Preheat the oven to 200°C, fan 180°C, gas 6.
2. Mix the chili powder, paprika, oregano, cumin, and salt in a small bowl and set aside.
3. Put the chicken strips, peppers, onion, garlic, oil, and lime juice in a large bowl and mix to distribute the oil and lime juice thoroughly. Sprinkle in the spice mixture and toss to coat the chicken and vegetables.

4. Spread the seasoned chicken and veggies in a single layer in a baking dish/pan. Bake for 20-25 minutes, stirring halfway through the baking time until the chicken is cooked through and tender. If you enjoy a little char on your fajitas, you can place the pan under the grill for 3 to 5 minutes at the end before serving.
5. Garnish with fresh coriander and serve.

Nutrition:
Calories: 456 **Fat:** 33g **Carbohydrates:** 22g **Protein:** 22g

286. Keto Salmon with Lemon Sauce

Preparation Time: 10 minutes	Cooking Time: 30 minutes	Servings: 2

Ingredients

- 120 ml vegetable stock
- 160 ml double cream
- 1 tablespoon fresh chives
- 2 tablespoon fresh parsley
- ½ lemon juice
- ½ teaspoon salt
- Black pepper
- 2 tablespoons olive oil
- 450 grams salmon
- 1 tablespoon butter
- 450 grams spinach

Directions

Lemon sauce

1. Pour the vegetable stock into a small saucepan and bring to a boil over high heat. Boil for a few minutes to slightly reduce the stock.
2. Add the cream, chives, parsley, lemon juice, salt, and pepper to the stock, and whisk to combine. Reduce the temperature to low, keep uncovered, and whisk occasionally. The sauce will thicken as the salmon is being prepared.

Salmon

1. In a large, non-stick pan, heat the olive oil over a medium-high heat for a couple of minutes. Season the salmon on both sides with salt and pepper. Place the salmon in the pan (skin side down, if applicable) and sear for about 4 minutes until golden and crispy.
2. Gently flip with a spatula and reduce the heat to medium. Cook for another 3-5 minutes, until golden crisp on the outside, and a light pink color inside. Transfer to a serving platter and keep warm.

Serving

1. Melt the butter in a large frying pan or wok, over a medium heat. Increase the temperature to medium-high and add the spinach. Toss with tongs for a couple of minutes until wilted. Remove from heat, and season with salt and pepper.
2. To serve, drizzle the lemon sauce over the salmon, with the sautéed spinach on the side.

Nutrition:
Calories: 422 **Carbohydrates:** 23g **Fat:** 80 g **Protein:** 56 g

287. Chicken with parmesan and mushrooms

Preparation Time: 10 minutes	Cooking Time: 30 minutes	Servings: 4

Ingredients

- 2 tablespoons avocado oil
- 650 grams boneless chicken thighs
- 230 grams baby bella (Italian portobello) mushrooms
- 4 garlic cloves
- 350 ml double cream
- 40 grams grated parmesan cheese
- 1 teaspoon fresh parsley

Directions

1. Over a medium heat, in a large pan, warm the avocado oil. Season the chicken thighs with salt and pepper. Fry in the pan, until browned or cooked through; remove chicken to a plate with a slotted spoon, reserving juices in the pan.
2. Add garlic to the frying pan and stir-fry until soft; add mushrooms and sauté until softened, for about 5-7 minutes.
3. On a low heat, add the cream, stirring well. Allow to simmer for about 10 minutes stirring often. Stir in parmesan cheese until melted. Add additional salt and pepper to taste.
4. Add chicken back into skillet and coat with sauce. Serve garnished with parsley.

 Nurtition:
Calories: 455 **Fat:** 34g **Carbohydrates:** 20g **Protein:** 14g

288. Keto Pizza

Preparation Time: 15 minutes	Cooking Time: 30 minutes	Servings: 4

Ingredients

- Crust
- 170 grams mozzarella cheese
- 2 tablespoons cream cheese
- 85 grams almond flour
- 1 teaspoon white wine vinegar
- 1 egg
- Olive oil
- Topping
- 230 grams Italian sausage
- 1 tablespoon butter
- 120 ml. unsweetened tomato sauce
- ½ teaspoon dried oregano
- 170 grams mozzarella cheese

Directions

1. Preheat the oven to 200°C, fan 180°C, gas 6.
2. Heat mozzarella and cream cheese in a non-stick pan on a medium heat or in a bowl in the microwave. Stir until they melt together. Add the other ingredients and mix well. Tip: use a hand mixer with dough hooks.
3. Moisten your hands with olive oil and flatten the dough on baking paper, making a circle about 8" (20 cm) in diameter. You can also use a rolling pin to flatten the dough between two sheets of baking paper.

4. Remove the top baking sheet (if used). Prick the crust with a fork (all over) and bake in the oven for 10–15 minutes until golden brown. Remove from the oven.
5. While the crust is baking, sautée the ground sausage meat in olive oil or butter.
6. Spread a thin layer of tomato sauce on the crust. Top the pizza with meat and plenty of cheese. Bake for 10–15 minutes or until the cheese has melted.
7. Sprinkle with oregano and enjoy!

 Nutrition:
Calories: 600 **Fat:** 23g **Protein:** 17g **Carbohydrates:** 22g

289. Beef & Mushroom Chili

Preparation Time: 15 minutes	Cooking Time: 3 hours 10 minutes	Servings: 8

Ingredients:

- 1kg. grass-fed minced beef
- 1 onion
- 60 grams green pepper
- 60 grams carrot
- 120 grams mushrooms
- 2 garlic cloves
- 1 can sugar-free tomato paste
- 60 grams red chili powder
- 6 grams ground cumin
- 6 grams ground cinnamon
- 6 grams red pepper flakes
- 6 grams ground allspice
- Salt
- Pepper
- 250 ml. of water
- 70 grams sour cream

Directions:

1. Cook the beef for 8-10 minutes.
2. Stir in the remaining ingredients, except for sour cream and boil.
3. Cook on low, covered, for 3 hours.
4. Top with sour cream and serve.

 Nutrition:
Calories: 333 **Carbohydrates:** 5.9g **Fat:** 8.2g **Protein:** 25.1g

290. Steak with Cheese Sauce

Preparation Time: 15 minutes	Cooking Time: 17 minutes	Servings: 4

Ingredients:

- 500 grams grass-fed filet mignon
- Salt
- Ground black pepper
- 2 tablespoons butter
- 65 grams onion
- 110 grams blue cheese
- 120 grams double cream
- 1 garlic clove
- Ground nutmeg

Directions:

1. Cook onion for 5-8 minutes. Add the blue cheese, cream, garlic, nutmeg, salt, and black pepper and stir well to combine.
2. Cook for about 3-5 minutes.

3. Season the filet mignon steaks with salt and black pepper.
4. Cook the steaks for 4 minutes per side.
5. Transfer and set aside. Top with cheese sauce, then serve.

Nutrition:
Calories: 521 **Carbohydrates:** 3g **Fat:** 33g **Protein:** 44.7g

291. Steak with Blueberry Sauce

 Preparation Time:
15 minutes
 Cooking Time:
20 minutes
 Servings:
4

Ingredients:

- For Sauce:
- 2 tablespoons butter
- 2 tablespoons onion
- 2 garlic cloves
- 1 teaspoon thyme
- 220 ml. beef broth/stock
- 2 tablespoons lemon juice
- 90 grams blueberries
- For Steak:
- 2 tablespoons butter
- 4 grass-fed flank steaks
- Salt
- Ground black pepper

Directions:

For the sauce:
1. Sauté the onion for 2-3 minutes.
2. Add the garlic and thyme and sauté for 1 minute.
3. Stir in the broth and simmer for 10 minutes.

For the steak:
1. Season with salt and black pepper.
2. Cook steaks for 3-4 minutes per side.
3. Transfer and put aside.
4. Add sauce into the pan and stir.
5. Stir in the lemon juice, blueberries, salt, and black pepper and cook for 1-2 minutes.
6. Put blueberry sauce over the steaks. Serve.

Nutrition:
Calories: 467 **Carbohydrates:** 4.6g **Fat:** 19g **Protein:** 49.5g

292. Grilled Steak

 Preparation Time:
15 minutes
 Cooking Time:
12 minutes
 Servings:
6

Ingredients:

- 1 teaspoon lemon zest
- 1 garlic clove
- 1 tablespoon red chili powder
- 1 tablespoon paprika
- 1 tablespoon ground coffee
- Salt
- Pepper
- 2 grass-fed skirt steaks

Directions:

1. Mix all the ingredients except steaks. Marinate the steaks and keep aside for 30-40 minutes.
2. Grill the steaks for 5-6 minutes per side. Remove then cool before slicing. Serve.

Nutrition:
Calories: 473 **Carbohydrate:** 17g **Fat:** 23g **Protein:** 60.8g

293. Roasted Tenderloin

 Preparation Time:
10 minutes
Cooking Time:
50 minutes
 Servings:
10

Ingredients:

- 2kg. grass-fed beef tenderloin roast
- 4 garlic cloves
- Salt
- Black Pepper
- 1 tablespoon rosemary

Directions:

1. Preheat the oven to 200°C, fan 180°C, gas 6.
2. Place beef meat into the prepared roasting pan.
3. Massage it with garlic, rosemary, salt, and black pepper and oil.
4. Roast the beef for 45-50 minutes.
5. Remove, cool, slice, and serve.

Nutrition:
Calories: 669 **Carbohydrates:** 15g **Protein:** 39.5g **Fat:** 13.9g

294. Garlicky Prime Rib Roast

 Preparation Time:
15 minutes
 Cooking Time:
1 hour 35 minutes
Servings:
15

Ingredients:

- 10 garlic cloves
- 2 teaspoons dried thyme
- 2 tablespoons olive oil
- Salt
- Pepper
- 1 grass-fed prime rib roast

Directions:

1. Mix the garlic, thyme, oil, salt, and black pepper. Marinate the rib roast with garlic mixture for 1 hour.
2. Preheat the oven to 220°C, fan 200°C, gas 8.
3. Roast for 20 minutes. Lower to 200° C, fan 200°C, gas 6 and roast for 65-75 minutes.
4. Remove then cooldown for 10-15 minutes, slice, and serve.

Nutrition:
Calories: 499 **Carbohydrates:** 12g **Protein:** 61.5g **Fat:** 25.9g

295. Beef Taco Bake

 Preparation Time:
15 minutes
Cooking Time:
1 hour
 Servings:
6

Ingredients:

- For Crust:
- 3 organic eggs
- 120 grams cream cheese
- ½ teaspoon taco seasoning
- 40 ml. double cream
- 200 grams cheddar cheese
- For Topping:
- 500 grams grass-fed minced beef
- 120 grams green chilies
- 30 grams sugar-free tomato sauce

- 3 teaspoons taco seasoning
- 170 grams cheddar cheese

Directions:

1. Preheat the oven to 220°C, fan 200°C, gas 8.
2. For the crust: beat the eggs, and cream cheese, taco seasoning, and cream.
3. Place cheddar cheese in a baking dish. Spread cream cheese mixture over the cheese.
4. Bake for 25-30 minutes. Remove then set aside for 5 minutes.

For topping:

1. Cook the beef for 8-10 minutes.
2. Stir in the green chilies, tomato sauce, and taco seasoning and transfer.
3. Place the beef mixture over the crust and sprinkle with cheese. Bake for 18-20 minutes.
4. Remove then slice and serve.

 Nutrition:
Calories: 569 **Carbohydrates:** 3.8g **Fat:** 12g **Protein:** 38.7g

296. Meatballs with Curry

 Preparation Time: 15 minutes | **Cooking Time:** 25 minutes | **Servings:** 6

Ingredients

- 2 garlic cloves
- 1 red chilli, deseeded
- 1 thick slice white bread
- small pack mint leaves, reserving some to serve
- 400 grams lamb mince
- 1 egg, lightly beaten
- 1 tbsp vegetable oil
- 1 large onion, roughly chopped
- 1 tablespoon masala curry paste
- 400 grams chopped tomato
- 400 ml. lamb stock
- 100 grams baby spinach leaves
- cooked basmati rice and cucumber & mint raita, to serve (optional)

Directions

1. Place the garlic, chilli, bread and mint in a food processor and pulse until finely chopped. Tip into a bowl and mix with the lamb, egg and seasoning. using damp hands, shape into 16 small meatballs.
2. Heat half the vegetable oil in a large non-stick frying pan. Fry the meatballs in batches over a high heat until golden, then set aside.
3. Heat the remaining oil in the frying pan, add the onion and cook for 3-4 mins until beginning to soften. Add the curry paste and fry for 1 min, then tip in the tomatoes and stock and bring to a simmer.
4. Add the meatballs and simmer for 15 mins until the sauce is thickened. Stir through the spinach until just wilted. Scatter over the remaining mint leaves, and serve with rice and cucumber & mint raita, if you like.

 Nutrition:
Calories: 444 **Carbohydrate:** 8.6g **Fat:** 12g **Protein:** 17g

297. Meatballs in Cheese Sauce

 **Preparation Time:** 20 minutes | **Cooking Time:** 25 minutes | **Servings:** 5

Ingredients:

Meatballs:

- 60 grams panko breadcrumbs
- 1 large egg
- 1 teaspoon each: garlic powder and onion powder
- ½ teaspoon each: red pepper flakes, salt and black pepper
- 1 tablespoon low sodium soy sauce
- 130 grams grated parmesan cheese
- 2 tablespoons chopped parsley
- 500 grams minced beef

Sauce:

- olive oil, for cooking
- 60 grams of each: chopped onions, chopped green peppers, and chopped mushrooms
- 2 tablespoons each: all-purpose flour and chopped parsley
- 1 teaspoon garlic powder
- 130ml. low sodium beef stock (or chicken)
- 1 tablespoon low sodium soy sauce
- 60 grams sour cream
- 130 grams shredded edam cheese

Directions:

1. In a medium mixing bowl, mix together the breadcrumbs, egg, garlic powder, onion powder, salt, red pepper flakes, black pepper, soy sauce, parmesan, and parsley. The mixture will resemble a coarse breading.
2. Add the minced beef and mix until *just* combined. You don't want to overwork the meat. Roll into 23-27 meatballs. Mine were about 1 ½ tablespoon each.
3. Heat 1 tablespoon of oil in a large pan over medium-high heat. Add the meatballs to the pan but do not overcrowd the pan. Cook in batches if they don't all fit.
4. Sear the meatballs for 5-6 minutes, flipping to brown all sides evenly and cook the meatballs all the way through. Remove the meatballs to a plate. Repeat until all the meatballs are cooked.
5. Depending on how much oil is left in your pan, you'll want to have 2 tablespoons worth before adding the onions and sautéing for 2 minutes or until the onions begin to turn translucent.
6. Add the peppers and mushrooms and continue to cook until everything softens a bit, about 2-3 minutes. Sprinkle the flour and garlic powder over the veggies and push the veggies around the pan to coat evenly and cook for about 1 minute to cook out the raw taste of flour. Gradually whisk in the stock and cook. Add 60ml. of water and soy sauce, and continue to whisk.
7. You want to whisk continuously so you don't have lumps, about 2-3 minutes. When the sauce begins to thicken just a bit, add the sour cream, whisking it in if necessary.
8. Add in the cheese and stir continuously using a wooden spoon until it melts. Allow the sauce to start bubbling and allow for it to thicken; about 3-5 minutes.

9. Remove from the stove, add the meatballs and cover them in the sauce. Sprinkle with parsley and serve in baguettes, over pasta, mashed potatoes, or rice.

 Nutrition:
Calories: 555 **Carbohydrate:** 6.6g **Protein:** 38.6g **Fat:** 24.8g

298. Chocolate Chili

Preparation Time: 15 minutes	**Cooking Time:** 260 grams hours	**Servings:** 8

Ingredients:

- Olive oil
- 1 small onion
- 1 green pepper
- 4 garlic cloves
- 1 jalapeño pepper
- 1 teaspoon dried thyme
- 2 tablespoons red chili powder
- 1 tablespoon ground cumin
- 1kg. lean minced pork
- 250 grams fresh tomatoes
- 120 grams sugar-free tomato paste
- 1½ tablespoons cacao powder
- 250 ml. chicken broth
- 120 ml. of water
- Salt
- Black pepper
- 110 grams cheddar cheese

Directions:

1. Sauté the onion and pepper for 5-7 minutes.
2. Add the garlic, jalapeño pepper, thyme, and spices and sauté for 1 minute.
3. Add the pork and cook for 4-5 minutes. Stir in the tomatoes, tomato paste, and cacao powder and cook for 2 minutes.
4. Add the broth and water, boil. Simmer, covered for 2 hours. Stir in the salt and black pepper. Remove then top with cheddar cheese and serve.

 Nutrition:
Calories: 369 **Carbohydrate:** 9.1g **Protein:** 23.3g **Fat:** 22.9g

299. Pork Stew

Preparation Time: 15 minutes	**Cooking Time:** 45 minutes	**Servings:** 6

Ingredients:

- 1kg. boneless pork roast
- 60 grams all-purpose flour
- 2 1/2 teaspoons salt
- 1 1/2 teaspoons black pepper
- 3 tablespoons extra virgin olive oil
- 2 small leeks, white and green part thinly sliced
- 130 grams chopped shallots
- 4 large garlic cloves, chopped
- 220 ml. white wine
- 5 medium carrots, peeled and cut into 3/4 inch pieces
- 4 medium Yukon Gold potatoes, peeled and cut into 1-inch cubes
- 220 ml. chicken stock
- 1 can chopped tomatoes
- 2 tablespoons balsamic vinegar
- 2 bay leaves
- 1 teaspoon dried basil
- 1 teaspoon dried organo
- 1 teaspoon dried thyme

- 100 grams Italian portobello mushrooms, cut in half
- Chopped parsley for garnish

Directions:

1. In a medium bowl, toss pork cubes in flour, 1/2 teaspoon salt, and 1/2 teaspoon black pepper.
2. Heat olive oil in a large dutch oven over a medium high heat. Place one half on the pork in an even layer in the dutch oven. Do not overcrowd. Brown for 2-3 minutes. Turn each piece and brown for a further 2-3 minutes. Transfer browned pork to a plate. Repeat with remaining pork, transferring to plate when browned.
3. Add leeks, shallots, and garlic to dutch oven and saute 2-3 minutes until the leeks have wilted. Add wine and stir to deglaze the pan, scraping the bottom of the pot to remove browned bits.
4. Add carrots, potatoes, chicken stock, tomatoes, vinegar, bay leaves, basil, oregano, thyme, two teaspoons salt, and one teaspoon pepper to Dutch oven. Bring to a boil, mixing well. Reduce heat to low and simmer for 5 minutes.
5. Add pork to the stew, cover, and simmer for 30 to 40 minutes. Add mushrooms and continue simmering for 10 to 15 minutes or until vegetables are tender. Adjust seasoning with salt and pepper to taste. Serve immediately garnished with chopped parsley.

 Nutrition:
Calories: 777 **Carbohydrates:** 22g **Fiber:** 12g
Protein: 41g **Fat:** 10.4g

300. Pork & Chilly Stew

Preparation Time: 15 minutes	**Cooking Time:** 2 hours & 10 minutes	**Servings:** 8

Ingredients:

- 3 tablespoons unsalted butter
- 250 grams pounds boneless pork ribs
- 1 large onion
- 4 garlic cloves
- 160 ml. chicken broth/stock
- 2 cans sugar-free tomatoes
- 120 grams canned roasted poblano chilies
- 2 teaspoons dried oregano
- 1 teaspoon ground cumin
- Salt
- 30 grams coriander
- 2 tablespoons lime juice

Directions:

6. Cook the pork, onions, and garlic for 5 minutes.
7. Add the broth, tomatoes, poblano chilies, oregano, cumin, and salt, then boil.
8. Then simmer, cover for 2 hours.
9. Mix in the fresh coriander and lime juice then remove from the heat. Serve.

 Nutrition:
Calories: 369 **Carbohydrates:** 36g **Fat:** 21g **Protein:** 39.6g

SNACK

301. Chips

Preparation Time: 10 Minutes	Cooking Time: 20 Minutes	Servings: 4

Ingredients:

- Oil spray (make sure its avocado)

What you need for the coating:

- 1 tablespoon of paprika
- ½ of a tablespoon of cayenne pepper for a little bit of a kick
- ½ of a tablespoon of onion powder
- ¼ teaspoon nutritional yeast
- ½ tablespoon of garlic powder

What you need for the chip:

- A bag of pork rinds (take note that whatever bag you choose will change the nutrition information at the end of the recipe)

Directions:

1. Add the coating ingredients to a spice grinder and blend until everything becomes smooth.
2. Spray your pork rinds with oil as it will make the coating stick better.
3. Transfer the rinds to a plastic bag and pour the toppings in before you begin to shake it.

Nutrition:
Calories: 124 Fat: 2.7g Carbohydrates: 2g Protein: 14g

302. Pickle

Preparation Time: 20 Minutes	Cooking Time: 20 Minutes	Servings: 3

Ingredients:

- 1 can of tuna (go for a version that is light flaked)
- 30 grams of mayo (it needs to be sugar-free if you can get it and a light version)
- 1 tablespoon dill
- 5 or 6 pickles depending on what you need

Directions:

1. Cut your pickles in half so that they are lengthwise.
2. Seed your pickles.

3. Drain the tuna and then add the dill, mayo, and tuna in a bowl before mixing.
4. Spoon the tuna mixture onto the pickle. It will only take you five minutes.
5. You can get up to four servings from these ingredients.

Nutrition:
Calories: 133 Protein: 6g Carbohydrates: 3.6g Fat: 0.6g

303. Cucumber Sushi

Preparation Time: 15 minutes	Cooking Time: 20 minutes	Servings: 10

Ingredients

- 2 medium cucumbers, halved
- 1/4 avocado, thinly sliced
- 1/2 red pepper, thinly sliced
- 1/2 yellow pepper, thinly sliced
- 2 small carrots, thinly sliced

FOR THE DIPPING SAUCE

- 90 grams mayonnaise
- 1 tablespoon sriracha
- 1 teaspoon. soy sauce

Directions

6. Using a small spoon, remove seeds from center of cucumbers until they are completely hollow.
7. Press avocado into the center of cucumber, using a butter knife. Next, slide the peppers and carrots into the cuecumber until the cucumber is completely full of veggies.
8. Make dipping sauce: combine mayo, sriracha, and soy sauce in a small bowl. Whisk to combine.
9. Slice cucumber rounds into 1" thick pieces and serve with sauce on the side.

Nutrition:
Calories: 190 Carbohydrates: 5g Fat: 15 g Protein: 3g

304. Brussel Sprout Chips

Preparation Time: 5 minutes	Cooking Time: 18-20 minutes	Servings: 2

Ingredients

- 500 grams brussel sprouts
- 1 tablespoon olive oil
- 2 tablespoons parmesan cheese, grated

1 teaspoon garlic powder
 Black pepper

 Salt
 Caesar dressing, optional

Directions

1. Preheat the oven to 200°C, fan 180°C, gas 6. In a large bowl, toss brussel sprouts with oil, Parmesan, and garlic powder and season with salt and pepper. Spread in an even layer on a medium baking tray.
2. Bake 10 minutes, toss, and bake 8 to 10 minutes more, until crisp and golden. Garnish with more Parmesan and serve with caesar dressing for dipping.

Nutrition:
Calories: 220   **Fat:** 25 g   **Carbohydrates:** 4g   **Protein:** 3g

305. Keto Taquitos

🥣 **Preparation Time:** 15 minutes	🕐 **Cooking Time:** 45 minutes	🍽 **Servings:** 12

Ingredients

 2 tablespoons extra-virgin olive oil
- 1/2 onion, finely chopped
- 4 cloves garlic, minced
- 1 teaspoon ground cumin
- 1 teaspoon chili powder
- 160 grams shredded chicken
- 3 tablespoons red enchilada sauce

- 4 tablespoons freshly chopped coriander, plus more for garnish
- Kosher salt
- 220 grams grated cheddar
- 220 grams grated Monterey jack
- Sour cream, for serving (optional)

Directions

3. Preheat oven to 180°C and line two baking trays with baking paper. In a medium pan over a medium heat, heat oil. Add onion and cook until slightly soft, 3 minutes.
4. Add garlic and spices and cook until fragrant, 1 to 2 minutes more. Add chicken and enchilada sauce, then bring mixture to a simmer.
5. Stir in coriander, season with salt, and remove from the heat.
6. Make taquito shells: In a medium bowl, mix together cheeses. Divide mixture into 12 3 ½" piles on a prepared baking tray. Bake until cheese is melty and slightly golden around the edges, about 10 minutes. Let cool for 2 to 4 minutes, then peel shells off parchment.
7. Add a small pile of chicken to each and roll tightly. Repeat until all taquitos are made.
8. Garnish with coriander and serve with sour cream, for dipping.

Nutrition:
Calories: 330   **Fat:** 4g   **Protein:** 3g   **Carbohydrates:** 11g

306. Bacon Asparagus Bites

🥣 **Preparation Time:** 10 minutes	🕐 **Cooking Time:** 30 minutes	🍽 **Servings:** 6

Ingredients

 6 slices bacon, cut into thirds
- 220 grams cream cheese, softened to room temperature
- 1 garlic clove, chopped

- Freshly ground black pepper
- Kosher salt
- 9 asparagus spears, blanched

Directions

1. Preheat the oven to 200°C, fan 180°C, gas 6 and line 1 medium baking tray with baking paper.
2. Cook bacon: In a large pan over a medium heat, cook the bacon until most of the fat is cooked out, but is not crisp. Remove from the pan and drain on a kitchen paper lined plate.
3. In a small bowl, combine cream cheese with garlic and season with salt and pepper. Stir until combined.
4. Assemble bites: Spread about 1/2 tablespoon cream cheese onto each strip of bacon. Place asparagus in the center and roll bacon until bacon ends meet. Once all bites are made, place on prepared baking tray and bake for 5 minutes, until bacon is crisp and cream cheese is warmed through. Serve.

Nutrition:
Calories: 234   **Fat:** 5g   **Protein:** 5g   **Carbohydrates:** 3g

307. Avocado Boats with Crab

🥣 **Preparation Time:** 5 minutes	🕐 **Cooking Time:** 10 minutes	🍽 **Servings:** 4

Ingredients

 500 grams crab meat
- 220 grams Greek yogurt
- 1/2 red onion, chopped
- 2 tablespoons chopped chives
- 3 tablespoons lemon juice

- 1/2 tsp. cayenne pepper
- kosher salt
- 130 grams shredded Cheddar
- 2 avocados, halved and pitted

Directions

1. In a medium bowl, stir together crab meat, yogurt, red onion, chives, lemon juice, and cayenne and season with salt.
2. Scoop out avocados to create bowls, leaving a small border. Dice scooped out avocado and fold into crab mixture.
3. Preheat grill. Fill avocado bowls with crab mixture and top with cheddar. Broil until cheese is just melted, about 1 minute. Serve immediately.

Nutrition:
Calories: 350   **Fat:** 11 g   **Protein:** 5 g   **Carbohydrates:** 12g

308. Pinwhee Delight

🥣 **Preparation Time:** 5 Minutes	🕐 **Cooking Time:** 5 Minutes	🍽 **Servings:** 20

Ingredients:

- 1 block of cream cheese
- 10 slices of salami (genoa) and pepperoni
- 5 tablespoons pickles (make sure they are finely chopped)

Directions:

1. Have your cream cheese brought to room temperature.
2. Whip the cream cheese until it becomes fluffy.
3. Spread your cream cheese in a rectangle that is a quarter-inch thick. Make sure to use an appropriately sized cling film.
4. Put pickles on top of cream cheese
5. Place the salami over the cream cheese in layers that are over-lapping so that each cream cheese layer is covered.
6. Place another layer of the cling film over the layer of salami and press down. Be gentle.
7. Flip your whole rectangle over so that the bottom cream cheese layer is now facing the top instead.
8. Peel back your cking film very carefully from the top cream cheese layer.
9. You should begin rolling this into a log shape, slowly removing the bottom layer of your cling film as you go along.
10. Place the pinwheel in tight cling film.
11. Place in the fridge overnight or if you can't wait at least four hours.
12. Slice, whatever thickness you would like it.

 Nutrition:
Calories: 133 **Fat:** 4.2g **Carbohydrates:** 0.8g **Protein:** 1g

309. Zesty olives

Preparation Time: 5 Minutes	Cooking Time: 5 Minutes	Servings: 6

Ingredients:

- 30 grams of oil (make sure that it is extra virgin olive oil)
- ¼ teaspoon pepper flakes
- 1 thinly sliced garlic clove
- 1 tablespoon lemon juice
- 1 strip of zest from a lemon
- 120 grams of olives
- 2 sprigs of thyme
- 1 tablespoon orange juice
- 1 strip of zest from an orange

Directions:

1. Get a saucepan.
2. Heat your oil over a medium-high heat.
3. Add zest, thyme, garlic and cook it.
4. Be sure that you stir occasionally.
5. Cook for a few minutes, and you will notice that the garlic is golden.
6. You will then need to stir in the olives and cook them as well.
7. Stir them as they cook but only cook for 2 minutes. You want them to be warmed.
8. Turn off your heat.
9. Stir in your juice.
10. Place in a dish.

 Nutrition:
Calories: 180 **Fat:** 20g **Carbohydrates:** 2g **Protein:** 4g

310. Deviled Eggs Keto Style!

 Preparation Time: 5 Minutes	Cooking Time: 5 Minutes	Servings: 20

Ingredients:

- 10 large eggs (hard boiled)
- 1 avocado (make sure it is ripe)
- 1 lemon (you will need to juice this)
- 1 tablespoon mustard (use Dijon)
- Paprika (use smoked)

Directions:

1. Slice your eggs in half and take out the yolks.
2. Combine your yolks, avocado, and lemon juice in a bowl and stir thoroughly.
3. Spoon the mixture into the egg white halves.
4. Sprinkle the top with paprika.

 Nutrition:
Calories: 250 **Fat:** 4g **Carbohydrates:** 6g **Protein:** 3g

311. Cucumber

 Preparation Time: 5 Minutes	Cooking Time: 0 Minutes	Servings: 1

Ingredients:

- 120 grams of cucumber (make sure they are sliced)
- 10 olives (Kalamata olives. Use large ones)

Directions:

1. Mix them in a bowl, and there you go!

 Nutrition:
Calories: 71 **Fat:** 4.8g **Carbohydrates:** 5g **Protein:** 1.29g

312. Nutty Yogurt

 Preparation Time: 5 Minutes	Cooking Time: 0 Minute	Servings: 1

Ingredients:

- 56 grams of yogurt (use whole milk Greek yogurt)
- ½ teaspoon cinnamon
- 1 tablespoon walnuts

Directions:

1. Place the yogurt in a dish.
2. Add the walnuts.
3. Add the cinnamon.

Nutrition:
Calories: 160 **Fat:** 12.5g **Protein:** 8g **Carbohydrates:** 6g

313. Creamy Boat

 Preparation Time: 5 Minutes | **Cooking Time:** 0 Minutes | **Servings:** 4

Ingredients:

- 2 stalks of celery
- 2 tablespoons cream cheese

Directions:

1. Clean the celery and cut it into pieces.
2. Place the pieces on a plate before adding cream cheese to them.
3. Repeat this process if necessary.

 Nutrition:
Calories: 113 **Fat:** 10.1g **Carbohydrates:** 4g **Protein:** 2.3g

314. Parmesan Cheese Strips

 Preparation Time: 15 minutes | **Cooking Time:** 5-7 minutes | **Servings:** 12

Ingredients:

- 120 grams parmesan cheese
- 1 teaspoon dried basil

Directions:

1. Preheat the oven to 190°C, fan 170°C, gas 5.
2. Form small piles of the parmesan cheese on the baking tray.
3. Flatten and sprinkle dried basil on top of the cheese.
4. Bake for 5 to 7 minutes.
5. Serve.

 Nutrition:
Calories: 455 **Fat:** 2g **Protein:** 2g **Carbohydrates:** 6.21g

315. Peanut Butter Power Granola

 Preparation Time: 15 minutes | **Cooking Time:** 35 minutes | **Servings:** 12

Ingredients:

- 120 grams desiccated coconut
- 160 grams almonds
- 150 grams pecans
- 10 grams swerve sweetener
- 10 grams vanilla whey protein powder
- 10 grams peanut butter
- 10 grams sunflower seeds
- 10 grams butter
- 20 ml. water

Directions:

1. Preheat the oven to 220°C, fan 200°C, gas 8.
2. Combine the almonds and pecans using a food processor. Transfer and add the sunflower seeds, coconut, vanilla, sweetener, and protein powder.

3. Dissolve the peanut butter and butter in the microwave.
4. Mix the melted butter in the nut mixture. Put in the water to create a lumpy mixture.
5. Scoop out the batter and place it on the baking tray. Bake for 30 minutes. Serve!

 Nutrition:
Calories: 338 **Fat:** 30g **Carbohydrates:** 5g **Protein:** 9.6g

316. Homemade Graham Crackers

 Preparation Time: 15 minutes | **Cooking Time:** 60 minutes to 1 hour | **Servings:** 10

Ingredients:

- 1 egg
- 250 grams almond flour
- 43 grams swerve brown
- 6 grams cinnamon
- 5 grams baking powder
- 2 teaspoons melted butter
- 1 teaspoon vanilla extract
- Salt

Directions:

1. Preheat the oven to 220°C, fan 200°C, gas 8.
2. Mix the almond flour, cinnamon, sweetener, baking powder, and salt.
3. Put in the egg, melted butter, and vanilla extract. Mix to form a dough.
4. Roll out the dough evenly. Cut the dough into the shapes.
5. Bake for 20 to 30 minutes. Cool for 30 minutes and then put back in for another 30 minutes, 200°C. Serve.

 Nutrition:
Calories: 156 **Fat:** 13.35g **Carbohydrates:** 6.21g **Protein:** 5.21g

317. Keto No-Bake Cookies

 Preparation Time: 15 minutes | **Cooking Time:** 2 minutes | **Servings:** 18

Ingredients:

- 83 grams natural peanut butter
- 120 grams coconut, unsweetened
- 1 tablespoon real butter
- 4 drops of vanilla essence

Directions:

1. Melt the butter in the microwave. Remove and add the peanut butter. Stir.
2. Add the sweetener and coconut. Mix. Spoon it onto a tray lined with baking paper
3. Freeze for 10 minutes. Cut and serve.

 Nutrition:
Calories: 98 **Fat:** 1g **Carbohydrates:** 12g **Protein:** 5g

318. Swiss Cheese Crunchy Nachos

 **Preparation Time:** 15 minutes	**Cooking Time:** 12-3 minutes	**Servings:** 2

Ingredients:

- 70 grams Swiss cheese
- 70 grams cheddar cheese
- 220 grams cooked bacon

Directions:

1. Preheat the oven to 220°C, fan 200°C, gas 8.
2. Spread the Swiss cheese on baking paper. Sprinkle with bacon and top it with the cheddar cheese.
3. Bake for 10 minutes. Cool and cut into triangle strips.
4. Grill for 2 to 3 minutes. Serve.

 Nutrition:
Calories: 280 **Fat:** 21.8g **Protein:** 18.6g **Carbohydrates:** 2.44g

319. Homemade Thin Mints

Preparation Time: 15 minutes	**Cooking Time:** 20-30 minutes	**Servings:** 20

Ingredients:

- 1 egg
- 250 grams almond flour
- 43 grams cocoa powder
- 43 grams swerve sweetener
- 2 tablespoons butter, melted
- 1 teaspoon baking powder
- ½ teaspoon Vanilla extract
- ¼ teaspoon Salt
- 1 tablespoon coconut oil
- 50 grams sugar-free dark chocolate
- 1 teaspoon peppermint extract

Directions:

1. Preheat the oven to 220°C, fan 200°C, gas 8.
2. Mix the cacao powder, sweetener, almond flour, salt, and baking powder. Then put the beaten egg, vanilla extract, and butter.
3. Knead the dough and roll it on the baking paper. Cut into a cookie. Bake the cookies for 20 to 30 minutes.
4. For the coating, dissolve the oil and chocolate. Stir in the peppermint extract.
5. Dip the cookie in the coating, chill, and serve.

 Nutrition:
Calories: 116 **Fat:** 10.41g **Carbohydrates:** 6.99g **Protein:** 8g

320. Mozzarella Cheese Pockets

Preparation Time: 15 minutes	**Cooking Time:** 25 minutes	**Servings:** 8

Ingredients:

- 1 egg
- 8 mozzarella cheese sticks
- 250 grams mozzarella cheese

- 90 grams almond flour
- 30 grams cream cheese
- 60 grams crushed pork rinds

Directions:

6. Grate the mozzarella cheese.
7. Mix the almond flour, mozzarella, and the cream cheese. Microwave for 30 seconds.
8. Put in the egg and mix to form a dough.
9. Put the dough in between 2 wax papers and roll it into a semi-rectangular shape.
10. Cut them into smaller rectangle pieces and wrap them around the cheese sticks.
11. Roll the stick onto crushed pork rinds.
12. Bake for 20 to 25 minutes at 200°C, fan 180°C, gas 6. Serve.

 Nutrition:
Calories: 272 **Fat:** 22g **Carbohydrates:** 2.4g **Protein:** 17g

321. No-Bake Coconut Cookies

Preparation Time: 15 minutes	**Cooking Time:** 10 minutes	**Servings:** 8

Ingredients:

- 400 grams unsweetened shredded coconut
- 60 grams sweetener
- Coconut oil
- Salt
- 2 teaspoons Vanilla
- Topping: coconut shreds

Directions:

1. Process all the ingredients in a food processor. Form into cookie shapes. Add the topping.
2. Chill and serve.

 Nutrition:
Calories: 329 **Carbohydrates:** 4.1g **Protein:** 2.1g **Fat:** 30g

322. Cheesy Cauliflower Breadsticks

Preparation Time: 15 minutes	**Cooking Time:** 30 minutes	**Servings:** 8

Ingredients:

- 4 eggs
- 250 grams cauliflower, riced
- 250 grams mozzarella cheese
- 4 cloves chopped garlic
- 3 teaspoons oregano
- Salt
- Pepper

Directions:

1. Preheat the oven to 200°C, fan 180°C, gas 6.
2. Process cauliflower in a food processor. Microwave for 10 minutes. Cool and drain; put the eggs, oregano, garlic, salt, pepper, and mozzarella. Mix.

3. Separate the mixture into individual sticks. Bake for 25 minutes. Remove and sprinkle mozzarella on top. Bake again for 5 minutes. Serve.

 Nutrition:
Calories: 121 **Carbohydrates:** 4g **Protein:** 13g **Fat:** 11g

323. Easy Peanut Butter Cups

Preparation Time: 15 minutes	**Cooking Time:** 0 minutes	**Servings:** 12

Ingredients:
- 60 grams peanut butter
- 30 grams butter
- 30 grams cacao butter
- 43 grams powdered swerve sweetener
- ½ teaspoon vanilla extract
- 120 grams sugar-free dark chocolate

Directions:
1. Melt the peanut butter, butter, and cacao butter in a pan on a low heat.
2. Add the vanilla and sweetener. Put the mixture in the muffin cups. Chill. Melt the chocolate over a bain marie.
3. Take out the muffin tin and drizzle the chocolate on top. Chill again for 15 minutes. Serve.

 Nutrition:
Calories: 200 **Fat:** 19g **Carbohydrates:** 6g **Protein:** 2.9g

324. Fried Green Beans Rosemary

Preparation Time: 10 minutes	**Cooking Time:** 5 minutes	**Servings:** 2

Ingredients:
- 150 grams green beans
- 2 teaspoons minced garlic
- 2 tablespoons Rosemary
- Salt
- 1 tablespoon butter

Directions:
1. Warm-up an Air Fryer to 220° C.
2. Put the chopped green beans then brush with butter. Sprinkle salt, minced garlic, and rosemary over then cook for 5 minutes. Serve.

 Nutrition:
Calories: 277 **Fat:** 6.3g **Protein:** 0.7g **Carbohydrates:** 4.5g

325. Crispy Broccoli Popcorn

Preparation Time: 15 minutes	**Cooking Time:** 10 minutes	**Servings:** 4

Ingredients:
- 220 grams broccoli florets
- 220 grams coconut flour
- 4 egg yolks
- Salt
- Pepper
- 1 stack butter

Directions:
1. Melt butter, then let it cool. Break the eggs into the butter.
2. Add the coconut flour to the liquid, then season with salt and pepper. Mix.
3. Warm-up an Air Fryer to 200°Celsius.
4. Dip a broccoli floret in the coconut flour mixture, then place it in the Air Fryer.
5. Cook the broccoli florets 6 minutes. Serve.

 Nutrition:
Calories: 202 **Fat:** 17.5g **Protein:** 5.1g **Carbohydrates:** 7.8g

326. Cheesy Cauliflower Croquettes

Preparation Time: 10 minutes	**Cooking Time:** 16 minutes	**Servings:** 4

Ingredients:
- 220 grams cauliflower florets
- 2 tablespoons garlic
- 60 grams onion
- ¾ teaspoon mustard
- ½ teaspoon salt
- ½ teaspoon pepper
- 2 tablespoon butter
- 100 grams cheddar cheese

Directions:
1. Microwave the butter. Let it cool.
2. Process the cauliflower florets using a processor. Transfer to a bowl then add the chopped onion and cheese.
3. Add the minced garlic, mustard, salt, and pepper, then pour melted butter over. Shape the cauliflower batter into medium balls.
4. Warm-up an Air Fryer to 200° C and cook for 14 minutes. Serve.

 Nutrition:
Calories: 160 **Fat:** 13g **Protein:** 6.8g **Carbohydrates:** 5.1g

327. Spinach in Cheese Envelopes

Preparation Time: 15 minutes	**Cooking Time:** 30 minutes	**Servings:** 8

Ingredients:
- 220 grams cheddar cheese
- 164-gram coconut flour
- 3 egg yolks
- 2 eggs
- 60 grams cheese
- 120 grams steamed spinach
- Salt
- Pepper
- Onion powder

Directions:
1. Whisk cream cheese, add egg yolks. Stir in coconut flour until it becomes a soft dough.

2. Put the dough on a flat surface then roll until thin. Cut the thin dough into 8 squares.
3. Beat the eggs, then place in a bowl. Add salt, pepper, and grated cheese.
4. Put chopped spinach and onion into the egg batter.
5. Put spinach filling on a square dough then fold until becoming an envelope. Glue with water.
6. Warm-up an Air Fryer to 200° C. Cook for 12 minutes.
7. Remove and serve!

 Nutrition:
Calories: 365   **Fat:** 34.6g   **Protein:** 10.4g   **Carbohydrates:** 4.4g

328. Cheesy Mushroom Slices

Preparation Time: 8-10 minutes	Cooking Time: 15 minutes	Servings: 8

Ingredients:

- 220 grams mushrooms
- 2 eggs
- 100 grams almond flour
- 70 grams cheddar cheese
- 2 tablespoons butter
- Salt
- Pepper

Directions:

1. Process chopped mushrooms in a food processor then add eggs, almond flour, and cheddar cheese.
2. Put salt and pepper then pour melted butter into the food processor. Transfer.
3. Warm-up an Air Fryer to 190° Celsius.
4. Put the loaf pan on the Air Fryer's rack then cook for 15 minutes. Slice and serve.

 Nutrition:
Calories: 365   **Fat:** 34.6g   **Protein:** 10.4g   **Carbohydrates:** 4.4g

329. Asparagus Fries

Preparation Time: 10 minutes	Cooking Time: 10 minutes	Servings: 4

Ingredients:

- 10 organic asparagus spears
- 1 roasted red pepper
- 1 tablespoon Organic roasted red pepper
- ¼ Almond flour
- ½ teaspoon Garlic powder
- ½ teaspoon Smoked paprika
- 2 tablespoons parsley
- 60 grams Parmesan cheese, full fat
- 2 organic eggs
- 3 tablespoons mayonnaise, full fat

Directions:

1. Preheat the oven to 200°C, fan 180°C, gas 6.
2. Process cheese in a food processor, add garlic and parsley, and pulse for 1 minute.
3. Add almond flour, pulse for 30 seconds, transfer, and add the paprika.

4. Whisk eggs into a shallow dish.
5. Dip asparagus spears into the egg batter, then coat with parmesan mixture and place it on a baking tray. Bake in the oven for 10 minutes.
6. Put the mayonnaise in a bowl, add red pepper and whisk, then chill. Serve with prepared dip.

 Nutrition:
Calories: 453   **Fat:** 33.4 g   **Protein:** 19.1g   **Carbohydrates:** 5.5g

330. Kale Chips

Preparation Time: 5 minutes	Cooking Time: 12 minutes	Servings: 4

Ingredients:

- 1 organic kale
- Salt
- Olive oil

Directions:

1. Preheat the oven to 220°C, fan 200°C, gas 8.
2. Put kale leaves into a large plastic bag and add oil. Shake and then spread on a large baking tray.
3. Bake for 12 minutes. Serve with salt.

 Nutrition:
Calories: 163   **Fat:** 10 g   **Protein:** 2 g   **Carbohydrates:** 14 g

331. Guacamole

 Preparation Time: 10 minutes	Cooking Time: 0 minutes	Servings: 4

Ingredients:

- 2 organic avocados pitted
- 1/3 organic red onion
- 1 organic jalapeño
- ½ teaspoon salt
- ½ teaspoon ground pepper
- 2 tablespoons tomato salsa
- 1 tablespoon lime juice
- ½ organic coriander

Directions:

1. Slice the avocado flesh horizontally and vertically.
2. Mix in onion, jalapeno, and lime juice in a bowl.
3. Put salt and black pepper, add salsa, and mix. Fold in coriander and serve.

 Nutrition:
Calories: 16.5   **Fat:** 1.4 g   **Protein:** 0.23 g   **Carbohydrates:** 0.5 g

332. Courgette Noodles

Preparation Time: 5 minutes	Cooking Time: 6 minutes	Servings: 2

Ingredients:

- 2 courgettes, spiralized into noodles
- 2 tablespoons butter, unsalted

- 1 ½ tablespoon garlic
- 90 grams Parmesan cheese
- Salt
- ¼ teaspoon ground black pepper
- ¼ teaspoon red chili flakes

Directions:

1. Sauté butter and garlic for 1 minute.
2. Put zucchini noodles, cook for 5 minutes, then put salt and black pepper.
3. Transfer then top with cheese and sprinkle with red chili flakes. Serve.

 Nutrition:
Calories: 298 **Fat:** 26.1 g **Protein:** 5 g **Carbohydrates:** 2.3 g

333. Cauliflower Souffle

Preparation Time: 10 minutes	**Cooking Time:** 12 minutes	**Servings:** 6

Ingredients:

- 1 cauliflower, florets
- 2 eggs
- 2 tablespoons double cream
- 60 grams cream cheese
- 60 grams sour cream
- 60 grams Asiago cheese
- 120 grams cheddar cheese
- 30 grams chives
- 2 tablespoons butter, unsalted
- 6 bacon slices, sugar-free
- 120 ml. of water

Directions:

4. Pulse eggs, cream, sour cream, cream cheese, and cheeses in a food processor.
5. Add cauliflower florets, pulse for 2 seconds, then add butter and chives and pulse for another 2 seconds.
6. Put water in a pot and add a trivet stand.
7. Put the cauliflower batter in a greased round casserole dish then put the dish on the trivet stand.
8. Cook for 12 minutes on high. Remove, top with bacon, and serve.

 Nutrition:
Calories: 342 **Fat:** 28 g **Protein:** 17g **Carbohydrates:** 5 g

334. No-Churn Ice Cream

Preparation Time: 10 minutes	**Cooking Time:** 0 minutes	**Servings:** 3

Ingredients:

- Pinch salt
- 120 grams double cream
- ¼ teaspoon xanthan gum
- 2 tablespoon zero-calorie sweetener powder
- 1 teaspoon vanilla extract
- 1 tablespoon vodka

Directions:

1. Place the xanthan gum, cream, vanilla extract, sweetener, vodka, and salt into a jar and mix.
2. Blend the batter in the immersion blender for 2 minutes.

3. Put the batter back in the jar, cover it, and chill for 4 hours. Stir the cream batter at 40 minutes intervals.
4. Serve.

 Nutrition:
Calories: 291 **Carbohydrates:** 3.2g **Protein:** 1.6g **Fat:** 29.4g

335. Cheesecake Cupcakes

Preparation Time: 10 minutes	**Cooking Time:** 15 minutes	**Servings:** 12

Ingredients:

- 1 teaspoon vanilla extract
- 60 grams almonds
- 50 grams granulated no-calorie sucralose sweetener
- 30 grams melted butter
- 2 eggs
- 250 grams pack softened cream cheese

Directions:

1. Preheat the oven to 220°C, fan 200°C, gas 8.
2. Mix butter and almonds and put into the bottom of the muffin cups.
3. Mix vanilla extract, cream cheese, sucralose sweetener, and egg in an electric mixer. Put this batter to the top of the muffin cups.
4. Bake for 17 minutes. Cool and serve.

 Nutrition:
Calories: 209 **Carbohydrates:** 3.5g **Protein:** 4.9g **Fat:** 20g

336. Chocolate Peanut Butter Cups

Preparation Time: 15 minutes	**Cooking Time:** 3 minutes	**Servings:** 12

Ingredients:

- 30 grams peanuts, salted
- 120 ml. coconut oil
- Salt
- 60 grams natural peanut butter
- ¼ teaspoon vanilla extract
- 2 tablespoons double cream
- 1 teaspoon liquid stevia
- 1 tablespoon cocoa powder

Directions:

1. Melt coconut oil for 5 minutes, then add peanut butter, salt, double cream, cocoa powder, vanilla extract, and liquid stevia to the pan. Stir.
2. Place the batter into muffin molds. Put the salted peanuts on top. Chill for an hour. Serve.

Nutrition:
Calories: 246 **Carbohydrates:** 3.3g **Protein:** 3.4g **Fat:** 26g

337. Peanut Butter Cookies

Preparation Time: 15 minutes	**Cooking Time:** 15 minutes	**Servings:** 12

Ingredients:

- 1 teaspoon vanilla extract, sugar-free
- 120 grams peanut butter
- 1 egg
- 60 grams natural sweetener, low-calorie

Directions:

1. Preheat the oven to 220°C, fan 200°C, gas 8.
2. Mix peanut butter, vanilla extract, sweetener, and egg to form a dough.
3. Mold the dough into balls. Bake for 15 minutes. Cool and serve.

 Nutrition:
Calories: 133 **Carbohydrates:** 12.4g **Protein:** 5.9g **Fat:** 11.2g

338. Low-Carb Almond Coconut Sandies

Preparation Time: 15 minutes	Cooking Time: 12 minutes	Servings: 18

Ingredients:

- 1 teaspoon stevia powder
- 120 grams coconut, unsweetened
- 5 grams Himalayan Sea salt
- 120 grams ground almonds
- 1 tablespoon vanilla extract
- 80 ml. melted coconut oil
- 2 tablespoons water
- 1 egg white

Directions:

1. Preheat the oven to 220°C, fan 200°C, gas 8.
2. Mix Himalayan Sea salt, unsweetened coconut, stevia powder, almonds, vanilla extract, coconut oil, water, and egg white. Put aside for 10 minutes.
3. Mold into little balls. Press down on the balls. Bake for 15 minutes. Cool and serve.

 Nutrition:
Calories: 107 **Carbohydrates:** 2.7g **Protein:** 1.9g **Fat:** 10.5g

339. Crème Brûlée

Preparation Time: 15 minutes	Cooking Time: 34 minutes	Servings: 4

Ingredients:

- 5 tablespoons natural sweetener, low calorie
- 4 egg yolks
- 250 grams double cream
- 1 teaspoon vanilla extract

Directions:

1. Preheat the oven to 220°C, fan 200°C, gas 8. Mix the vanilla extract and egg yolks together.
2. Add and simmer 15 grams of natural sweetener and cream in the pan and stir. Put the ramekins with batter in a glass baking dish and add hot water.

3. Bake for 30 minutes. Put 15 grams. natural sweetener on top. Serve.

 Nutrition:
Calorie: 466 **Carbohydrates:** 16.9g **Protein:** 5.1g **Fat:** 48.4g

340. Chocolate Fat Bomb

 Preparation Time: 15 minutes	Cooking Time: 0 minutes	Servings: 10

Ingredients:

1. 220 grams chocolate pudding mix, sugar-free
2. 250 grams cream cheese
3. Coconut oil

Directions:

1. Mix the chocolate pudding mix, cream cheese, and coconut oil using an electric mixer.
2. Put this batter into a mold to form into mounds. Cover and chill for 30 minutes. Serve.

 Nutrition:
Calories: 231 **Carbohydrates:** 3.5g **Protein:** 1.9g **Fat:** 24.3g

341. Cocoa Mug Cake

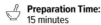 Preparation Time: 15 minutes	Cooking Time: 5 minutes	Servings: 2

Ingredients:

- 2 tablespoons coconut oil, melted
- 6 tablespoons almond flour
- 2 eggs
- 3 tablespoons cocoa powder, unsweetened
- Salt
- 2 teaspoons natural sweetener, low-calorie
- ½ teaspoon baking powder

Directions:

1. Mix salt, almond flour, baking powder, cocoa powder and natural sweetener.
2. Beat the eggs using an electric mixer. Add the coconut oil and stir. Put this egg batter into the bowl containing baking powder. Whisk.
3. Put the batter into mugs. Microwave to high for 1 minute. Serve.

 Nutrition:
Calories: 338 **Carbohydrates:** 8.6g **Protein:** 12.3g **Fat:** 30.9g

342. Dark Chocolate Espresso Paleo and Keto Mug Cake

 Preparation Time: 15 minutes	Cooking Time: 5 minutes	Servings: 2

Ingredients:

- 1 tablespoon brewed espresso
- 120 grams dark chocolate chips
- 1 egg
- 1 tablespoon coconut oil
- Baking soda
- 2 tablespoons water
- 1 tablespoon coconut flour
- 1 tablespoon almond flour

Directions:

1. Put both the coconut oil and chocolate chips in a mug.
2. Add the baking soda, water, coconut flour, and almond flour.
3. Microwave for 1 minute and 30 seconds. Cool and serve.

 Nutrition:
Calories: 793 **Carbohydrates:** 83.7g **Protein:** 14g **Fat:** 52.2g

343. Keto Matcha Mint Bars

Preparation Time: 15 minutes	**Cooking Time:** 0 minutes	**Servings:** 12

Ingredients:

- 6 drops stevia
- 120 grams almond flour
- 3 tablespoon melted butter
- 1 tablespoon cocoa powder, unsweetened
- 3 tablespoon warmed coconut oil
- 130 grams coconut butter
- 1 teaspoon peppermint extract
- 1 teaspoon vanilla extract
- 120 grams coconut butter
- 2 ripe avocados
- 1 tablespoon matcha
- 3 tablespoons stevia powder

Directions:

1. Mix almond flour, stevia powder, cocoa powder, and butter. Press down on it till a crust is formed. Let it chill for 15 minutes.
2. For the filling:
3. Mix stevia powder, coconut butter, vanilla extract, matcha, avocados, and peppermint extract using an electric mixer. Put this on the crust. Let it chill.
4. Mix liquid stevia, coconut oil, cocoa powder, and peppermint extract into the crust. Chill for 30 minutes.

 Nutrition:
Calories: 276 **Carbohydrates:** 12.6g **Protein:** 4.3g **Fat:** 26.1g

344. Keto No-Churn Blueberry Maple Ice Cream

Preparation Time: 15 minutes	**Cooking Time:** 0 minutes	**Servings:** 2

Ingredients:

- Salt
- 120 grams double cream
- ¼ teaspoon xanthan gum
- 250 grams blueberries, frozen
- ½ teaspoon maple extract
- 2 tablespoons natural sweetener, low calorie
- 1 tablespoon vodka
- a pinch of Salt

Directions:

1. Combine cream, salt, blueberries, xanthan gum, natural sweetener, maple extract, and vodka in a jar.
2. Process this mixture for 75 seconds with an immersion blender.
3. Chill in 35 minutes, stirring occasionally. Serve.

 Nutrition:
Calories: 304 **Carbohydrates:** 13.4g **Protein:** 1.8g **Fat:** 29.6g

345. Keto Raspberry Cake and White Chocolate Sauce

Preparation Time: 15 minutes	**Cooking Time:** 45 minutes	**Servings:** 4

Ingredients:

- 5 ounces cacao butter
- 4 teaspoons vanilla extract
- 4 eggs
- 300 grams raspberries
- 260 grams grass-fed ghee
- 1 teaspoon baking powder
- 1 teaspoon apple cider vinegar
- 120 grams green banana flour
- 90 grams coconut cream
- 90 grams granulated sweetener
- 120 grams cacao butter
- 2 tablespoons pure vanilla extract
- 90 grams coconut cream
- Salt

Directions:

1. Mix the butter and the sweetener. Pour in the grass-fed ghee into the mix, blend.
2. Beat the eggs in a different bowl.
3. Preheat the oven to 220°C, fan 200°C, gas 8. Grease a baking dish.
4. Add the mixed eggs into the butter and sweetener mixture. Mix well.
5. Pour in the banana flour and mix. Then the vanilla extract, apple cider, coconut cream, baking powder, and mix again.
6. Spoon around the sliced raspberries. Then, sprinkle flour in the baking dish.
7. Put the mixture into the dish then bake for 45 minutes. Cool down.

For the sauce:

1. Mix cacao butter with 2 tablespoons pure vanilla extract. Add coconut cream and beat. Put salt and beat.
2. Chop the remaining berries and throw them in the mix. Pour the mixture on the cake. Serve cold.

 Nutrition:
Calories: 325 **Fat:** 12g **Carbohydrates:** 3g **Protein:** 40g

346. Keto Chocolate Chip Cookies

Preparation Time: 15 minutes	**Cooking Time:** 10 minutes	**Servings:** 4

Ingredients:

- 90 grams unsweetened coconut powder
- 7 tablespoons Keto chocolate chips
- 5 tablespoons butter
- 2 tablespoons baking powder
- 2 eggs
- 90 grams confectioner's swerve
- 200 grams almond flour
- 1 teaspoon vanilla extract

Directions:

1. Preheat the oven to 220°C, fan 200°C, gas 8.
2. Melt half chocolate chips, then add the butter. Mix.
3. Mix the eggs into chocolate and butter mixture.
4. Add the vanilla extract, coconut powder, confectioners swerve, and almond flour. Mix well.
5. Then add chocolate chip cookies. Followed by the baking powder and mix until dough forms.
6. Roll the dough out and cut out cookies, top with chocolate chips.
7. Bake for 8 to 10 minutes. Serve.

 Nutrition:
Calories: 287 **Fat:** 19g **Carbohydrates:** 6.5g **Protein:** 6.8g

347. Keto Beef and Sausage Balls

Preparation Time: 15 minutes	**Cooking Time:** 20 minutes	**Servings:** 3

Ingredients:

For the meat:
- 1 kg. minced beef
- 1 kg. sausage (remove meat from skins)
- 2 eggs
- 60 grams Keto mayonnaise
- 50 grams ground pork rinds
- 60 grams Parmesan cheese
- Salt
- Pepper
- 60 grams butter
- 50 ml. Olive oil

For the sauce:
- 3 chopped onions
- 2 pounds mushrooms
- 5 cloves garlic
- 380 grams beef broth/stock
- 120 grams sour cream
- 60 grams mustard
- Worcestershire sauce
- Salt
- Pepper
- Parsley
- 15 grams Arrowroot powder

Directions:

1. Put meat, egg, and onions in a bowl, mix. Then add the beef, parmesan, egg, mayonnaise, sausage, pork rind in the bowl. Season with salt and pepper. Warm-up oil in a pan.
2. Mold the beef mixture into balls, fry for 7-10 minutes. Put aside.
3. Fry the chopped onions, then the garlic and mushrooms, cook for 3 minutes. Then, add the broth. Mix in mustard, sour cream, and Worcestershire sauce.
4. Boil for 2 minutes, then add in the meatballs. Season with salt and pepper, simmer. Serve.

 Nutrition:
Calories: 592 **Fat:** 53.9g **Carbohydrates:** 1.3g **Protein:** 25.4g

348. Keto Coconut Flake Balls

Preparation Time: 15 minutes	**Cooking Time:** 0 minutes	**Servings:** 2

Ingredients:

- 1 Vanilla Shortbread Collagen Protein Bar
- 1 tablespoon lemon juice
- ¼ teaspoon ground ginger
- 60 grams unsweetened coconut flakes
- ½ teaspoon ground turmeric

Directions:

1. Combine the protein bar, ginger, turmeric, and ¾ of the total flakes into a food processor.
2. Remove and add a spoon of water and roll till dough forms.
3. Roll into balls and sprinkle the rest of the coconut flakes on them. Serve.

 Nutrition:
Calories: 204 **Fat:** 11g **Carbohydrates:** 4.2g **Protein:** 1.5g

349. Keto Chocolate Greek Yoghurt Cookies

Preparation Time: 15 minutes	**Cooking Time:** 30 minutes	**Servings:** 3

Ingredients:

- 3 eggs
- 1/8 teaspoon tartar
- 5 tablespoons softened Greek yogurt

Directions:

1. Beat the egg whites, the tartar, and mix.
2. In the yolks, add in the Greek yogurt, and mix.
3. Combine both egg whites and yolk batter into a bowl.
4. Bake for 25-30 minutes at 220°C.
5. Serve.

Nutrition:
Calories: 287 **Fat:** 19g **Carbohydrates:** 6.5g **Protein:** 6.8g

350. Keto Coconut Flavored Ice Cream

Preparation Time: 15 minutes	**Cooking Time:** 0 minutes	**Servings:** 4

Ingredients:

- 250 ml. coconut milk
- 30 grams xylitol
- ¼ teaspoon salt
- 2 teaspoons vanilla extract
- 1 teaspoon coconut extract

Directions:

1. Add the coconut milk in a bowl, with the sweetener, extracts, and salt.
2. Mix well to combine.
3. Pour this mixture in the ice cube trays and put it in the freezer.
4. Serve.

 Nutrition:
Calories: 244 **Fat:** 48g **Carbohydrates:** 6g **Protein:** 15g

351. Chocolate-Coconut Cookies

Preparation Time: 15 minutes	**Cooking Time:** 20 minutes	**Servings:** 4

Ingredients:

- 2 eggs
- 60 grams of cocoa powder
- 60 grams flour
- 60 grams of coconut oil
- 30 grams grated coconut
- Stevia

Directions:

1. Preheat the oven to 200°C, fan 180°C, gas 6. Crack eggs and separate whites and yolks, mix separately.
2. Add salt to the yolks. Warm-up the oil in a pan, add cocoa, egg whites, and mix.
3. Add in the salted yolks; then add stevia. Followed by the coconut flour and mix until dough forms.
4. On a flat surface, sprinkle grated coconut. Roll the dough around in the coconut, mix. Mold into cookies.
5. Bake for 15 minutes at 200°C, serve.

 Nutrition:
Calories: 260 **Fat:** 26g **Carbohydrates:** 4.5g **Protein:** 1g

352. Keto Buffalo Chicken Meatballs

Preparation Time: 15 minutes	**Cooking Time:** 20 minutes	**Servings:** 3

Ingredients:

- 500 grams ground chicken
- 1 large egg
- 2 tablespoons hot sauce
- 60 grams almond flour
- Salt
- 10 grams pepper
- 60 grams melted butter
- 1 large onion
- 1 teaspoon garlic

Directions:

1. Combine meat, egg, and onions in a bowl. Pour in almond flour, garlic, salt, and pepper in.
2. Preheat the oven to 220°C, fan 200°C, gas 8 and grease a baking tray.
3. Mold the egg mixture into balls and place on the baking tray.
4. Bake for 18-20 minutes.
5. Melt butter in the microwave for few seconds; mix it with hot sauce.
6. Pour the sauce over the meatballs. Serve.

 Nutrition:
Calories: 360 **Fat:** 26g **Carbohydrates:** 4.5g **Protein:** 1g

353. Eggplant and Chickpea Bites

Preparation Time: 15 minutes	**Cooking Time:** 60 minutes	**Servings:** 6

Ingredients:

- 3 large aubergines
- Spray oil
- 2 large cloves garlic
- 2 tablespoons coriander powder
- 2 tablespoons cumin seeds
- 400 grams canned chickpeas
- 2 tablespoons chickpea flour
- Lemon zest and lemon juice of 1 lemon
- 3 tablespoons polenta

Directions:

1. Preheat the oven to 220°C, fan 200°C, gas 8.
2. Grease the aubergine halves and place them on the meat side up on a baking tray. Sprinkle with coriander and cumin seeds, and then place the cloves of garlic on the plate. Roast for 40 minutes, put aside.
3. Add chickpeas, chickpea flour, zest, and lemon juice. Crush roughly and mix well.
4. Form about twenty pellets and place them on a baking tray. Put in the fridge for 30 minutes.
5. Reduce the temperature of the oven to 180ºC. Remove the meatballs from the fridge and coat in the polenta. Roast for 20 minutes.
6. Serve with lemon wedges.

 Nutrition:
Calories: 70 **Carbohydrates:** 4g **Fat:** 5g **Protein:** 2g

354. Baba Ganouj

Preparation Time: 15 minutes	**Cooking Time:** 1 hour 20 minutes	**Servings:** 3

Ingredients:

- 1 large aubergine
- 1 head of garlic
- 30 ml of olive oil
- Lemon juice

Directions:

1. Preheat the oven to 220°C, fan 200°C, gas 8.
2. Place the aubergine on a plate, skin side up. Roast, about 1 hour.
3. Place the garlic cloves in a square of aluminum foil. Fold the edges of the sheet. Roast with the aubergine, for about 20 minutes. Let cool.
4. Purée the pods with a garlic press.
5. Puree the flesh of the aubergine. Add the garlic puree, the oil, and the lemon juice.
6. Serve.

Nutrition:
Calories: 99   **Carbohydrates:** 6g   **Fat:** 6g   **Protein:** 2g

355. Spicy Crab Dip

Preparation Time: 15 minutes	**Cooking Time:** 15 minutes	**Servings:** 3

Ingredients:

- 250 grams cream cheese
- 2 onions, chopped
- 1 tablespoon lemon juice
- 2 tablespoons Worcestershire sauce
- Black pepper
- Cayenne pepper
- 2 tablespoons milk
- 180 grams crabmeat

Directions:

1. Preheat the oven to 220°C, fan 200°C, gas 8.
2. Pour the cream cheese into a bowl. Add the onions, lemon juice, Worcestershire sauce, black pepper, and cayenne pepper. Mix. Stir in the milk and crab meat.
3. Cook uncovered for 15 minutes. Serve.

 Nutrition:
Calories: 134   **Carbohydrates:** 4g   **Fat:** 12g   **Protein:** 4g

356. Parmesan Cheese "Potatoes"

Preparation Time: 15 minutes	**Cooking Time:** 10 minutes	**Servings:** 3

Ingredients:

- 75 grams Parmesan cheese
- 1 tablespoon Chia seeds
- 2 tablespoons whole flaxseeds
- 2 ½ tablespoons pumpkin seeds

Directions:

1. Preheat the oven to 180°C, fan 160°C, gas 6.
2. Combine both the cheese and seeds in a bowl.
3. Put small piles of the mixture onto baking paper on a baking tray.
4. Bake for 8 to 10 minutes.
5. Remove and serve.

 Nutrition:
Calories: 165   **Carbohydrates:** 18g   **Fat:** 9g   **Protein:** 3g

357. Chili Cheese Chicken with Crispy and Delicious Cabbage Salad

Preparation Time: 15 minutes	**Cooking Time:** 70 minutes	**Servings:** 5

Ingredients:

Chili Cheese Chicken:
- 200 grams of chicken
- 200 grams tomatoes
- 100 grams of cream cheese
- 125 grams cheddar
- 40 grams jalapenos
- 60 grams of bacon

Crispy Cabbage Salad:
- 0.5 pcs cumin
- 200 grams Brussel sprouts
- 2 grams of almonds
- 3 tangerines
- 11 teaspoon olive oil
- 1 teaspoon apple cider vinegar
- Salt
- 10 grams pepper
- 11 teaspoon lemon

Directions:

For Chilli Cheese Chicken:
1. Preheat the oven to 200°C, fan 180°C, gas 6.
2. Half the tomatoes and place on the bottom of a baking dish.
3. Add the chicken fillets and half of the cream cheese on top of each chicken fillet, then sprinkle with cheddar.
4. Add the jalapenos and then bake for 25 minutes.
5. Place bacon on a baking tray with baking paper and bake for 10 minutes.

For Crispy Cabbage Salad:
1. Blend the Brussel sprouts and cumin in a food processor.
2. Make the dressing with the juice from 1 tangerine, olive oil, apple cider vinegar, salt, pepper, and lemon juice.
3. Place the cabbage in a dish and pour the dressing over it.
4. Chop almonds, cut the remaining tangerines into slices, and place them on the salad.
5. Sprinkle the bacon over the chicken dish. Serve.

 Nutrition:
Calories: 515   **Carbohydrates:** 35g   **Fat:** 23g   **Protein:** 42

358. Keto Pumpkin Pie Sweet and Spicy

Preparation Time: 15 minutes	**Cooking Time:** 60 minutes	**Servings:** 5

Ingredients:

Pie Bottom:
- 110 grams of almond flour
- 50 grams sucrine
- Salt
- 1 scoop protein powder
- 1 egg
- 80 grams butter

The Filling:
- 1 pcs Hokkaido (pumpkin)
- 3 egg yolks
- 60 grams of coconut fat
- 5 grams vanilla powder
- 15 grams of protein powder
- ¼ teaspoon ground cinammon
- 2 grams sucrine
- ½ teaspoon black cardamom
- ½ teaspoon cloves

Directions:

1. Preheat the oven to 175°C, fan 155°C.
2. Combine all the dry ingredients and then add the wet ones.

3. Mix and shape it into a dough lump.
4. Place on baking paper, then flatten the dough. Prick holes, place the baking paper on a baking try and bake for 8-10 minutes.

For filling:
1. Cut the meat of Hokkaido and cook for 15-20 minutes.
2. Process it with the other ingredients.
3. Pour the stuffing into the baked tray and bake again for 25-30 minutes.
4. Cool and serve.

 Nutrition:
Calories: 229   **Carbohydrates:** 4g   **Fat:** 22g   **Protein:** 8g

359. Blackened Tilapia with Courgette Noodles

Preparation Time: 15 minutes	Cooking Time: 10 minutes	Servings: 5

Ingredients:
- 2 courgettes
- Salt
- 2 garlic cloves
- 120 grams Pico de Gallo
- 200 grams fish
- 2 teaspoons olive oil
- ½ teaspoon cumin
- ¼ teaspoon garlic powder
- 10 grams paprika
- Pepper

Directions:
1. Mix half the salt, pepper, cumin, paprika, and garlic powder together.
2. Rub it onto the fish thoroughly.
3. Cook for 3 minutes each side and remove from the heat.
4. Cook the courgettes and garlic, with the remaining salt for 2 minutes.
5. Place the noodles on a plate with the fish on top of the noodles. Serve.

 Nutrition:
Calories: 220   **Carbohydrates:** 27g   **Fat:** 2g   **Protein:** 24g

360. Pepper Nachos

Preparation Time: 15 minutes	Cooking Time: 10 minutes	Servings: 2

Ingredients:
- 2 peppers
- 120 grams minced beef
- ¼ teaspoon cumin
- 30 grams guacamole
- Salt
- 120 grams cheese
- ¼ teaspoon chili powder
- 1 tablespoon vegetable oil
- 2 tablespoons sour cream
- 30 grams Pico de Gallo

Directions:
1. Place the peppers in a microwave dish, sprinkle salt and splash water on them and microwave for 4 minutes then cut them into 4 pieces.

2. Toast the chili powder and cumin in a pan for 30 seconds.
3. Put the salted beef in the pan, stir, and cook for 4 minutes.
4. Add all the pieces of pepper, then the cheese and cook for 1 minute.
5. Serve with Pico de Gallo, guacamole, and cream.

 Nutrition:
Calories: 475   **Carbohydrates:** 19g   **Fat:** 24g   **Protein:** 50g

361. Radish, Carrot & Coriander Salad

Preparation Time: 15 minutes	Cooking Time: 0 minutes	Servings: 2

Ingredients:
- 400 grams carrots
- 30 grams coriander
- 60 grams radish
- ½ teaspoon salt
- 6 onions
- ¼ teaspoon black pepper
- 3 tablespoons lemon juice
- 3 tablespoons orange juice
- 2 tablespoons olive oil

Directions:
1. Mix all the ingredients together until they are thoroughly combined.
2. Chill and serve.

 Nutrition:
Calories: 123   **Carbohydrates:** 7g   **Fat:** 3g   **Protein:** 3g

362. Asparagus-Mushroom Frittata

Preparation Time: 15 minutes	Cooking Time: 25 minutes	Servings: 2

Ingredients:
- 1 tablespoon olive oil
- 1 garlic clove
- 30 grams onion
- 250 grams button mushrooms
- 1 asparagus
- 1 tablespoon thyme
- 6 eggs
- 60 grams feta cheese
- Salt
- Black pepper

Directions:
1. Cook the onions for 5 minutes in a pan.
2. Add the mushrooms and garlic then cook for 5 minutes.
3. Mix in thyme, salt, pepper, and asparagus and cook for 3 minutes.
4. Beat eggs and cheese in a bowl and pour it in the pan and cook for a further 2 to 3 minutes.
5. Then finally bake in the oven for 10 minutes at 180°C.

 Nutrition:
Calories: 129   **Carbohydrates:** 2g   **Fat:** 7g   **Protein:** 9g

363. Shrimp Avocado Salad

 Preparation Time: 15 minutes | **Cooking Time:** 0 minutes | **Servings:** 1

Ingredients:

- 2 onions
- 1 tomato
- 2 limes, juice
- 1 avocado
- Salt
- Pepper
- 1 jalapeno
- 500 grams shrimp/prawn
- 1 tablespoon coriander

Directions:

1. Mix the onion, lime juice, salt and pepper, and let it stand 5 minutes.
2. In another bowl, add chopped shrimp, avocado, tomato, jalapeno, and onion mixture.
3. Season with salt and pepper, toss and serve.

 Nutrition:
Calories: 365 **Carbohydrates:** 15g **Fat:** 17g **Protein:** 25g

364. Smoky Cauliflower Bites

 Preparation Time: 15 minutes | **Cooking Time:** 25 minutes | **Servings:** 2

Ingredients:

- 1 cauliflower
- 2 garlic cloves
- 2 tablespoon olive oil
- 2 tablespoons parsley
- 1 teaspoon Paprika
- Salt

Directions:

1. Mix cauliflower, olive oil, paprika, and salt.
2. Preheat your oven to 220°C.
3. Bake for 10 minutes.
4. Then add the garlic and bake for a further 10 to 15 minutes.
5. Serve with parsley.

 Nutrition:
Calories: 69 **Carbohydrates:** 8g **Fat:** 3g **Protein:** 1g

365. Avocado Crab Boats

Preparation Time: 15 minutes | **Cooking Time:** 2 minutes | **Servings:** 2

Ingredients:

- 12oz crab meat
- 3 tablespoons lemon juice
- 60 grams Greek yogurt
- Pepper
- 1/2 onion
- Salt
- 2 tablespoons chives
- 130 grams cheddar cheese
- 2 avocados

Directions:

1. Mix the crab meat, yogurt, onion, chives, lemon juice, cayenne, and salt.
2. Scoop out the avocado flesh, fill the avocado skins with meat mixture, and top with cheddar cheese.
3. Microwave for 2 minutes and serve.

 Nutrition:
Calories: 325 **Carbohydrates:** 8g **Fat:** 28g **Protein:** 0g

366. Coconut Curry Cauliflower Soup

 Preparation Time: 15 minutes | **Cooking Time:** 40 minutes | **Servings:** 2

Ingredients:

- Olive oil
- 2 to 3 teaspoons curry powder
- 1 onion
- 2 teaspoons ground cumin
- 3 garlic cloves
- ½ teaspoon turmeric powder
- 1 teaspoon ginger
- 30 ml. coconut milk
- 220 grams tomatoes
- 120 grams vegetable broth/stock
- 1 cauliflower
- Salt
- Pepper

Directions:

1. Mix olive oil and onion in a pan, sauté for 3 minutes.
2. Add garlic, ginger, curry powder, cumin, and turmeric powder and sauté for 5 minutes.
3. Then add coconut milk, tomatoes, vegetable broth, and cauliflower.
4. Cook on low for 20 minutes.
5. Blend the mixture thoroughly in a blender, and warm-up the soup for 5 minutes in a pan.
6. Season with salt and pepper.
7. Serve.

 Nutrition:
Calories: 112 **Carbohydrates:** 4g **Fat:** 3g **Protein:** 0g

367. Parmesan Asparagus

Preparation Time: 15 minutes | **Cooking Time:** 15 minutes | **Servings:** 4

Ingredients:

- 2 kg. asparagus
- Salt
- 200 grams butter
- 220 grams parmesan cheese grated
- Pepper

Directions:

1. Boil asparagus for 3 minutes.
2. Drain and put aside.
3. Preheat the oven to 220°C, fan 200°C, gas 8.

4. Arrange asparagus into the pan and pour on the butter, then sprinkle pepper, salt, and parmesan cheese on top.
5. Bake for 10 to 15 minutes.
6. Serve.

 Nutrition:
Calories: 166 **Carbohydrates:** 5g **Fat:** 5g **Protein:** 6g

368. Cream Cheese Pancakes

Preparation Time: 15 minutes	**Cooking Time:** 10 minutes	**Servings:** 12

Ingredients:
- 220 grams cream cheese
- Vanilla extract
- 4 eggs
- Butter

Directions:
1. Blend cream cheese and eggs in a blender, put aside.
2. Grease pan with butter.
3. Cook the batter for 2 minutes.
4. Serve with a sprinkle of cinnamon.

 Nutrition:
Calories: 344 **Carbohydrates:** 3g **Fat:** 29g **Protein:** 17g

369. Sugar-Free Mexican Spiced Dark Chocolate

Preparation Time: 15 minutes	**Cooking Time:** 0 minutes	**Servings:** 1

Ingredients:
- 20 grams cocoa powder
- ¼ teaspoon ground cinammon
- ½ teaspoon chilli powder
- 1/8 teaspoon nutmeg
- Black pepper
- Salt
- 40 grams melted butter
- ¼ teaspoon vanilla extract
- 25 drops liquid stevia

Directions:
1. Mix cocoa powder, cinnamon, chilli powder, nutmeg, black pepper, and salt.
2. Put aside.
3. Stir melted butter with vanilla extract and stevia and then mix the butter mixture with dry ingredients.
4. Put the mixture in chocolate molds.
5. Chill and serve.

 Nutrition:
Calories: 163 **Carbohydrates:** 8g **Fat:** 5g **Protein:** 1g

370. Tuna in Cucumber Cups

Preparation Time: 15 minutes	**Cooking Time:** 0 minutes	**Servings:** 10

Ingredients:
- 150 grams Mayonnaise
- Dill
- Black pepper
- 1 can tuna
- 1 cucumber
- Black pepper
- Salt

Directions:
1. Mix the cucumber flesh with the remainder of the ingredients and then fill the holes in the slices of cucumber.
2. Garnish with fresh dill.
3. Serve.

 Nutrition:
Calories: 187 **Protein:** 3g **Fat:** 2g **Carbohydrates:** 2g

371. Parmesan Crisps

Preparation Time: 15 minutes	**Cooking Time:** 10 minutes	**Servings:** 2

Ingredients:
- 150 grams Provolone cheese
- Jalapeno pepper
- 90 grams Parmesan cheese

Directions:
1. Preheat the oven to 200°C, fan 180°C, gas 6.
2. Grease a baking tray then set the parmesan cheese into 8 mounds.
3. Lay the slices of jalapeno over the parmesan cheese mounds.
4. Put one square provolone over the 8 parmesan mounds.
5. Bake for 9 minutes and serve.

 Nutrition:
Calories: 160 **Protein:** 15g **Fat:** 9g **Carbohydrates:** 2g

372. Onion Rings

Preparation Time: 15 minutes	**Cooking Time:** 15 minutes	**Servings:** 2

Ingredients:
- 2 Eggs
- 120 grams Parmesan cheese
- 1 tablespoon double cream
- 220 grams coconut flour
- 500 grams pork rinds
- 1 white onion

Directions:
1. Warm-up oven to 200° Celsius.
2. Arrange the first bowl with the coconut flour, the second bowl with mixed whipping cream and beaten egg, and in the third bowl, with crushed pork rinds and grated parmesan cheese, mix.
3. Dip the rings into the coconut flour, then into the egg-cream mixture, and lastly, into the mix of cheese and pork rinds.
4. Bake for fifteen minutes.
5. Serve.

Nutrition:
Calories: 205 **Fat:** 18g **Protein:** 12g **Carbohydrates:** 4g

373. Cold Crab Dip

Preparation Time: 15 minutes	**Cooking Time:** 0 minutes	**Servings:** 12

Ingredients:

- 1 teaspoon lemon juice
- 2 tablespoons chives
- ½ teaspoon Old Bay seasoning
- 45 grams sour cream
- 250 grams crab meat
- 150 grams cream cheese

Directions:

1. Mix the cream cheese, lemon juice, seasoning, and sour cream.
2. Fold in the crab meat, then the chives.
3. Serve.

 Nutrition:
Calories: 244 **Fat:** 4g **Carbohydrates:** 4g **Protein:** 5g

374. Baked Coconut Shrimp

Preparation Time: 15 minutes	**Cooking Time:** 20 minutes	**Servings:** 4

Ingredients:

- 500 grams shrimp/prawns
- Black pepper
- 220 grams coconut flakes
- Salt
- ¼ teaspoon garlic powder
- 3 Eggs
- ¼ teaspoon paprika
- 3 tablespoons coconut flour

Directions:

1. Preheat the oven to 200°C, fan 180°C, gas 6.
2. In the first bowl, put the beaten eggs, in the second bowl, put the coconut flakes, and in the last bowl, put a mix of the garlic powder, salt, paprika, pepper, and coconut flour.
3. Dip each shrimp into the flour mixture first, then into the egg wash, and then roll them in the coconut flakes.
4. Bake for ten minutes. Serve.

 Nutrition:
Calories: 440 **Protein:** 3g **Fat:** 32g **Carbohydrates:** 5g

375. Spicy Deviled Eggs

Preparation Time: 15 minutes	**Cooking Time:** 0 minutes	**Servings:** 24

Ingredients:

- 1 tablespoon sriracha sauce
- 1 tablespoon chili powder
- 1 tablespoon chives
- 1 tablespoon Dijon mustard
- 80 grams mayonnaise
- Black pepper
- 12 eggs
- Salt

Directions:

1. Boil the eggs, allow to cool.
2. Mash the yolks into a paste.
3. Mix in the salt, mayonnaise, chili powder, sriracha sauce, pepper, and the mustard.
4. Refill the egg whites with this mixture. Serve with chopped chives on top.

 Nutrition:
Calories: 173 **Protein:** 3g **Carbohydrates:** 1g **Fat:** 5g

376. Bacon-Wrapped Scallops

Preparation Time: 15 minutes	**Cooking Time:** 20 minutes	**Servings:** 4

Ingredients:

- 16 Toothpicks
- Salt
- 2 tablespoons olive oil
- Black pepper
- 150 grams Sea scallops
- 3/4 slices Bacon

Directions:

1. Preheat the oven to 200°C, fan 180°C, gas 6. Grease a baking tray.
2. Use 1/2 of a bacon slice to wrap around each scallop and stick in the toothpick.
3. Brush on the olive oil and season with salt and pepper.
4. Bake for fifteen minutes. Serve.

 Nutrition:
Calories: 225 **Protein:** 13g **Fat:** 16g **Carbohydrates:** 2g

377. Buffalo Chicken Jalapeno Poppers

Preparation Time: 15 minutes	**Cooking Time:** 30 minutes	**Servings:** 5

Ingredients:

- Ranch dressing
- Onions
- 4 slices of bacon
- 10 Jalapeno peppers
- 2 tablespoons garlic powder
- 220 grams cream cheese
- 350 grams chicken
- 11 teaspoon buffalo wing sauce
- ½ tablespoon onion powder
- 250 grams Blue cheese
- 200 grams Mozzarella cheese
- Salt

Directions:

1. Preheat the oven to 220°C, fan 200°C, gas 8. Lay the half pieces of the jalapeno peppers on the baking tray.
2. Fry the onion powder, ground chicken, garlic, and salt for 15 minutes.
3. Blend in the mozzarella cheese, wing sauce, and one-quarter of the crumbled blue cheese. Combine into the pepper halves, then top with bacon and blue cheese.
4. Bake for 30 minutes then serve.

Nutrition:
Calories: 250   **Protein:** 15g   **Fat:** 20g   **Carbohydrates:** 4g

378. Baked Garlic Parmesan Wings

 | **Preparation Time:** 15 minutes | **Cooking Time:** 60 minutes | **Servings:** 6 |

Ingredients:
- 10 grams parsley
- Salt
- 1 teaspoon onion powder
- 1kg. chicken wings
- 50 grams butter
- 220 grams parmesan cheese
- 2 tablespoons garlic powder
- 2 tablespoons baking powder
- Pepper

Directions:
1. Preheat the oven to 250°C, fan 230°C, gas 9.
2. Sprinkle the pepper and salt on the wings and let them sit for ten minutes. Then put baking powder over the wings, toss.
3. Bake the wings for 30 minutes.
4. Adjust the oven temperature to 200° Celsius and then bake again for 30 minutes.
5. Meanwhile, mix the chopped garlic, parmesan cheese, onion powder, garlic powder, parsley, and melted butter.
6. Toss wings in the sauce. Serve.

 Nutrition:
Calories: 459   **Protein:** 32g   Fat:40g   **Carbohydrates:** 2g

379. Sausage Stuffed Mushrooms

 | **Preparation Time:** 15 minutes | **Cooking Time:** 30 minutes | **Servings:** 20 |

Ingredients:
- Salt
- 2 tablespoons butter
- 2 sausages (remove meat from skins)
- 2 tablespoons garlic powder
- Black pepper
- 1 onion, chopped
- 20 baby Bella mushrooms
- 130 grams cheddar cheese

Directions:
1. Preheat the oven to 220°C, fan 200°C, gas 7.
2. Fry sausage meat with butter in a pan, remove from the pan and put aside.
3. Cook the mushroom stalks, garlic, and chopped onion in the same pan, with the leftover liquid, for 5 minutes.
4. Mix in the salt, cheddar cheese, pepper, and sausage. Fill all of the mushroom caps with this mixture.
5. Bake for 20 minutes.
6. Serve.

 Nutrition:
Calories: 187   **Protein:** 5g   **Fat:** 4g   **Carbohydrates:** 2g

DESSERT

380. Raspberry Mousse

 Preparation Time: 10 minutes   **Cooking Time:** 10 minutes   **Servings:** 4

Ingredients:

- 200 grams raspberries
- 40 grams of granulated erythritol
- 40 ml. of unsweetened almond milk
- 1 teaspoon fresh lemon juice
- 1 teaspoon liquid stevia
- Salt

Directions:

1. In a food processor, add all the listed ingredients and pulse until smooth.
2. Transfer the mixture into serving glasses and refrigerate to chill before serving.

Nutrition:
Calories: 125   **Carbohydrates:** 4.3 g   **Fat:** 4g   **Protein:** 5g

381. Egg Custard

 Preparation Time: 15 minutes   **Cooking Time:** 55 minutes   **Servings:** 8

Ingredients:

- 6 organic eggs
- 60 ml. yacon syrup
- 500 ml. of unsweetened almond milk
- ¼ teaspoon of ground ginger
- ¼ teaspoon of ground cinnamon
- ¼ teaspoon of ground nutmeg
- ¼ teaspoon of ground cardamom
- 1/8 teaspoon of ground cloves
- 1/8 teaspoon of ground all spice

Directions:

1. Preheat your oven to 190° C, fan 170°C, gas 5 .
2. Grease 8 small ramekins.
3. In a bowl, add the eggs and salt and beat well.
4. Arrange a sieve over a medium bowl.
5. Through a sieve, strain the egg mixture into a bowl.
6. Add the Yacon syrup into the eggs and stir to combine.
7. Add the almond milk and spices and beat until well combined.
8. Transfer the mixture into prepared ramekins.
9. Now, place ramekins in a large baking dish.
10. Add hot water in the baking dish, about 2-inch high, around the ramekins.
11. Place the baking dish in the oven and bake for about 30–40 minutes or until a toothpick inserted in the center comes out clean.
12. Remove ramekins from the oven and set aside to cool.
13. Refrigerate to chill before serving.

Nutrition:
Calories: 104   **Fat:** 3.8g   **Carbohydrates:** 6g   **Protein:** 3.8g

382. Mocha Ice Cream

 Preparation Time: 15 minutes   **Cooking Time:** 15 minutes   **Servings:** 2

Ingredients:

- 120 grams unsweetened coconut milk
- 30 grams double cream
- 2 tablespoons of granulated erythritol
- 15 drops of liquid stevia
- 2 tablespoons of cacao powder
- 1 tablespoon of instant coffee
- ¼ teaspoon of xanthan gum

Directions:

1. In a container, add the ingredients (except xanthan gum) and with an immersion blender, blend until well combined.
2. Slowly, add the xanthan gum and blend until a slightly thicker mixture is formed.
3. Transfer the mixture into an ice cream maker and process according to manufacturer's instructions.
4. Now, transfer the ice cream into an airtight container and freeze for at least 4–5 hours before serving.

Nutrition:
Calories: 246   **Carbohydrates:** 6.2g   **Fat:** 23.1g   **Protein:** 2.8g

383. Vanilla Crème Brule

 Preparation Time: 20 minutes    **Cooking Time:** 1 hour 20 minutes    **Servings:** 4

Ingredients:

- 250 grams of double cream
- 1 vanilla bean (halved with seeds scraped out)
- 4 organic egg yolks
- 1/3 teaspoon stevia powder
- 1 teaspoon vanilla extract
- Salt
- 4 tablespoons granulated erythritol

Directions:

1. Preheat the oven to 190°C, fan 170°C, gas 5.
2. In a pan, add the cream over a medium heat and cook until heated through.
3. Stir in the vanilla bean seeds and bring to a gentle boil.
4. Reduce the heat to very low and cook, covered for about 20 minutes.
5. Meanwhile, in a bowl, add the remaining ingredients (except erythritol) and beat until a thick and pale mixture forms.
6. Remove the cream from the heat and through a fine-mesh strainer, strain into a heat-proof bowl.
7. Slowly, add the cream in egg yolk mixture beating continuously until well combined.
8. Divide the mixture evenly into 4 ramekins.
9. Arrange the ramekins into a large baking dish.
10. In the baking dish, add hot water to the level of about halfway up the side of the ramekins.
11. Bake for about 30–35 minutes.
12. Remove the dish from the oven and then let cool slightly.
13. Refrigerate the ramekins for at least 4 hours.
14. Just before serving, sprinkle the ramekins with erythritol evenly.
15. Holding a kitchen torch about 4–5-inches from the top, caramelize the erythritol for about 2 minutes.
16. Set aside for 5 minutes before serving.

 Nutrition:
Calories: 264 **Fat:** 26.7g **Carbohydrates:** 2.4g **Protein:** 3.9g

384. Lemon Soufflé

| 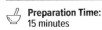 **Preparation Time:** 15 minutes | **Cooking Time:** 35 minutes | **Servings:** 4 |

Ingredients:

- 2 large organic eggs (whites and yolks separated)
- 60 grams of granulated erythritol (divided)
- 120 grams of ricotta cheese
- 1 tablespoon of fresh lemon juice
- 2 teaspoons of lemon zest (grated)
- 1 teaspoon of poppy seeds
- 1 teaspoon of organic vanilla extract

Directions:

1. Preheat your oven to 220°Celsius.
2. Grease 4 ramekins.
3. Add egg whites and beat in a clean glass bowl until it has a foam-like texture.
4. Add 2 tablespoons of erythritol and beat the mixture until it is stiff.

5. In another bowl, add ricotta cheese, egg yolks, and the remaining erythritol until it is mixed thoroughly.
6. Put the lemon juice and lemon zest in the bowl and mix well.
7. Add the poppy seeds and vanilla extract and mix again.
8. Add the whipped egg whites into the ricotta mixture and gently stir.
9. Place the mixture evenly into prepared ramekins.
10. Bake for about 20 minutes.
11. Remove from the oven and serve immediately.

 Nutrition:
Calories: 130 **Fat:** 7.7g **Carbohydrates:** 4g **Protein:** 10.4g

385. Cottage Cheese Pudding

| **Preparation Time:** 10 minutes | **Cooking Time:** 45 minutes | **Servings:** 6 |

Ingredients:

Pudding

- 120 grams of cottage cheese
- 120 ml. double cream
- 3 organic eggs
- 90 ml. of water
- 60 grams of granulated erythritol
- 1 teaspoon organic vanilla extract

Topping

- 43 grams of double cream
- 43 grams of fresh raspberries

Directions:

1. Preheat the oven to 190°C, fan 170°C, gas 5.
2. Grease the ramekins.
3. Add all the ingredients (except cinnamon) and pulse in a blender until smooth.
4. Transfer the mixture into prepared ramekins evenly.
5. Now, place the ramekins in a large baking dish.
6. Add hot water in the baking dish, about 1-inch up the sides of the ramekins.
7. Bake for about 35 minutes.
8. Serve warm, topped with double cream and raspberries.

 Nutrition:
Calories: 226 **Fat:** 19.6g **Carbohydrates:** 3.7g **Protein:** 9g

386. Cream Cake

| **Preparation Time:** 15 minutes | **Cooking Time:** 1 hour and 5 minutes | **Servings:** 12 |

Ingredients:

- 250 grams of almond flour
- 2 teaspoons organic baking powder
- 60 grams of butter (chopped)
- 56 grams of cream cheese (softened)
- 120 grams of sour cream
- 120 grams of granulated erythritol
- 1 teaspoon organic vanilla extract
- 4 large organic eggs

Directions:

1. Preheat the oven to 190°C, fan 170°C, gas 5.
2. Generously, grease a 9-inch Bundt pan.
3. Add almond flour and baking powder in a large bowl and mix well. Set aside.
4. In a microwave-safe bowl, add butter and cream cheese and microwave for about 30 seconds.
5. Remove from microwave and stir well.
6. Add sour cream, erythritol, and vanilla extract and mix until well combined.
7. Add the cream mixture into the bowl of the flour mixture and mix until well combined.
8. Add eggs and mix until well combined.
9. Transfer the mixture into the prepared pan evenly.
10. Bake for about 50 minutes or until a toothpick inserted in the center comes out clean.
11. Remove from the oven and put onto a wire rack to cool for about 10 minutes.
12. Carefully, invert the cake onto a wire rack to cool completely.
13. Just before serving, dust the cake with powdered erythritol.
14. Cut into 12 equal-sized slices and serve.

 Nutrition:
Calories: 258 **Fat:** 24.3g **Carbohydrates:** 5.5g **Protein:** 7.2g

387. Sugar-Free Lemon Bars

Preparation Time: 15 minutes	**Cooking Time:** 45 minutes	**Servings:** 8

Ingredients:

- 60 grams butter, melted
- 200 grams almond flour, divided
- 120 grams powdered erythritol, divided
- 3 medium-size lemons
- 3 large eggs

Directions:

1. Prepare the parchment paper and baking tray. Combine butter, 120 grams of almond flour, 30 grams of erythritol, and salt. Stir well. Bake for about 20 minutes. Then set aside to let it cool.
2. Zest of 1 lemon and juice of all the lemons in a bowl.
3. Add the eggs, 90 grams of erythritol, 90 grams of almond flour, and salt. Stir together to create the filling.
4. Put the filling on top, then cook for 25 minutes.
5. Cut into small pieces and serve with lemon slices.

 Nutrition:
Calories: 272 **Carbohydrates:** 4 g **Fat:** 26 g **Protein:** 8 g

388. Creamy Hot Chocolate

Preparation Time: 5 minutes	**Cooking Time:** 5 minutes	**Servings:** 4

Ingredients:

- 90 grams dark chocolate, chopped
- 64 ml. unsweetened almond milk
- 70 grams double cream
- 1 tablespoon erythritol
- 60 grams vanilla extract

Directions:

1. Combine the almond milk, erythritol, and cream in a small saucepan.
2. Heat over a medium heat and cook for 1-2 minutes.
3. Add vanilla extract and chocolate. Stir continuously until the chocolate melts.
4. Pour into cups and serve.

 Nutrition:
Calories: 193 **Carbohydrates:** 4g **Fat:** 18g **Protein:** 2g

389. Delicious Coffee Ice Cream

Preparation Time: 10 minutes	**Cooking Time:** 5 minutes	**Servings:** 1

Ingredients:

- 180 grams coconut cream, frozen into ice cubes
- 1 ripe avocado, chopped and frozen
- 60 grams coffee expresso
- 2 tablespoons sweetener
- 1 teaspoon vanilla extract
- 1 tablespoon water
- Coffee beans

Directions:

1. Take out the frozen coconut cubes and avocado from the fridge. Slightly melt them for 5-10 minutes.
2. Add the sweetener, coffee expresso, and vanilla extract to the coconut avocado mix and whisk with an immersion blender until it becomes creamy (for about 1 minute).
3. Pour in the water and blend for 30 seconds.
4. Top with coffee beans and enjoy!

 Nutrition:
Calories: 596 **Carbohydrates:** 20.5 g **Fat:** 61 g **Protein:** 6.3 g

390. Fatty Bombs with Cinnamon and Cardamom

Preparation Time: 10 minutes	**Cooking Time:** 35 minutes	**Servings:** 10

Ingredients:

- 120 grams unsweetened coconut, shredded
- 90 grams unsalted butter
- ¼ teaspoon green cinnamon
- ¼ ground cardamom
- ½ teaspoon teaspoon vanilla extract

Directions:

1. Roast the unsweetened coconut (choose a medium-high heat) until it begins to turn lightly brown.
2. Combine the room-temperature butter, half of the shredded coconut, cinnamon, cardamom, and vanilla extract in a separate dish. Cool the mix in the fridge for about 5-10 minutes.
3. Form small balls and cover them with the remaining shredded coconut.
4. Cool the balls in the fridge for about 10-15 minutes.

 Nutrition:
Calories: 258 **Carbohydrates:** 15g **Fat:** 10g **Protein:** 3g

391. Fudgy Brownie

 **Preparation Time:** 10 minutes | **Cooking Time:** 4 hours | **Servings:** 8

Ingredients:

- 60 grams butter
- 220 grams unsweetened baking chocolate
- 130 grams almond flour
- 90 grams powdered erythritol
- 2 tablespoon cocoa powder
- 2 large eggs (at room temperature)
- 1 teaspoon vanilla extract (optional)
- 1/4 teaspoon sea salt (only if using unsalted butter)
- 120 grams walnuts (optional, chopped)

Directions:

1. Preheat the oven to 170°C, fan 150°C, gas 5. Line an 8x8 in (20x20 cm) tray with baking paper, with the edges of the paper over the sides.
2. Melt the butter and chocolate together in a double boiler sauce-pan, stirring occasionally, until smooth. Remove from the heat.
3. Stir in the vanilla extract.
4. Add the almond flour, powdered sweetener, cocoa powder, sea salt, and eggs. Stir together until uniform. The batter will be a little grainy looking.
5. Transfer the batter to the lined tray. Smooth the top with a spatula or the back of a spoon. If desired, sprinkle with chopped walnuts and press into the top.
6. Bake for about 13-18 minutes, until an inserted toothpick comes out almost clean with just a little batter on it that balls up between your fingers. (Do NOT wait for it to come out totally clean, and don't worry about any butter pooled on top - just watch the actual brownie part to be super soft but not fluid.)
7. Cool completely before moving or cutting. There may be some butter pooled on top - do not drain it, it will absorb back in after cooling.

 Nutrition:
Calories: 174   Carbohydrates:4g   **Fat:** 16 g   **Protein:** 3g

392. Chocolate Spread with Hazelnuts

 Preparation Time: 5 minutes | **Cooking Time:** 5 minutes | **Servings:** 6

Ingredients:

- 2 tablespoons cocoa powder
- 150 grams hazelnuts, roasted and without shells
- 30 grams unsalted butter
- 32 ml. of coconut oil

Directions:

1. Whisk all the spread ingredients in a blender. Serve.

 Nutrition:
Calories: 271   **Carbohydrates:** 2 g   **Fat:** 28 g   **Protein:** 4 g

393. Quick and Simple Brownie

 Preparation Time: 20 minutes | **Cooking Time:** 5 minutes | **Servings:** 2

Ingredients:

- 3 tablespoons Keto chocolate chips
- 1 tablespoon unsweetened cacao powder
- 2 tablespoons salted butter
- 2 ¼ tablespoon powdered sugar

Directions:

1. Combine the chocolate chips together with the butter and melt them in a microwave for 10-15 minutes. Remove, and set aside to cool.
2. Add the cacao powder and powdered sugar to the sauce and whisk well until you have a dough.
3. Place the dough on a baking tray, form the Brownie.
4. Preheat the oven to 220°C, fan 200°C, gas 7.
5. Put the dough inside the oven and bake for 10 minutes.

 Nutrition:
Calories: 100   **Carbohydrates:** 9 g   **Fat:** 30 g   **Protein:** 13 g

394. Cute Peanut Balls

 Preparation Time: 20 minutes | **Cooking Time:** 20 minutes | **Servings:** 18

Ingredients:

1. 120 grams salted peanuts, chopped
2. 120 grams peanut butter
3. 120 grams powdered sweetener
4. 250 grams keto chocolate chips

Directions:

1. Combine the chopped peanuts, peanut butter, and sweetener in a separate dish. Stir well and make a dough. Divide it into 18 pieces and form small balls.

2. Put them in the fridge for 10-15 minutes.
3. Use a microwave to melt your chocolate chips.
4. Plunge each ball into the melted chocolate.
5. Return your balls to the fridge.
6. Cool for about 20 minutes.

 Nutrition:
Calories: 194   **Carbohydrates:** 7g   **Fat:** 17g   **Protein:** 7g

395. Chocolate Mug Muffins

Preparation Time: 5 minutes	**Cooking Time:** 2 minutes	**Servings:** 4

Ingredients:

- 4 tablespoon almond flour
- 1 teaspoon baking powder
- 4 tablespoons granulated erythritol
- 2 tablespoons cocoa powder
- ½ teaspoon vanilla extract
- Salt
- 2 eggs beaten
- 3 tablespoon butter, melted
- 1 teaspoon coconut oil, for greasing the mug
- 60 grams sugar-free dark chocolate, chopped

Directions:

1. Mix the dry ingredients in a separate bowl. Add the melted butter, beaten eggs, and chocolate to the bowl. Stir thoroughly.
2. Divide your dough into 4 pieces. Put these pieces in the greased mugs and put them in the microwave. Cook for 1-1.5 minutes (700 watts).
3. Let them cool for 1 minute and serve.

 Nutrition:
Calories: 208   **Carbohydrates:** 2 g   **Fat:** 19 g   **Protein:** 5 g

396. Keto Peanut Butter Cup Style Fudge

Preparation Time: 10 minutes	**Cooking Time:** 30 minutes	**Servings:** 36

Ingredients:

- 60 grams natural peanut butter
- 30 grams butter
- 120 grams powdered swerve sweetener
- 1 teaspoon vanilla extract
- Salt
- 3 tablespoons peanuts, chopped
- Salt

Directions:

1. Line a baking tray with baking pepper for easy removal.
2. Add peanut butter, vanilla, and butter in a pan and heat over medium heat until melted and smooth.
3. Turn off the heat and stir in sweetener and salt, mix to combine well.
4. Spread the mixture in the prepared baking tray in even layered.
5. Chill for 20-30 minutes, cut into 36 slices.

6. Sprinkle with sea salt or other toppings of your choice, keep in an airtight container.

 Nutrition:
Calories: 247   **Fat:** 10g   **Carbohydrates:** 22g   **Protein:** 41g

397. Keto and Dairy-Free Vanilla Custard

Preparation Time: 11 minutes	**Cooking Time:** 5 minutes	**Servings:** 4

Ingredients:

- 6 egg yolks
- 64 ml. unsweetened almond milk
- 1 teaspoon vanilla extract
- 32 ml. melted coconut oil

Directions:

1. Mix egg yolks, almond milk, vanilla in a metal bowl.
2. Gradually stir in the melted coconut oil.
3. Boil water in a saucepan, place the mixing bowl over the saucepan. To form a bain Marie.
4. Whisk the mixture constantly and vigorously until thickened for about 5 minutes.
5. Remove from the saucepan, serve hot or chill in the fridge.

 **Nutrition:**
Calories: 222   **Fat:** 24g   **Carbohydrates:** 11g   **Protein:** 3g

398. Keto Triple Chocolate Mug Cake

Preparation Time: 3 minutes	**Cooking Time:** 1 minute	**Servings:** 3

Ingredients:

- 1 ½ tablespoon coconut flour
- ½ teaspoon baking powder
- 2 tablespoons cacao powder
- 2 tablespoons powdered sweetener
- 1 medium egg
- 5 tablespoons double cream
- 2 tablespoons sugar-free chocolate chips
- ¼ teaspoon vanilla extract optional

Directions:

1. Mix all the dry ingredients, - coconut flour, baking powder, cacao powder, in a bowl.
2. Whisk together the egg, cream, and vanilla extract, pour the mixture into the dry ingredients.
3. Add the chocolate chips into the mixture and let the batter rest for a minute.
4. Grease the ramekins with the melted butter, pour the batter into the ramekins.
5. Place in the microwave and microwave for 1 minute until cooked through.

 Nutrition:
Calories: 250   **Carbohydrates:** 9.7g   **Protein:** 6g   **Fat:** 22g

399. Keto Cheesecake Stuffed Brownies

Preparation Time: 11 minutes	Cooking Time: 30 minutes	Servings: 16

Ingredients:

For the Filling:
- 250 grams cream cheese
- 30 grams sweetener
- 1 large egg

For the Brownie:
- 85 grams low carb milk chocolate
- 5 tablespoons butter
- 3 large eggs
- 60 grams sweetener
- 30 grams cocoa powder
- 60 grams almond flour

Directions:

1. Preheat the oven to 200°C, fan 180°C, gas 6, line a brownie pan with baking paper.
2. In a mixing bowl, whisk together cream cheese, egg, and sweetener until smooth, set aside.
3. Place chocolate and butter in a microwave-safe bowl and microwave at 30 second intervals.
4. Whisk frequently until smooth, allow to cool for a few minutes.
5. Whisk together the remaining eggs and sweetener until fluffy.
6. Mix in the almond flour plus cocoa powder until soft peaks form.
7. Mix in the chocolate and butter mixture and beat with a hand mixer for a few seconds.
8. Fill the prepared pan with ¾ of the batter, then top with the cream cheese and the brownie batter.
9. Bake the cheesecake brownie until mostly set, for about 25-30 minutes.
10. The jiggling parts of the cake will firm when you remove it from the oven.

Nutrition:
Calories: 177 **Fat:** 13g **Carbohydrates:** 12g **Protein:** 5g

400. Keto Raspberry Ice Cream

Preparation Time: 45 minutes	Cooking Time: 0 minutes	Servings: 8

Ingredients:

- 250 grams double cream
- 120 grams raspberries
- 60 grams powdered erythritol
- 1 pasteurized egg yolk

Directions:

1. Process all the ice cream ingredients in a food processor.
2. Add blended mixture into the ice cream maker.
3. Turn on the ice cream machine and churn according to the manufacturer's directions.
4. Serve

Nutrition:
Calories: 120 **Fat:** 23g **Carbohydrates:** 4g **Protein:** 0g

401. Chocolate Macadamia Nut Fat Bombs

Preparation Time: 11 minutes	Cooking Time: 0 minutes	Servings: 4

Ingredients:

- 40 grams sugar-free dark chocolate
- 1 tablespoon
- Salt
- 40 grams raw macadamia nuts, halves

Directions:

1. Put three macadamia nut halves in each of 8 wells of the mini muffin pan.
2. Microwave the chocolate chips for about a few seconds.
3. Whisk until smooth, add coconut oil and salt, mix until well combined.
4. Fill the mini muffin pan with the chocolate mixture to cover the nuts completely.
5. Refrigerate the muffin pan until chilled and firm for about 30 minutes.

Nutrition:
Calories: 153 **Fat:** 1g **Carbohydrates:** 2g **Protein:** 4g

402. Keto Peanut Butter Chocolate Bars

Preparation Time: 11 minutes	Cooking Time: 0 minutes	Servings: 8

Ingredients:

For the Bars:
- 85 grams superfine almond flour
- 60 grams butter
- 45 grams Swerve, icing sugar style
- 60 grams peanut butter
- 1 teaspoon vanilla extract

For the Topping:
- 90 grams sugar-free chocolate chips

Directions:

1. Combine all the ingredients for the bars and spread into a small 6-inch pan.
2. Microwave the chocolate in the microwave oven for 30 seconds and whisk until smooth.
3. Pour the melted chocolate in over the bars ingredients.
4. Refrigerate for at least an hour or 2 until the bars firmed. Keep in an airtight container.

Nutrition:
Calories: 246 **Fat:** 23g **Carbohydrates:** 7g **Protein:** 7g

403. Salted Toffee Nut Cups

 Preparation Time: 11 minutes | **Cooking Time:** 10 minutes | **Servings:** 5

Ingredients:

- 140 grams low-carb milk chocolate
- 3 tablespoons plus 2 tablespoons sweetener
- 2 tablespoons cold butter
- 15 grams, walnuts, chopped
- Sea salt to taste

Directions:

1. Microwave the chocolate in 45 seconds intervals and continue whisk until chocolate melted.
2. Line the cupcake pan with 5 paper liners and add chocolate to the bottom of the cupcake.
3. Spread the chocolate to coat the bottom of the cupcake evenly, freeze to harden.
4. In a heat-proof bowl, heat the cold butter and sweetener in the microwave for 3 minutes.
5. Stir the butter every 20 seconds to prevent from burning.
6. Mix in the 28 grams. of sweetener and whisk to thicken. Fold in the walnuts.
7. Fill the chocolate cups with the toffee mixture quickly.
8. Top the cupcakes with the remaining chocolate and refrigerate to firm for 20-30 minutes.
9. Remove from the cups and sprinkle with sea salt!

Nutrition:
Calories: 194   **Fat:** 18g   **Carbohydrates:** 2g   **Protein:** 2.5g

404. Crisp Meringue Cookies

 Preparation Time: 10 minutes | **Cooking Time:** 40 minutes | **Servings:** 8

Ingredients:

- 4 large egg whites
- ¼ teaspoon cream of tartar
- ½ teaspoon almond extract
- 6 tablespoons Swerve Confectioners
- Pinch of salt

Directions:

1. Preheat the oven to 100C, fan 80°C..
2. Whip egg whites, cream of tartar in a mixers bowl on a medium speed until foamy.
3. While whipping, gradually add the swerve confectioners, 60 grams tsp,. at a time.
4. When all the swerve has been added, then turn the mixer up to high speed and whip.
5. Add in the almond extract and whip until very stiff.
6. Pour the batter in a piping bag with a French star tip and pipe the batter onto the lined baking tray.
7. Sheet. Bake the meringue for 40 minutes.
8. Serve immediately, enjoy!

Nutrition:
Calories: 234   **Fat:** 14g   **Carbohydrates:** 12g   **Protein:** 4g

405. Instant Pot Matcha Cheesecake

 Preparation Time: 11 minutes | **Cooking Time:** 55 minutes | **Servings:** 6

Ingredients:

Cheesecake:
- 450 grams cream cheese, room temperature
- 60 grams sweetener
- 2 teaspoons coconut flour
- ½ teaspoon vanilla extract
- 2 tablespoons double cream
- 1 tablespoon matcha powder
- 2 large eggs, room temperature

Directions:

1. In a mixing bowl, combine cream cheese, Swerve, coconut flour, vanilla extract, cream, and matcha powder until well combined. Stir in the eggs one at a time.
2. Add the cheesecake batter into the prepared springform tin.
3. Pour 60 ml. of water into the bottom of the Instant Pot. Put the trivet in the instant pot.
4. Place the springform on the top of the trivet, sealing, and securing the instant pot's lid.
5. Set the instant pot on high pressure, set the timing for 35 minutes.
6. Once the cooking time is up, release the pressure naturally.
7. Transfer the cheesecake on a cooling rack and allow it to cool the cake for 30 minutes.
8. Top with your favorite toppings, enjoy!

Nutrition:
Calories: 350   **Fat:** 33.2g   **Carbohydrates:** 5.8g   **Protein:** 8.4g

406. Matcha Skillet Souffle

 Preparation Time: 5 minutes | **Cooking Time:** 5 minutes | **Servings:** 1

Ingredients:

- 3 large eggs
- 2 tablespoons sweetener
- 1 teaspoon vanilla extract
- 1 tablespoon matcha powder
- 1 tablespoon butter
- 7 whole raspberries
- 1 tablespoon coconut oil
- 1 tablespoon unsweetened cocoa powder
- 30 grams double cream

Directions:

1. Grill, then heat-up a heavy-bottom pan over a medium heat.
2. Whip the egg whites with one tablespoon of Swerve confectioners. Once the peaks form add in the matcha powder and whisk again.
3. With a fork, break up the yolks. Mix in the vanilla, then add a little amount of the whipped whites. Carefully fold the remaining of the whites into the yolk mixture.

4. Dissolve the butter in a pan, put the souffle mixture into the pan. Reduce the heat to low and top with raspberries. Cook until the eggs double in size and set.
5. Transfer the pan to the oven and keep an eye on it. Cook until golden brown.
6. Melt the coconut oil and combine with cocoa powder and the remaining Swerve.
7. Drizzle the chocolate mixture across the top. Serve

 Nutrition:
Calories 578 **Fat:** 44g **Carbohydrates:** 5.g **Protein:** 19g

407. Flourless Keto Brownies

Preparation Time: 10 minutes	Cooking Time: 25 minutes	Servings: 4

Ingredients:

- 141 grams low-carb milk chocolate
- 4 tablespoons butter
- 3 large eggs
- 60 grams Swerve
- 30 grams mascarpone cheese
- 30 grams unsweetened cocoa powder, divided
- Salt

Directions:

1. Preheat the oven to 190°C, fan 170°C, gas 5 and line a baking tray with baking paper.
2. In a glass bowl over a medium heat, melt the 5 oz. chocolate for 30 seconds, stirring until smooth.
3. Stir in the butter and microwave the bowl for another ten seconds. Repeat the process until smooth. Put aside.
4. Beat the eggs and sweetener in a large mixing bowl until eggs become pale and the mixture fluffy.
5. Stir in the mascarpone cheese and whisk until smooth.
6. Gently sift in half of the cocoa powder and salt, combine.
7. Sift the remaining cocoa powder and whisk until combined and form the mixture into a batter.
8. Heat the chocolate again if it firmed and whisk in the mixture until creamy.
9. Add the mixture to the prepared baking tin/dish and bake until firm for about 25 minutes.
10. Allow to cool before serving, enjoy!

 Nutrition:
Calories: 130 **Fat:** 8g **Carbohydrates:** 2.9g **Protein:** 2.18g

408. Tropical Chocolate Mousse Bites

Preparation Time: 5 minutes	Cooking Time: 2 minutes	Servings: 1

Ingredients:

- 300 sugar-free dark chocolate
- 30 ml. coconut oil
- 60 grams double cream
- 1 tablespoon shredded coconut
- 1 tablespoon lemon zest

Directions:

1. Chill the molds in the freezer.
2. Microwave the chocolate and coconut oil in 10-second intervals, stirring continuously until smooth.
3. In a separate mixing bowl, whip the cream until medium-stiff peaks form.
4. Stir in the lemon zest and shredded coconut and fold into the cream.
5. Gradually stir in the 1/3 of the melted chocolate into the cream until well combined, reserving 2/3 for the molds. Place the mousse in the fridge to cool.
6. Pour the remaining melted chocolate into the chilled molds to form a thick layer on the sides.
7. Refrigerate the molds for 10-15 minutes.
8. Fill the cooled ice molds with the mousse batter, leaving some space for the chocolate topping.
9. Pour the remaining melted chocolate over the mousse and refrigerate and molds for 10-15 minutes.
10. Keep in the airtight container in the fridge.

 Nutrition:
Calories: 175 **Fat:** 13.75g **Carbohydrates:** 1.02g **Protein:** 1.98g

409. Coconut Raspberry Slice

Preparation Time: 11 minutes	Cooking Time: 20 minutes	Servings: 12

Ingredients:

- 110 grams butter melted
- 50g coconut flour
- 4 tablespoons granulated sweetener
- 2 teaspoons vanilla
- 1 teaspoon baking powder
- 8 eggs - medium
- 120 grams frozen raspberries

Directions:

1. Mix the melted butter, coconut flour, sweetener, vanilla, and baking powder in a bowl until smooth.
2. Add in the eggs, whisk in between each one.
3. Add the mixture to a rectangle baking dish, lined with baking parchment.
4. Top with each frozen raspberry evenly onto the cake.
5. Bake the raspberry fingers at 180°/220° C for 20-25 minutes until cooked through in the center.
6. Allow cooling, for raspberry fingers, cut down in the center, then cut across.

 Nutrition:
Calories: 146 **Fat:** 11.5g **Carbohydrates:** 6g **Protein:** 4.7g

410. White Chocolate Bark

Preparation Time: 11 minutes	Cooking Time: 10 minutes	Servings: 12

Ingredients:

- 60 grams cacao butter
- 43 grams sweetener

- 1 teaspoon vanilla powder
- ½ teaspoon hemp seed powder
- Pinch of Salt
- 1 teaspoon toasted pumpkin seeds

Directions:

1. Finely chop, measure cacao butter and melt in a double boiler over a pan of boiling water.
2. Mix the remaining ingredients in a bowl. Grease a plate or bowl with coconut oil.
3. Mix the melted butter into the remaining ingredients, combine well.
4. Pour the mixture into the greased plate or bowl, freeze until firm for 15 minutes.
5. Remove the dish from the freezer and break the frozen mix into 12 even pieces.
6. Chill and serve.

 Nutrition:
Calories: 258 **Fat:** 33g **Carbohydrates:** 24g **Protein:** 3g

411. Keto Hot Chocolate

Preparation Time: 5 minutes	**Cooking Time:** 10 minutes	**Servings:** 1

Ingredients:

- 60 grams double cream, divided
- ½ teaspoon vanilla extract, divided
- 40 ml. water
- 2 tablespoons cocoa powder, unsweetened
- 4 teaspoons erythritol or comparable measure of preferred sweetener, divided

Directions:

1. Mix half of the cream, half of the erythritol, and half of the vanilla extract in a bowl. Using a hand mixer, beat the mixture until it becomes light and fluffy.
2. Set to chill in the refrigerator while you prepare the cocoa.
3. Warm a medium saucepan over a medium-low heat and combine 60 ml. of water, the cocoa powder, and the remainder of the erythritol. Stir.
4. Turn the heat up to medium.
5. Once smooth, add the remaining cream and water. Stir continuously to combine.
6. Stir the vanilla into the mixture and allow it to get nice and hot, to your preference.
7. Pour the mixture into your favorite mug and serve topped with about 60 ml. of your cream in the refrigerator.

 Nutrition:
Calories: 320 **Carbohydrates:** 9g **Fat:** 31g **Protein:** 1g

412. Carrot Cake Chia Pudding

Preparation Time: 15 minutes	**Cooking Time:** 0 minutes	**Servings:** 4

Ingredients:

- 60 grams chia seeds
- ½ teaspoon erythritol or comparable measure of preferred sweetener
- 1 ½ teaspoon cinnamon, ground
- ¼ teaspoon nutmeg, ground
- ¼ teaspoon ginger, ground
- 130 grams carrot, grated
- 1 teaspoon vanilla extract
- 130 grams Greek yogurt, plain
- 60 grams pecans, toasted
- 220 ml. almond milk, unsweetened

Directions:

1. Mix chia seeds with seasonings, carrot, and almond milk in a bowl. Stir to combine thoroughly.
2. Let chill for 30 minutes so the chia seeds can swell. The mixture will become very thick like a pudding.
3. Remove the mixture from the refrigerator and stir the yogurt into it.
4. Top with toasted pecans.
5. Serve chilled!

 Nutrition:
Calories: 123 **Carbohydrates:** 6g **Fat:** 15g **Protein:** 9g

413. Carrot Cake Energy Balls

Preparation Time: 15 minutes	**Cooking Time:** 0 minutes	**Servings:** 8

Ingredients:

- 60 grams coconut, shredded & unsweetened
- 64 ml. sugar-free maple syrup
- 60 grams carrot, grated
- ½ teaspoon cinnamon, ground
- 130 grams almond flour
- 40 grams coconut flour
- 1/8 teaspoon ginger, grated
- 1/8 teaspoon nutmeg
- 3 tablespoons erythritol or comparable measure of preferred sweetener

Directions:

1. Combine all the ingredients, except for the shredded coconut, and pulse until a thick dough is formed.
2. If the dough is too wet, add a little extra flour and pulse. If the dough is too dry, add a bit more of water and pulse.
3. Once the dough has reached the desired consistency, take about a tablespoon of dough at a time and roll it into a smooth ball.
4. Roll each ball through the shredded coconut to coat thoroughly and set on the baking tray in an even layer.
5. Once you've rolled out all your balls, set them in the refrigerator for 30 minutes to become firm.
6. Keep stored in the refrigerator, in an airtight container for a snack, or serve chilled to guests!

 Nutrition:
Calories: 158 **Carbohydrates:** 22g **Fat:** 9g **Protein:** 2g

414. Caramel Pecan Muffins

Preparation Time: 10 minutes	Cooking Time: 20 minutes	Servings: 8

Ingredients:

For the Muffins:
- 60 grams coconut flour
- 64 ml. coconut milk, canned & unsweetened
- 60 grams almond flour
- 60 grams scoops vanilla protein powder of choice
- 1 ½ tablespoons coconut oil, melted
- 1 egg, beaten
- 1 teaspoon baking powder
- Sea salt
- 2 tablespoons erythritol or comparable measure of preferred sweetener

For the Filling:
- 64 ml. water
- 60 grams erythritol
- 1 egg, yolk only
- 2 tablespoons coconut oil
- ½ teaspoon vanilla extract
- ¼ teaspoon yacon syrup
- ¼ teaspoon sea salt
- ¼ teaspoon cinnamon, ground
- 60 grams pecans, chopped

Directions:

1. Preheat the oven to 190°C, fan 170°C, gas 5.
2. In a large sauté pan, combine all the filling ingredients (except the pecans). Warm them over a medium heat, continually stirring until it begins to bubble.
3. Allow the filling to bubble for about 30 seconds, remove from the heat, and set the pan on a trivet. The mixture should have a slight thickness but will be a little thinner than the traditional caramel.
4. Stir the pecans into the filling until thoroughly incorporated and set aside.
5. In a large mixing bowl, combine all dry ingredients for the muffins, whisking to combine.
6. In a smaller bowl, combine the wet ingredients for the muffins and whisk to combine.
7. Mix the wet and the dry ingredients.
8. Once the mixture is smooth, scoop a little batter into each cup to cover the bottoms.
9. Spoon a teaspoon of the filling into each muffin liner, then top each with the bowl's remaining batter.
10. Add a small dollop of caramel to each muffin's top and, using a toothpick, give each a quick swirl to give the muffin a swirled and delicious top.
11. Bake for 18 to 22 minutes, then cool for about 10 minutes before removing from the tin.
12. Serve warm!

 Nutrition:
Calories: 369 **Carbohydrates:** 12g **Fat:** 10g **Protein:** 5g

415. Cinnamon Roll Cookies

Preparation Time: 25 minutes	Cooking Time: 6 minutes	Servings: 16

Ingredients:

For the Cookies:
- 60 grams coconut flour
- 60 grams erythritol or comparable measure of preferred sweetener
- ¼ teaspoon xanthan gum
- ½ teaspoon vanilla extract
- 100 grams almond flour
- 1 tablespoon egg whites
- 1/8 teaspoon baking soda
- 1/8 teaspoon sea salt
- 3 tablespoons butter, cubed

For the Filling:
- ½ tablespoon butter, melted
- ½ teaspoon cinnamon, ground
- 2 teaspoon erythritol or comparable measure of preferred sweetener
- For the Frosting:
- 1 tablespoon coconut oil
- 1 teaspoon erythritol or comparable measure of preferred sweetener
- 1/8 teaspoon vanilla extract
- 3 tablespoons cream cheese

Directions:

1. Mix all the dry ingredients for the cookie dough in a bowl.
2. Drop the cubes of butter into the dough and use your hands to crumble it into the mixture of dry ingredients.
3. Stir the wet ingredients into the dough mix and combine until a smooth dough begins to form. You may need to let it stand for about five minutes once it's soft to allow it to firm up.
4. On a baking tray, place a piece of baking paper.
5. Place the cookie dough onto the baking paper and shape it into a long rectangular sheet. You may need to place baking paper on top of the dough to make it easier to roll out. Try to ensure that it is of even thickness (about half an inch) all the way through.
6. Chill the baking tray, then allow the dough to chill and firm up for about 20 minutes.
7. Grease the dough with melted butter, then put the filling ingredients over the dough, spreading them evenly.
8. Take hold of one of the short sides of the dough and roll it up tightly.
9. Cut the dough into disks about a quarter of an inch thick and place onto a baking tray lined with parchment paper.
10. Chill the baking sheet for another 20 minutes and preheat the oven to 190° C.
11. Bake the cookies for 7 minutes or until an inserted toothpick comes out clean.
12. Mix all the ingredients for the frosting and dip, drizzle into the cookies.
13. Serve and enjoy!

 Nutrition:
Calories: 358 **Carbohydrates:** 14g **Fat:** 5g **Protein:** 2g

416. Courgette Cookies

 **Preparation Time:** 10 minutes **Cooking Time:** 12 minutes **Servings:** 10

Ingredients:

- 1 egg, beaten
- 1 teaspoon vanilla extract
- 60 grams courgette, grated & drained
- 130 grams almond flour
- ¼ teaspoon Psyllium husk powder or xanthan gum
- ½ teaspoon baking powder
- 1 teaspoon cinnamon, ground
- 60 grams sugar-free chocolate chips
- Sea salt
- ¼ teaspoon nutmeg, ground
- 40 grams butter softened
- 85 grams erythritol or comparable measure of preferred sweetener

Directions:

1. Preheat the oven to 190°C, fan 170°C, gas 5 and line a baking tray with baking paper.
2. In a medium mixing bowl, combine sweetener, eggs, vanilla, and butter. Mix until thoroughly combined.
3. Add courgette to the bowl and mix once more.
4. Stir the psyllium husk powder (or xanthan gum), cinnamon, nutmeg, salt, and baking powder into the bowl and form a smooth batter.
5. Using your spoon or spatula, fold the sugar-free chocolate chips into the batter.
6. Make 10 evenly sized blobs of dough on your cookie sheet, taking care to space them evenly. Flatten each chunk just a little bit, so the dough is more cookie shaped.
7. Bake for 11 to 12 minutes or until the edges begin to crisp up.
8. Let stand for about 10 minutes, then move to a cooling rack.
9. Serve and enjoy!

 Nutrition:
Calories: 120 **Carbohydrates:** 2 g **Fat:** 10 g **Protein:** 2 g

417. Mint Chocolate Pie

 Preparation Time: 15 minutes **Cooking Time:** 0 minutes **Servings:** 10

Ingredients:

- 60 grams almond flour
- 60 grams erythritol or comparable measure of preferred sweetener, powdered
- 60 grams mint, fresh & chopped
- 2 drops green food coloring
- 250 grams double cream, divided
- 2 teaspoons gelatin powder, unflavored
- 3 tablespoons water
- 4 eggs, yolks only
- 4 tablespoons butter, melted
- 5 tablespoons erythritol or comparable measure of preferred sweetener, granulated
- 6 tablespoons cocoa powder, unsweetened

Directions:

1. Mix almond flour, granulated erythritol, and cocoa powder in a bowl. Whisk to combine thoroughly.
2. Stir butter into the mixture until nice and crumbly.
3. Press the mixture into a pie plate, making sure to push it up the dish's sides.
4. Set the crust to chill in the refrigerator until you're ready for it.
5. Warm 60 grams of the cream cheese and the mint on a medium heat, stirring thoroughly to keep smooth.
6. When the mixture is hot, kill the heat, cover the pan, and let it stand on a cold burner or trivet for 30 minutes.
7. Pour the cream cheese mixture through a strainer into a mixing bowl. Use a plastic or silicone spatula to push the cream through the strainer without the leaves. Set the cream aside.
8. Whisk the water and gelatin until it's fully dissolved on a medium heat. Slowly stir the cream mixture into the water and continue to whisk until the mixture is entirely smooth and hot all the way through.
9. In another bowl, beat the egg yolks and powdered erythritol. Beat until smooth.
10. Take 200 grams of the cream mixture and slowly stir it into the egg yolks, constantly whisking so they don't seize.
11. Once the cream's cup is thoroughly mixed in, mix the egg mixture into the remainder of the cream overheat and whisk until it thickens to a puddling-like consistency.
12. Stir the food coloring (optional) into the mix and beat until peaks form in the cream.
13. Fill the pie crust with the creamy mixture and use your spoon or spatula to smooth the top.
14. Chill for about three hours, then slice and serve chilled!

 Nutrition:
Calories: 161 **Carbohydrates:** 2g **Fat:** 14g **Protein:** 5g

418. Truffle Balls

 Preparation Time: 15 minutes **Cooking Time:** 0 minutes **Servings:** 12

Ingredients:

- 60 grams butter, melted
- 60 grams erythritol or comparable measure of preferred sweetener
- 140 grams almond flour
- 1 ½ teaspoon vanilla extract
- 1 pinch salt
- 1 tablespoon coconut oil
- 150 grams sugar-free chocolate, chopped
- 6 tablespoons cocoa powder

Directions:

1. In a medium mixing bowl, combine the erythritol, almond flour, salt, and cocoa powder. Whisk to combine
2. Stir the butter and vanilla into the mixture and allow the dough to form.
3. Mix until the desired consistency is reached.

4. Use a spoon, take enough dough out of the bowl to form one-inch balls, roll them in your palms, and lay them in one even layer on the parchment paper.
5. Chill the balls about an hour to allow them to be firm enough to stand up to chocolate dipping.
6. In a double boiler or a heat-resistant glass bowl over boiling water (a bain Marie), warm the chocolate and the coconut oil, continually stirring to make a coating.
7. Once the mixture is smooth, remove it from the heat and place it on a trivet.
8. Gently dip and roll each ball in the coating (using 2 forks is a great way to move the balls and pull them out without burning your fingers), then place back on the paper.
9. Once all the balls are coated, place all the truffles into the refrigerator for about an hour to stiffen.
10. If you have chocolate coating leftover, set it to cool until the truffles are done chilling.
11. Put back the batter to the double boiler to melt once again, then drizzle the remaining chocolate on top of the truffle balls.
12. Chill and serve.

 Nutrition:
Calories: 240   Carbohydrates: 14g   Fat: 8g   Protein: 2g

419. Peanut Butter Chocolate Cupcakes

Preparation Time: 15 minutes	Cooking Time: 20 minutes	Servings: 12

Ingredients:
- 130 grams peanut flour
- 100 grams cocoa powder, unsweetened
- 2 teaspoons baking powder
- Salt
- 4 egg whites
- 100 grams erythritol or comparable measure of preferred sweetener, powdered
- ½ teaspoon stevia powdered
- ½ tablespoons vanilla extract
- 12 tablespoons butter, melted
- 100 ml. almond milk, unsweetened
- 120 grams sugar-free peanut butter

Directions:
1. Preheat the oven to 190°C, fan 170°C, gas 5, then line a muffin tin with paper liners.
2. In a bowl, mix the flour, baking powder, cocoa powder, and salt. Whisk to combine.
3. In another bowl, mix eggs, sweeteners, and vanilla.
4. Whisk the melted butter and almond milk in with the other wet ingredients.
5. Mix all the dry ingredients into the wet and create a smooth batter with no lumps.
6. Spoon the batter into the cups (they won't rise too much).
7. Bake for 18 to 20 minutes or until an inserted toothpick comes out clean.
8. Let cool for about five minutes in the muffin tin, then set them out on wire racks to cool completely.

9. Using 60 grams for each cupcake, frost with peanut butter.
10. Serve and enjoy!

 Nutrition:
Calories: 340   Carbohydrates: 6.5g   Fat: 30.5g   Protein: 12.5g

420. Keto Cheesecakes

Preparation Time: 15 minutes	Cooking Time: 10 minutes	Servings: 9

Ingredients:
- 2 tablespoons butter
- 1 tablespoon caramel syrup; sugar-free
- 3 tablespoons coffee
- 250 grams cream cheese
- 43 grams swerve
- 3 eggs

For the frosting:
- 250 grams mascarpone cheese
- 50 ml. caramel syrup
- 60 grams swerve
- 50 grams butter

Directions:
1. Pulse cream cheese with eggs, 60 grams butter, coffee, 1 teaspoon of caramel syrup, mix in a processor.
2. Scoop into a cupcake tray and bake for 15 minutes.
3. Chill for 3 hours.
4. Combine 50 grams butter, 50 grams caramel syrup, 60 grams swerve, and mascarpone cheese. Pour over cheesecakes and serve.

 Nutrition:
Calories: 254   Fat: 23   Carbohydrates: 3g   Protein: 5g

421. Easy Keto Dessert

Preparation Time: 15 minutes	Cooking Time: 35 minutes	Servings: 4

Ingredients:
- 43 grams cocoa powder
- 43 grams erythritol
- 1 egg
- 30 grams almond flour
- 30 grams walnuts
- ½ teaspoon baking powder
- 7 tablespoons ghee
- ½ teaspoon vanilla extract
- 1 tablespoon peanut butter
- Salt

Directions:
1. Warm-up 84 grams ghee and the erythritol, cook for 5 minutes.
2. Transfer, mix with salt, vanilla extract, and cocoa powder.
3. Add the egg and beat.
4. Add baking powder, walnuts, and almond flour; stir and pour into a pan.
5. Mix 1 teaspoon of ghee with peanut butter, warm-up in the microwave for a few seconds.
6. Drizzle over brownies mix in the pan and bake for 30 minutes.
7. Slice and serve.

Nutrition:
Calories: 223 **Fat:** 32g **Carbohydrates:** 21g **Protein:** 4g

422. Keto Brownies

Preparation Time: 15 minutes	**Cooking Time:** 20 minutes	**Servings:** 9

Ingredients:

- 180 grams of coconut oil
- 120 grams cream cheese
- 5 tablespoons swerve
- 6 eggs
- 2 tablespoons vanilla extract
- 90 grams of cocoa powder
- ½ teaspoon baking powder

Directions:

1. Blend eggs with coconut oil, cocoa powder, baking powder, vanilla, cream cheese, and swerve using a mixer.
2. Put into a lined baking dish, at 220° C, fan 200°C, gas 8 and bake for 20 minutes.
3. Chill and serve.

 Nutrition:
Calories: 178 **Fat:** 14g **Carbohydrates:** 3g **Protein:** 5g

423. Raspberry and Coconut

Preparation Time: 15 minutes	**Cooking Time:** 5 minutes	**Servings:** 12

Ingredients:

- 30 grams swerve
- 64 ml. coconut oil
- 60 grams raspberries; dried
- 60 grams coconut
- 60 grams coconut butter

Directions:

1. Blend dried berries using a processor.
2. Warm-up the butter over a medium heat.
3. Add oil, coconut, and swerve; cook for 5 minutes.
4. Pour half into a baking pan. Add raspberry powder.
5. Add in the rest of the butter mixture, chill and serve.

 Nutrition:
Calories: 234 **Fat:** 22g **Carbohydrates:** 4g **Protein:** 2g

424. Chocolate Pudding Delight

Preparation Time: 60 minutes	**Cooking Time:** 10 minutes	**Servings:** 2

Ingredients:

- 1/2 teaspoon stevia powder
- 2 tablespoons cocoa powder
- 2 tablespoons water
- 1 tablespoon gelatin
- 120 ml. coconut milk
- 2 tablespoons maple syrup

Directions:

1. Warm-up the coconut milk over a medium heat; add the stevia and cocoa powder and mix
2. Mix gelatin with water; then add to the pan once soft.
3. Mix, add maple syrup, chill for 45 minutes. Serve.

 Nutrition:
Calories: 140 **Fat:** 2g **Carbohydrates:** 4g **Protein:** 4g

425. Special Keto Pudding

Preparation Time: 4 hours & 15 minutes	**Cooking Time:** 10 minutes	**Servings:** 2

Ingredients:

- 120 grams of coconut milk
- 4 teaspoons gelatin
- 1/4 teaspoon ginger
- 1/4 teaspoon liquid stevia
- A pinch of nutmeg
- A pinch of cardamom

Directions:

1. In a bowl, mix 32 ml of milk with gelatin.
2. Put the remaining coconut milk in a pan and warm-up.
3. Add gelatin mix, cold, and chill for 4 hours.
4. Transfer to a food processor, add stevia, cardamom, nutmeg, and ginger then blend.
5. Serve cold.

 Nutrition:
Calories: 150 **Fat:** 1g **Carbohydrates:** 2g **Protein:** 6g

426. Peanut Butter Fudge

Preparation Time: 2 hours & 15 minutes	**Cooking Time:** 10 minutes	**Servings:** 12

Ingredients:

- 120 grams peanut butter
- 120 ml. of coconut oil
- 32 ml. almond milk
- 2 teaspoons vanilla stevia
- A pinch of salt

Topping:

- 2 tablespoons swerve
- 30 grams cocoa powder
- 2 tablespoons melted coconut oil

Directions:

1. Mix peanut butter with 120 grams of coconut oil; microwave until it melts.
2. Add a pinch of salt, almond milk, and stevia; mix and pour into a lined loaf tin.
3. Chill for 2 hours and slice.
4. Mix 60 ml. melted coconut with cocoa powder and swerve.
5. Drizzle the sauce on top and serve.

 Nutrition:
Calories: 265 **Fat:** 23g **Carbohydrates:** 14g **Protein:** 6g

427. Coconut Pear Cream

 Preparation Time: 5 minutes | **Cooking Time:** 4 hours | **Servings:** 4

Ingredients:
- 1 tablespoon lime juice
- 2 tablespoons coconut cream
- 4 pears
- 60 grams date sugar

Directions:
1. Mix all the ingredients and cook on a low heat of 95°C for 4 hours in the oven.
2. Blend using an immersion blender and serve.

Nutrition:

Calories: 208 **Fat:** 4g **Carbohydrates:** 45g **Protein:** 15g

428. Lemony Coconut Cream

 Preparation Time: 5 minutes | **Cooking Time:** 3 hours | **Servings:** 4

Ingredients:
- 250 ml. of coconut milk
- 120 grams of coconut sugar
- Juice of 1 lemon
- 2 tablespoons ground cinammon
- 60 grams coconut

Directions:
1. Mix all the ingredients together in a bowl.
2. Pre-heat the oven to 170 degrees C, fan 150°C.
3. Put the mixture in the oven and bake for 3 hours.
4. Serve cold.

Nutrition:
Calories: 345 **Fat:** 27g **Carbohydrates:** 70 **Protein:** 6

429. Blackberry Stew

 **Preparation Time:** 5 minutes | **Cooking Time:** 4 hours | **Servings:** 4

Ingredients:
- 250 grams blackberries
- 2 tablespoons coconut oil
- 43 ml. rose water
- 83 grams coconut sugar

Directions:
1. Mix all the ingredients together in a bowl.
2. Transfer the mixture into a saucepan and cook it on medium-low for 4 hours.
3. Serve

 Nutrition:
Calories: 246 **Fat:** 8g **Carbohydrates:** 39g **Protein:** 14g

430. Peach Jam

 Preparation Time: 5 minutes | **Cooking Time:** 6 hours | **Servings:** 8

Ingredients:
- 3 pounds peaches
- 120 ml. of water
- 1 teaspoon vanilla extract
- 120 grams date sugar

Directions:
1. Mix all the ingredients together in a bowl.
2. Transfer the mixture into a saucepan and cook it on medium-low for 6 hours.
3. Cool, place in a jar and chill before serving.

 Nutrition:
Calories: 117 **Fat:** 18g **Carbohydrates:** 12g **Protein:** 4g

431. Strawberry Bowls

 Preparation Time: 5 minutes | **Cooking Time:** 3 hours | **Servings:** 4

Ingredients:
- 2 kg. strawberries
- 60 grams honey
- 2 tablespoons lemon zest
- 120 ml. of coconut water

Directions:
1. Mix all the ingredients together in a bowl.
2. Transfer the mixture into a saucepan and cook it on a medium-low heat for 3 hours.
3. Serve

 Nutrition:
Calories: 215 **Fat:** 4g **Carbohydrates:** 32g **Protein:** 2g

432. Pineapple Stew

 Preparation Time: 5 minutes | **Cooking Time:** 3 hours | **Servings:** 4

Ingredients:
- Half a pineapple
- 250 ml. apple juice
- 30 grams of coconut sugar

Directions:
1. Mix all the ingredients together in a bowl.
2. Transfer the mixture into a saucepan and cook on a medium-low heat for 2 hours.
3. Serve

 Nutrition:
Calories: 165 **Fat:** 12g Carbohydrates:16g **Protein:** 3g

433. Rhubarb Compote

Preparation Time: 5 minutes	Cooking Time: 4 hours	Servings: 6

Ingredients:

- 1 kg. rhubarb
- 120 ml. of water
- 4 tablespoons honey
- 1 teaspoon vanilla extract

Directions:

1. Mix all the ingredients together in a bowl.
2. Transfer the mixture into a saucepan and cook on a medium-low heat for 2 hours.
3. Serve.

 Nutrition:
Calories: 188 **Fat:** 12g **Carbohydrates:** 15g **Protein:** 2g

434. Banana Bowls

Preparation Time: 5 minutes	Cooking Time: 2 hours	Servings: 4

Ingredients:

- 1 tablespoon coconut sugar
- 4 bananas
- 64 ml. coconut oil

Directions:

1. Mix all the ingredients and cook on low heat for 2 hours.
2. Serve.

 Nutrition:
Calories: 346 **Fat:** 27g **Carbohydrates:** 28g **Protein:** 1g

435. Grape Compote

Preparation Time: 10 minutes	Cooking Time: 2 hours	Servings: 4

Ingredients:

- 100 ml. grape juice
- 1 kg. green grapes
- 2 tablespoons coconut sugar

Directions:

1. Mix all the ingredients and cook on a low heat for 2 hours.
2. Serve.

 Nutrition:
Calories: 131 **Fat:** 12g **Carbohydrates:** 33g **Protein:** 2g

436. Apricot Pudding

Preparation Time: 5 minutes	Cooking Time: 4 hours	Servings: 6

Ingredients:

- 3 eggs
- 250 grams apricots
- 120 ml. of coconut milk
- ½ tablespoon baking soda
- 2 tablespoons lemon juice
- 150 grams coconut flour
- 2 tablespoons coconut sugar
- 43 grams coconut oil
- 1 teaspoon vanilla extract
- Olive oil

Directions:

1. Mix all the ingredients together in a bowl.
2. Transfer the mixture into a slow cooker and cook on medium-low for 4 hours.
3. Serve.

 Nutrition:
Calories: 298 **Fat:** 27g **Carbohydrates:** 12g **Protein:** 4g

437. Blueberries and Cream

Preparation Time: 5 minutes	Cooking Time: 3 hours	Servings: 4

Ingredients:

- 250 grams blueberries
- 60 grams coconut cream
- 60 grams of coconut sugar

Directions:

1. Mix all the ingredients in a bowl.
2. Transfer them into a saucepan and cook on a medium-low heat for 3 hours.
3. Leave aside to cool, and once cooled use a blender to blend the mixture.
4. Serve

 Nutrition:
Calories: 384 **Fat:** 22g **Carbohydrates:** 51g **Protein:** 3g

438. Pumpkin Cream

Preparation Time: 10 minutes	Cooking Time: 2 hours	Servings: 2

Ingredients:

- 120 grams pumpkin puree
- 64 ml. almond milk
- 1 teaspoon ground cinnamon
- 2 tablespoons coconut sugar
- 1 teaspoon vanilla extract

Directions:

1. Mix all the ingredients in a bowl.
2. Transfer them into a saucepan and cook on a medium-low heat for 2 hours.
3. Serve.

 Nutrition:
Calories 211 **Fat:** 14g **Carbohydrates:** 20g **Protein:** 2g

439. Maple Pumpkin Dessert

 Preparation Time: 5 minutes | **Cooking Time:** 3 hours | **Servings:** 6

Ingredients:

- 1 ½ teaspoon ground cinnamon
- ½ teaspoon baking soda
- 2 tablespoons lemon juice
- 43 ml pure maple syrup
- 120 grams pumpkin puree
- 380 ml coconut milk
- 1 teaspoon grated ginger
- 2 teaspoons vanilla extract
- 120 grams walnuts

Directions:

1. Mix all the ingredients in a bowl.
2. Transfer them into a saucepan and cook on a medium-low heat for 3 hours.
3. Serve.

 **Nutrition:**
Calories: 472 **Fat:** 33g **Carbohydrates:** 24g **Protein:** 8g

440. Coconut Pineapple Bowls

 Preparation Time: 5 minutes | **Cooking time:** 3 hours | **Servings:** 2

Ingredients:

- 120 grams pineapple chunks
- 2 tablespoons coconut flakes
- 120 ml. of coconut milk
- 1 tablespoon ground cinnamon

Directions:

1. Mix all the ingredients in a bowl.
2. Transfer them into a saucepan and cook on a medium-low heat for 3 hours.
3. Serve.

 **Nutrition:**
Calories: 343 **Fat:** 30g **Carbohydrates:** 21g **Protein:** 3g

441. Almond Papaya Mix

 Preparation Time: 10 minutes | **Cooking Time:** 2 hours | **Servings:** 8

Ingredients:

- 120 ml. of coconut milk
- 120 grams papaya
- 1 tablespoon almonds

Directions:

1. Mix all the ingredients and cook on a low heat in a pan for 2 hours.
2. Serve cold.

Nutrition:
Calories: 334 **Fat:** 23g **Carbohydrates:** 13g **Protein:** 22g

442. Cinnamon Crunch Cereal

 Preparation Time: 10 minutes | **Cooking Time:** 20 minutes | **Servings:** 5

Ingredients:

- For the Cereal
- 120 grams almond flour
- 2 teaspoons cinnamon
- 150 grams coconut
- 1 tablespoon erythritol sweetener
- 6 tablespoons butter
- For sugar topping
- 1 tablespoons erythritol sweetener
- ½ teaspoon ground cinnamon

Directions:

1. Preheat the oven to 200°C, fan 180°C, gas 6.
2. Put the flour, coconut, sweetener, and cinnamon in a processor. Pulse.
3. Add the butter pieces and pulse.
4. Pour the mixture into a pan and cover with sheet of baking paper. Flatten out the ingredients. Bake for 20-30 minutes.
5. Combine the topping ingredients. Sprinkle over the cereal.
6. Cooldown and serve.

Nutrition:
Calories: 236 **Carbohydrates:** 6g **Fat:** 20g **Protein:** 9g

443. Cinnamon Rolls

Preparation Time: 10 minutes | **Cooking time:** 20 minutes | **Servings:** 8

Ingredients:

- 150 grams Mozzarella
- 80 grams Almond Flour
- 2 tablespoons Cream Cheese
- 1 Egg
- ½ teaspoon baking powder
- Filling
- 2 tablespoons water
- 2 tablespoons sweetener
- 2 teaspoons cinnamon
- Frosting
- 2 tablespoons cream cheese
- 1 tablespoon Greek yogurt
- 2 drops vanilla extract

Directions:

1. Preheat the oven to 220°C, fan 200°C, gas 7.
2. Dissolve the shredded mozzarella and cream cheese in a microwave. Remove.
3. Stir in the egg.
4. Mix in the flour and baking powder. Make a ball of smooth dough, divided into 4 pieces.
5. Form long rolls, flatten thin.
6. For the cinnamon filling:
7. Boil water, then put in the sweetener and cinnamon.
8. Put the cinnamon paste over the flattened dough rolls.
9. Roll into a bun and cut sideways in half.
10. Place the buns in a nonstick dish.
11. Bake for 18 minutes.
12. Prepare the frosting by thoroughly mixing yogurt, sweetener, and cream cheese. Serve.

Nutrition:
Calories: 321 **Carbohydrates:** 10g **Fat:** 9g **Protein:** 4g

444. Chocolate Ice Cream

| **Preparation Time:** 10 minutes | **Cooking Time:** 15 minutes | **Servings:** 8 |

Ingredients:

- 250 grams double cream
- 4 egg yolks
- 10 packets no-calorie sweetener
- 10 grams dry cocoa powder
- 2 tablespoons chocolate sweetener
- 1 teaspoon vanilla extract

Directions:

1. Warm-up the cream over a low heat in a pan.
2. Stir in the egg yolks and heat on low for 7 minutes.
3. Remove and combine in the sweetener, chocolate powder, syrup, and vanilla.
4. Add the mixture to the ice cream maker. Freeze and serve.

 Nutrition:
Calories: 234 **Carbohydrates:** 2g **Fat:** 11g **Protein:** 7g

445. Strawberry Ice Cream

| **Preparation Time:** 10 minutes | **Cooking Time:** 0 minutes | **Servings:** 3 |

Ingredients:

- 120 grams strawberries
- 1 ½ tablespoon vanilla whey protein powder
- 1 tablespoon almond butter
- 2 tablespoons coconut oil
- 60 ml. heavy cream
- 2 tablespoons sweetener

Directions:

1. Mix all the ingredients in a bowl.
2. Transfer the ingredients into a blender, and pulse.
3. Freeze for 4 hours and serve.

 Nutrition:
Calories 221 **Carbohydrates:** 36g **Fat:** 11g **Protein:** 5g

446. Lava Cake

| **Preparation Time:** 10 minutes | **Cooking Time:** 10 minutes | **Servings:** 2 |

Ingredients:

- 4 tablespoons cocoa powder
- ½ teaspoon baking powder
- 1 egg
- 2 tablespoons double cream
- 3 tablespoons Stevia
- 1 teaspoon vanilla extract
- Salt

Directions:

1. Preheat the oven to 220°C, fan 200°C, gas 7.

2. Combine the stevia and cocoa powder, mix with eggs.
3. Stir in the baking powder, cream, and vanilla. Add salt.
4. Put the batter evenly into cups and bake for 10 minutes. Serve.

 Nutrition:
Calories: 660 **Carbohydrates:** 66g **Fat:** 41g **Protein:** 5g

447. Lemon Mousse

| **Preparation Time:** 5 hours & 15 minutes | **Cooking Time:** 0 minutes | **Servings:** 4 |

Ingredients:

- 120 grams double cream
- 1 pack lemon jelly
- 1 tablespoon lemon Juice
- 1 teaspoon erythritol
- Sweetener

Directions:

1. Whisk the cream until peaks start to form. Prepare the jelly and chill for 12 minutes.
2. Combine the jelly and cream mixture for 3 minutes. Flavor it with sweetener and lemon juice.
3. Chill for up to 5 hours and serve.

 Nutrition:
Calories: 250 **Carbohydrates:** 3g **Fat:** 27g **Protein:** 5g

448. Chocolate Almond Butter Fat Bombs

|  **Preparation Time:** 60 minutes | **Cooking Time:** 5 minutes | **Servings:** 4 |

Ingredients:

- 60 grams unsweetened chocolate
- 2 tablespoons butter
- 60 grams almond butter
- 1 tablespoon peanut butter
- 1 tablespoon coconut oil
- 1 teaspoon stevia

Directions:

1. Melt the chocolate (in a pain Marie on a stove), put into a silicone mold. Let it chill for 15 minutes.
2. Put everything into a mixer. Add the stevia then process.
3. Pour mixture into the silicone mold.
4. Chill for 45 minutes, serve.

 Nutrition:
Calories 123 **Carbohydrates:** 12g **Fat:** 60g **Protein:** 10g

449. White Chocolate

|  **Preparation Time:** 15 minutes | **Cooking Time:** 5 minutes | **Servings:** 10 |

Ingredients:

- 250 grams raw cacao butter
- 60 grams erythritol
- 15 grams vanilla protein powder

- 2 tablespoons vanilla extract
- A pinch of salt

Directions:
1. Melt the cacao butter on a low heat.
2. Cooldown for 15 minutes, then put it into a blender.
3. Stir in the remaining ingredients and process in the blender.
4. Pour the mixture into the chocolate bar molds.
5. Chill, serve.

 Nutrition:
Calories: 432   **Carbohydrates:** 2g   **Fat:** 52g   **Protein:** 5g

450. Coconut Peanut Butter Balls

 **Preparation Time:** overnight & 1 hour	**Cooking Time:** 0 minutes	**Servings:** 10

Ingredients:
- 3 tablespoons peanut butter
- 3 teaspoons cocoa powder
- 2 ½ teaspoons erythritol
- 2 teaspoons almond flour
- 120 grams coconut flakes

Directions:
1. Mix everything together, except for the coconut flakes. Chill for an hour.
2. Scoop the mixture out and roll it in the coconut. Chill overnight, serve.

 Nutrition:
Calories: 260   **Carbohydrates:** 4g   **Fat:** 12 g   **Protein:** 3 g

30 DAYS MEAL PLAN 1

DAYS	BREAKFAST	LUNCH/DINNER	SNACKS
1	Blueberry Nutty Oatmeal	Baked Salmon	Pickle
2	Crab Salad Stuffed Avocados	Buttered Cod	Deviled Eggs Keto Style!
3	Keto Goat Cheese Salmon Fat Bomb	Shrimp Scampi with Garlic	Nutty Yogurt
4	Fried Pork Rind Crusted Salmon Cakes	Roasted Lemon Chicken Sandwich	Chips
5	Bacon Hash	Cabbage Soup with Beef	Pinwheel Delight
6	Bagels with Cheese	Baked Salmon	Zesty olives
7	Baked Apples	Buttered Cod	Strawberry Rhubarb Custard
8	Crab Salad Stuffed Avocados	Chinese Pork Bowl	Crème Brûlée
9	Banana Pancakes	Roasted Lemon Chicken Sandwich	Pickle
10	Fried Pork Rind Crusted Salmon Cakes	Shrimp Scampi with Garlic	Vanilla Frozen Yogurt
11	Brunch BLT Wrap	Quick Pumpkin Soup	Ice Cream
12	Keto Goat Cheese Salmon Fat Bomb	Roasted Lemon Chicken Sandwich	Nutty Yogurt
13	Coconut Porridge Keto	Chinese Pork Bowl	Mocha Mousse
14	Crab Salad Stuffed Avocados	Baked Salmon	Zesty olives
15	Creamy Basil, Baked Sausage	Cabbage Soup with Beef	Crème Brûlée
16	Almond, Coconut, Egg Wraps	Baked Salmon	Pickle
17	Fried Pork Rind Crusted Salmon Cakes	Buttered Cod	Chocolate Muffins
18	Bacon and Cheese Frittata	Quick Pumpkin Soup	Deviled Eggs Keto Style!
19	Blueberry Nutty Oatmeal	Roasted Lemon Chicken Sandwich	Chips
20	Bacon Hash	Trout and Chili Nuts	Mocha Mousse
21	Bagels with Cheese	Buttered Cod	Pinwheel Delight
22	Keto Goat Cheese Salmon Fat Bomb	Chinese Pork Bowl	Crème Brûlée

DAYS	BREAKFAST	LUNCH/DINNER	SNACKS
23	Baked Eggs In The Avocado	Baked Salmon	Nutty Yogurt
24	Fried Pork Rind Crusted Salmon Cakes	Shrimp Scampi with Garlic	Chocolate Muffins
25	Keto Goat Cheese Salmon Fat Bomb	Quick Pumpkin Soup	Pickle
26	Blueberry Nutty Oatmeal	Roasted Lemon Chicken Sandwich	Vanilla Frozen Yogurt
27	Cheesy Bacon and Egg Cups	Cabbage Soup with Beef	Deviled Eggs Keto Style!
28	Blueberry Nutty Oatmeal	Buttered Cod	Chocolate Avocado Ice Cream
29	Fried Pork Rind Crusted Salmon Cakes	Tuna Salad	Chips
30	Crab Salad Stuffed Avocados	Fresh Avocado Soup	Pickle

30 DAYS MEAL PLAN 2

Day	Breakfast	Lunch	Snack	Dinner	Dessert
1	Almond Coconut Egg Wraps	Turkey & Cream Cheese Sauce	Parmesan Cheese Strips	Baked Courgette Noodles with Feta	Sugar-Free Lemon Bars
2	Bacon & Avocado Omelet	Baked Salmon & Pesto	Peanut Butter Power Granola	Brussel Sprouts with Bacon	Creamy Hot Chocolate
3	Bacon & Cheese Frittata	Keto Chicken with Butter & Lemon	Homemade Graham Crackers	Bunless Burger- Keto Style	Delicious Coffee Ice Cream
4	Bacon & Egg Breakfast Muffins	Garlic Chicken	Keto no Bake Cookies	Coffee BBQ Pork Belly	Fatty Bombs with Cinnamon and Cardamom
5	Bacon Hash	Salmon Skewers & Wrapped with Prosciutto	Swiss Cheese Crunchy Nachos	Garlic & Thyme Lamb Chops	Raspberry Mousse
6	Bagel with Cheese	Buffalo Drumsticks & Chilli Aioli	Homemade Thin Mints	Jamaican Jerk Pork Roast	Quick & Simple Brownie
7	Baked Apples	Slow Cooked Roasted Pork & Creamy Gravy	Mozzarella Cheese Pockets	Keto Meatballs	Cute Peanut Balls
8	Baked Eggs in the Avocado	Bacon-Wrapped Meatloaf	No-Bake Coconut Cookies	Mixed Vegetables Patties- Instant Pot	Chocolate Mug Muffins
9	Banana Pancakes	Lamb Chops & Herb Butter	Cheesy Cauliflower Breadsticks	Roasted Leg of Lamb	Chocolate Spreads with Hazelnuts
10	Breakfast Pot	Crispy Cuban Pork Roast	Easy Peanut Butter Cups	Salmon Pasta	Keto Peanut Butter Cup Style Fudge
11	Brunch BLT Wrap	Keto Barbecued Ribs	Fried Green Beans Rosemary	Pan Fried Cod	Keto and Fairy-Free Vanilla Custard
12	Cheesy Bacon & Egg Cups	Turkey Burgers & Tomato Butter	Crispy Broccoli Popcorn	Slow-Cooked Kalua Pork & Cabbage	Keto Triple Chocolate Mug Cake
13	Coconut Keto Porridge	Keto Hamburger	Cheesy Cauliflower Croquettes	Steak Pinwheels	Keto Cheesecake Stuffed Brownies
14	Cream Cheese Eggs	Chicken Wings & Blue Cheese Dressing	Spinach in Cheese Envelopes	Tangy Shrimp	Keto Raspberry Ice Cream
15	Creamy Basil Baked Sausage	Salmon Burgers with Lemon Butter & Mash	Cheesy Mushroom Slices	Chicken Salad with Champagne Vinegar	Chocolate Macadamia Nut Fat Bombs

Day	Breakfast	Lunch	Snack	Dinner	Dessert
16	Banana Waffles	Egg Salad Recipe	Asparagus Fries	Mexican Beef Salad	Keto Peanut Butter Chocolate Bars
17	Keto Cinnamon Coffee	Taco Stuffed Avocados	Kale Chips	Cherry Tomatoes Tilapia Salad	Salted Toffee Nut Cups
18	Keto Waffles & Blueberries	Buffalo Shrimp Lettuce Wraps	Guacamole	Crunchy Chicken Milanese	Crisp Meringue Cookies
19	Baked Avocado Eggs	Broccoli Bacon Salad	Zucchini Noodles	Parmesan Baked Chicken	Instant Pot Matcha Cookies
20	Mushroom Omelette	Keto Egg Salad	Cauliflower Souffle	Cheesy Bacon and Broccoli Chicken	Matcha Pan Souffle
21	Chocolate Sea Salt Smoothie	Loaded Cauliflower Salad	No-Churn Ice Cream	Buttery Garlic Chicken	Flourless Keto Brownies
22	Courgette Lasagna	Caprese Zoodles	Cheesecake Cupcakes	Creamy Slow Cooker Chicken	Tropical Chocolate Mousse Bites
23	Vegan Keto Scramble	Courgette Sushi	Chocolate Peanut Butter Cups	Braised Chicken Thighs with Kalamata Olives	Coconut Raspberry Slice
24	Bavarian Cream with Vanilla and Hazelnuts	Asian Chicken Lettuce Wraps	Low-Carb Almond Coconut Sandies	Baked Garlic and Paprika Chicken Legs	White Chocolate Bark
25	Vanilla Mousse	California Burger Bowls	Crème Brûlée	Chicken Curry with Masala	Keto Hot Chocolate
26	Blueberry Mousse	Parmesan Brussel Sprouts Salad	Chocolate Fat Bomb	Chicken Quesadilla	Carrot Cake Chia Pudding
27	Strawberry Bavarian	Chicken Taco Avocados	Cocoa Mug Cake	Slow Cooker BBQ Ribs	Carrot Cake Energy Balls
28	Almond Mousse	Keto Quesadillas	Dark Chocolate Espresso Paleo & Keto Mug Cake	Barbacoa Beef Roast	Caramel Pecan Muffins
29	Nougat	No-Bread Italian Subs	Keto Matcha Mint Bars	Beef & Broccoli Roast	Cinnamon Roll Cookies
30	Chocolate Crepes	Basil Avocado frail Salad Wraps & Sweet Potato Chips	Keto No-Churn Blueberry Maple Ice cream	Cauliflower and Pumpkin Casserole	Courgette Cookies

30 DAYS MEAL PLAN 3

Day	Breakfast	Lunch	Snack	Dinner	Dessert
1	Rusk with Walnut Cream	Cauliflower Leek Soup	Chocolate Fat Bomb	Thai Beef salad Tears of the Tiger	Mint Chocolate Pie
2	Bavarian Coffee with Hazelnuts	Sugar-free Blueberry Cottage Cheese Parfaits	Cocoa Mug Cake	Stuffed Apples with Shrimp	Chocolate Truffle Balls
3	Strawberry Butter Bavarian	Low-Calorie Cheesy Broccoli Leek Soup	Dark Chocolate Espresso Paleo & Keto Mug Cake	Grilled Chicken Salad with Oranges	Peanut Butter Chocolate Cupcakes
4	Cheese Platters	Low Carb Chicken Taco Soup	Keto Matcha Mint Bars	Red Curry with Vegetables	Caramel Pecan Muffins
5	Hazelnut Bavarian with Hot Coffee Drink	Keto Chicken & Veggies Soup	Keto No-Churn Blueberry Maple Ice Cream	Baked Turkey Breast with Cranberry Sauce	Cinnamon Roll Cookies
6	Muffins with Coffee Drink	Low Carb Seafood Soup with Mayo	Keto-Friendly Crackers	Italian Keto Casserole	Courgette Cookies
7	French toast with Coffee Drink	Keto Tortilla Chips	Parmesan Cheese Strips	Salmon Keto cutlets	Sugar-Free Lemon Bars
8	Almond Coconut Egg Wraps	Chicken Courgette Alfredo	Peanut Butter Power Granola	Baked Cauliflower	Creamy Hot Chocolate
9	Bacon & Avocado Omelette	Low Carbohydrates: Chicken Cheese	Homemade Graham Crackers	Risotto with Mushrooms	Delicious Coffee Ice Cream
10	Bacon & Cheese Frittata	Lemon Chicken Spaghetti Squash Boats	Keto no Bake Cookies	Low Carb Green Bean Casserole	Fatty Bombs with Cinnamon and Cardamom
11	Bacon & Egg Breakfast Muffins	Stuffed Portobello Mushrooms	Swiss Cheese Crunchy Nachos	Avocado Low Carb Burger	Raspberry Mousse
12	Bacon Hash	Low Carbohydrates: Mexican Stuffed Peppers	Homemade Thin Mints	Protein Gnocchi with Basil Pesto	Quick & Simple Brownie
13	Bagel with Cheese	Low Carb Broccoli Mash	Mozzarella Cheese Pockets	Summery Bowls with Fresh Vegetables and Protein Quark	Cute Peanut Balls
14	Baked Apples	Roasted Tri-Color Vegetables	No-Bake Coconut Cookies	Beef and Kale Pan	Chocolate Mug Muffins

Day	Breakfast	Lunch	Snack	Dinner	Dessert
15	Baked Eggs in the Avocado	Low Carb Broccoli Leek Soup	Cheesy Cauliflower Breadsticks	Salmon and Lemon Relish	Chocolate Spreads with Hazelnuts
16	Banana Pancakes	Turkey & Cream Cheese Sauce	Easy Peanut Butter Cups	Mustard Glazed Salmon	Keto Peanut Butter Cup Style Fudge
17	Breakfast Pot	Baked Salmon & Pesto	Fried Green Beans Rosemary	Turkey and Tomatoes	Keto and Dairy-Free Vanilla Custard
18	Brunch BLT Wrap	Keto Chicken with Butter & Lemon	Crispy Broccoli Popcorn	Grilled Squid and Tasty Guacamole	Keto Triple Chocolate Mug Cake
19	Cheesy Bacon & Egg Cups	Garlic Chicken	Cheesy Cauliflower Croquettes	Salmon Bowls	Keto Cheesecake Stuffed Brownies
20	Coconut Keto Porridge	Salmon Skewers & Wrapped with Prosciutto	Spinach in Cheese Envelopes	Shrimp & Cauliflower Delight	Keto Raspberry Ice Cream
21	Cream Cheese Eggs	Buffalo Drumsticks & Chili Aioli	Cheesy Mushroom Slices	Scallops and Fennel Sauce	Chocolate Macadamia Nut Fat Bombs
22	Creamy Basil Baked Sausage	Slow Cooked Roasted Pork & Creamy Gravy	Asparagus Fries	Salmon Stuffed with Shrimp	Keto Peanut Butter Chocolate Bars
23	Banana Waffles	Bacon-Wrapped Meatloaf	Kale Chips	Cheesy Pork Casserole	Salted Toffee Nut Cups
24	Keto Cinnamon Coffee	Lamb Chops & Herb Butter	Guacamole	Incredible Salmon Dish	Crisp Meringue Cookies
25	Keto Waffles & Blueberries	Crispy Cuban Pork Roast	Courgette Noodles	Thai beef salad Tears of the Tiger	Instant Pot Matcha Cookies
26	Baked Avocado Eggs	Keto Barbecued Ribs	Cauliflower Souffle	Stuffed Apples with Shrimp	Matcha Skillet Souffle
27	Mushroom Omelette	Turkey Burgers & Tomato Butter	No-Churn Ice Cream	Grilled Chicken Salad with Oranges	Flourless Keto Brownies
28	Chocolate Sea Salt Smoothie	Keto Hamburger	Cheesecake Cupcakes	Red Curry with Vegetables	Tropical Chocolate Mousse Bites
29	Courgette Lasagna	Chicken wings & Blue Cheese Dressing	Chocolate Peanut Butter Cups	Baked Turkey Breast with Cranberry Sauce	Coconut Raspberry Slice
30	Vegan Keto Scramble	Salmon Burgers with Lemon Butter & Mash	Low-Carb Almond Coconut Sandies	Italian Keto Casserole	White Chocolate Bark

30 DAYS MEAL PLAN 4

Day	Breakfast	Lunch	Snack	Dinner	Dessert
1	Cheese Crepes	Easy Keto Smoked Salmon Lunch Bowl	Keto Raspberry Cake & White Chocolate Sauce	Green Chicken Curry	Keto Cheesecakes
2	Ricotta Pancakes	Easy one-pan minced beef & green beans	Keto Chocolate Chips Cookies	Creamy Pork Stew	Keto Easy Dessert
3	Yogurt Waffles	Easy Spinach & Bacon Salad	Keto beef & Sausage balls	Salmon & Shrimp Stew	Keto Brownies
4	Broccoli Muffins	Easy Keto Italian Plate	Keto Coconut Flake Balls	Chicken Casserole	Raspberry & Coconut
5	Pumpkin Bread	Fresh broccoli & Dill Keto Salad	Keto Chocolate Greek Yoghurt Cookies	Creamy Chicken Bake	Chocolate Pudding Delight
6	Eggs in Avocado cups	Keto Smoked Salmon filled Avocados	Keto coconut flavored ice cream	Beef & Veggie Casserole	Special Keto Pudding
7	Cheddar Scramble	Low-carb Broccoli Lemon Parmesan Soup	Chocolate-coconut Cookies	Beef with Peppers	Peanut Butter Fudge
8	Bacon Omelette	Prosciutto & Mozzarella Bomb	Keto Buffalo Chicken Meatballs	Braised Lamb Shanks	Coconut Pear Cream
9	Green Veggies Quiche	Summer Tuna Avocado Salad	Eggplant & Chickpea Bites	Shrimp & Pepper Stir-Fry	Blackberry Stew
10	Chicken & Asparagus Frittata	Mushrooms & Goat Cheese Salad	Baba Ganouj	Veggies & Walnut Loaf	Peach Jam
11	Southwest Scrambled Egg Bites	Keto Bacon Sushi	Spicy Crab dip	Keto Sloppy Joes	Strawberry Bowls
12	Bacon Egg Bites	Cole Slaw Keto Wrap	Potatoes" of Parmesan Cheese	Low Carb Crack Slaw Egg Roll in a Bowl Recipe	Pineapple Stew
13	Omelette Bites	Keto Chicken Club Lettuce Wrap	Chilli cheese Chicken with crispy & delicious cabbage salad	Low Carb Beef Stir Fry	Rhubarb Compote
14	Cheddar & Bacon Egg Bites	Keto Broccoli Salad	Keto Pumpkin Pie sweet & spicy	One Pan Pesto Chicken & Veggies	Banana Bowls
15	Avocado Pico Egg Bites	Keto Sheet Pan Chicken & Rainbow Veggies	Blackened Tilapia with Courgette Noodles	Crispy Peanut Tofu & Cauliflower Rice Stir-Fry	Grapes Compote

Day	Breakfast	Lunch	Snack	Dinner	Dessert
16	Salmon Scramble	Skinny Bang-Bang Courgette Noodles	Pepper Nachos	Simple Keto Fried Chicken	Apricot Pudding
17	Mexican Scrambled Eggs	Keto Caesar Salad	Radish, Carrot & Cilantro Salad	Keto Butter Chicken	Blueberries & Cream
18	Caprese Omelette	Keto Buffalo Chicken Empanadas	Asparagus-Mushroom Frittata	Keto Shrimp Scampi Recipe	Pumpkin Cream
19	Sausage Omelette	Pepperoni & Cheddar Stromboli	Shrimp Avocado Salad	Keto Lasagna	Maple Pumpkin Dessert
20	Brown Hash with Courgette	Tuna Casserole	Smoky Cauliflower Bites	Creamy Tuscan Garlic Chicken	Coconut Pineapple Bowls
21	Crunchy Radish & Courgette Hash Browns	Brussel Sprout & Hamburger Gratin	Avocado Crab Boats	Ancho Macho Chilli	Cinnamon Crunch Cereals
22	Fennel Quiche	Carpaccio	Coconut Curry Cauliflower Soup	Chicken Supreme Pizza	Cinnamon Rolls
23	Turkey Hash	Keto Croque Monsieur	Parmesan Asparagus	Baked Jerked Chicken	Chocolate Ice Cream
24	Crustless Veggie Quiche	Keto wraps with Cream Cheese & Salmon	Cream Cheese Pancakes	Chicken Schnitzel	Strawberry ice Cream
25	Keto Courgette Bread	Savory Keto Broccoli Cheese Muffins	Sugar-free Mexican Spiced Dark Chocolate	Broccoli & Chicken Casserole	Lava Cake
26	Keto Almond Bread Recipe	Keto Rusk	Tuna in Cucumber Cups	Baked Fish with Lemon Butter	Lemon Mousse
27	Quick Keto Toast	Flaxseed hemp Flour Bun	Parmesan Crisp	Chicken Broccoli Alfredo	Chocolate Almond Butter Fat Bombs
28	Keto Loaf of Bread	Keto Muffins with Roquefort	Onion Rings	Grilled Cheesy Buffalo Chicken	White Chocolate
29	Blueberry Loaf	Keto Wrap	Cold Crab Dip	Middle Eastern Shawarma	Coconut Peanut Butter Balls
30	Simple Loaf of Bread	Savory Keto Muffins	Baked Coconut Shrimp	Tex Mex Casserole	No-bake Cheese Cake

Printed in Great Britain
by Amazon

29493095R10082